ON WHAT WE KNOW
WE DON'T KNOW

Sylvain Bromberger

ON WHAT WE KNOW
WE DON'T KNOW

*Explanation, Theory,
Linguistics, and
How Questions Shape Them*

The University of Chicago Press
Chicago and London

&

Center for Study of Language and Information
Stanford

The University of Chicago Press, Chicago 60637
The University of Chicago Press, Ltd., London
© 1992 by the Center for the Study of Language and Information
Leland Stanford Junior University
All rights reserved. Published 1992
Printed in the United States of America
99 98 97 96 95 94 93 92   5 4 3 2 1

CIP data and other information appear at the end of the book

To the memory of
Aristides de Sousa Mendes
Portuguese Consul in Bordeaux in June 1940
with gratitude

Contents

Introduction

The nine papers in this book cover topics as diverse as the nature of explanation, the ambiguity of the word *theory*, the varieties of ignorance, the limits of rationality in the choice of questions, and the ontology of linguistics. Each is self-contained and can be read independently of the others. They are arranged essentially unchanged in the order in which they chronologically appeared. The book as a whole can thus be approached simply as a collection of papers that were previously scattered across many publications and are now assembled under one cover for convenience.

However, the book can also be approached as a collection of papers that belong naturally together by virtue of a common idea and a common agenda based on that idea. Philosophers have always recognized that scientific progress consists in more than successive additions to a stock of truths and highly confirmed propositions. But what that "more" comes to has turned out to be surprisingly controversial and elusive. The idea common to these papers is that the "more" will be found in the truism that science seeks answers to questions. The common agenda then is simply to examine with some care what such seeking involves.

We find ourselves, as individuals and as communities, willy-nilly cast in a world not of our own making, in which we want to survive, if possible to thrive, and whose features we want to understand. We start out with little prior information about that world, but we are endowed with the ability to come to know that there are things about it that we don't know, that is, with the ability to formulate and to entertain questions whose answers we know we do not know. It is an enormously complex ability derived from many auxiliary

1

abilities. And it induces the wish to know the answer to some of these questions. Scientific research represents our most reasonable and responsible way of trying to satisfy that wish. That is its most tenable defining goal, and not, as others have held, the construction of doctrines that can be recast as interpreted formal systems, or the achievement of intellectual economy, or the refutation of conjectures, or the solution of puzzles, or the provision of means for practical success, or the contrivance of communal consensus, or the domination of certain institutions, or the elaboration of ever more encompassing systems, or the making of worlds. Those sorts of achievements represent at best accidental objectives.

However, in seeking its goal science repeatedly runs into difficulties. Many of these difficulties are physical in nature and call for the design of new and more powerful instruments. Others are psychological and call for the invention of devices that supplement our memory and our computational powers. Still others, and those are the ones that are relevant here, are intellectual and pertain to our ability to conceive, formulate, consider, connect, and assess questions, and to our ability to conceive, formulate, consider, connect, and assess answers. These sorts of difficulties often call for inspiration and creative intelligence. Careful observation and description are not enough.

The idea linking these papers can thus be put more explicitly. It is that this "more" that scientific endeavors add to truths and warranted beliefs consists of insights through which inspiration and creative intelligence manage to overcome such intellectual difficulties. And the agenda is to specify the character of these insights.

In the rest of this introduction I will briefly describe the content of each paper. I will first describe the specific topic to which it is addressed for readers who look at it simply as a self-contained paper. I will then describe how it fits in the overall agenda when that is not obvious from the nature of the topic.

"An Approach to Explanation" belongs to the vast philosophic literature that seeks to analyze the notion of explanation. What is at stake can best be appreciated by noting an odd disagreement among philosophers of science. Some, Pierre Duhem most notably among them, hold that empirical science does not and cannot provide explanations. Others, and that includes most contemporary philosophers of science, hold that, on the contrary, science can and does provide explanations. All sides agree that the notion of explanation connotes norms and desiderata, and all sides also agree that the question is whether those norms and desiderata are compatible with the primary positivistic demands for empirical evidence, inductive justification, consistency, generality, productivity, etc. The sides differ on what the connoted norms and desiderata come to, and so they reach different conclusions about their legitimacy. What is at stake, then, goes beyond what the notion of explanation (or the word that expresses it) connotes and affects our consciousness of scientific desiderata and norms, and our awareness of what science can or cannot aspire to achieve.

I will not summarize my own analysis of these connotations here, since the whole paper is near at hand, but I can prepare the ground with a few remarks about its general character.

The paper was written under the influence of so-called ordinary language philosophy. It therefore focuses unashamedly on our use of the verb *to explain* and of its nominalization *explanation* on the obvious ground that the most direct way to find out what the notion of explanation connotes is to examine how we apply the words *explain* and *explanation*.

The analysis starts from the observation of two facts: first, the purely grammatical fact that the verb *to explain* and its cognate *explanation of* admit interrogative sentences (in indirect speech form, i.e., without so-called wh-aux inversion) as their complements; second, the nongrammatical fact that though they admit a wide range of questions as complement, they normally exclude some. They admit most why-questions, how-questions, what-is questions as their object, but they do not normally admit, e.g., *what time it is*. (We normally tell but don't explain what time it is.)

The first of these facts, incidentally, is probably responsible for the vast diversity of analyses that occur in the philosophic literature. Most writers on the subject implicitly limit their attention to some subfamily of the family of questions admissible as object of *explain*, and limit themselves to different ones. So Duhem, for instance, limits himself to the *what is the physical structure underlying such and such phenomena* subfamily; Mill, Hempel and other adherents of the covering law view limit themselves to the *why* subfamily; others limit themselves to the *what causes* subfamily; others still to the *how possible* subfamily, or to the *what mechanisms are present when so*

and so occurs subfamily, and so on. They are like the blind men who
each reported (perhaps correctly) on a different part of the elephant.
But unlike the blind men, they follow a reasonable strategy, if one
assumes, as most of them seem to do, that their object should be to
display truth-conditions distinctive of answers admitted by *explain*
and its cognates. That cannot be done in one fell swoop for such a
heterogenous family. It is therefore more reasonable to concentrate
on some particularly challenging subfamily. Of course that does not
justify the widespread attitude that only one of these subfamilies is
legitimate.

The analysis I propose in "An Approach to Explanation" shifts
the focus to what is distinctive about the questions admissible as
objects of *to explain* and away from what is distinctive, if anything,
about the truth-conditions on their answers. I argue that the distinction is fundamentally cognitive in nature, that is, that it has to do
with intellectual states and not with subject matter. Explanations,
I argue, express answers to not just any questions but to questions
that present the kind of intellectual difficulty I call "p-predicaments."
(I also write of "b-predicaments" there, but that is immaterial for
this introduction.) A p-predicament, to a first approximation, is the
condition one is in when one is able to entertain a question, has reason to think that it is sound, i.e., that it has a right answer, but one
can think only of answers that one knows (or believes) to be false.

Though being in a p-predicament over some question is practically a chronic condition of philosophers, they have seldom acknowledged its importance in the advance of science. Insofar as they have
thought about p-predicaments at all, they have probably thought of
them as mere psychological blocks on a par with the exasperating
trouble we often experience when we try to remember something and
can't. Like many erotetic logicians who identify questions with an
exhaustive set of possible (i.e., true and false) direct answers, they
probably hold that anyone who understands a question must already
possess all its possible answers. On such a view, p-predicaments have
to be lapses of recovery power calling for no particular creativity.

But p-predicaments are not like that at all. They are more like ignorance than like inability to remember. They call not for retrieval
of something already in mind, but for the begetting of something
new. It is not true that one understands a question only if one already knows all the possible correct or incorrect answers. Overcom-

ing p-predicaments may, in fact, require drastic innovations. It is the sort of achievement that can motivate scientific revolutions. When Newton thought of gravity as explaining how tides occur, he did not just remember an answer, he created a new, and as it happens, true idea.

"A Theory about the Theory of Theory of Theory and about the Theory of Theories" is based on an issue which overlaps the issue that motivated "An Approach to Explanation." All philosophers of science agree that science can, does, and should come up with theories. They also generally agree that the notion of theory, like the notion of explanation, connotes certain desiderata, and therefore that science can, does, and should seek results that meet these desiderata. But this is as far as agreement usually goes. When it comes to saying what these desiderata are, we find again a wide divergence of views. And as in the case of explanation, that divergence is not just about what the concept signifies but also about what science can aspire to achieve while remaining true to the mandates of empirical evidence, inductive support, generality, productivity, etc.

As in the previous paper (the two were written at roughly the same time) I unashamedly search for what the notion connotes by looking at the word that expresses it. But the lexicographical situation turns out to be more complex.

The word *theory* is actually used in two syntactically different ways associated with two different sorts of things. It is used as a mass term to mention certain fields of inquiry (*probability theory, sound theory, physical theory*) and it is used as a count term to mention specific propositions (*the kinetic theory of gases, the theory of evolution*). (The labels *mass term* and *count term* are slightly misused here, but they will serve the purpose, and the discussion in the paper goes over the distinction in greater detail.) This is admittedly a slippery distinction for reasons that I describe toward the end of the paper. Even so, it cannot always be ignored with impunity.

Conflating the two can in fact be disastrous. I became vividly aware of this while studying Pierre Duhem's *La Théorie physique, son objet et sa structure*. In that book Duhem conflates "What is the object of physical theory?" ("Quel est l'objet de la théorie physique?") with "What is the object of a physical theory?" ("Quel est l'objet d'une théorie physique?") This innocent-sounding slip, by

blinding him to a difference between two modes of reasoning and two
sets of norms, misled him into arguing **on a priori philosophic
grounds** that empirical investigations on the structure of matter
were bound to fail.

The bulk of the paper is devoted to an analysis of these two uses
aimed at bringing out the desiderata connoted by each. The heart of
the matter can be put in very few words, though the analysis itself
requires many. The desiderata connoted by the first use (the mention
of fields of inquiry) affect proposals on how one might compute the
answer to some questions from answers to others; the desiderata
connoted by the second use (the mention of specific propositions)
affect explanatory hypotheses.

Each use, not surprisingly, connects with the overcoming of a
specific kind of intellectual difficulty.

We experience the difficulty associated with the first use (the
mention of fields of inquiry) when we want the answer to some question but can't get it by direct means. I can't describe that difficulty
more clearly here but I may be able to show what I have in mind
through an example of how it was once overcome. A long time ago,
Erastothenes wanted to know what the radius of the earth is but
had no direct way of finding out. Digging a hole to the center and
measuring its depth was impossible. But he was able to establish
it indirectly through calculation from easily obtained lengths of two
shadows and the distance between the gnomons casting these shadows. All he needed was a bit of theory—physical geometry. That
gave him a way out of the difficulty.

Overcoming this sort of difficulty can have dramatic effects.
Mach, and many of his contemporaries, for instance, rejected particle theory for a long time as being beyond the pale of empirical
science. They assumed that particle theories of matter, even if true,
raised questions whose answers were forever blocked by insupera-
ble obstacles, and that there was in fact no reason to believe that
the theories were true if these questions were really unanswerable.
However, further developments in physics and in chemistry eventually put scientists in a position to compute the answer to some of
these questions from readily obtainable data. At that point, Mach
changed his mind. So did many of his contemporaries. And the face
of science changed dramatically. Generalized Energetics, which had
been seen by many of these skeptics as the only acceptable frame-

work for physics and chemistry almost vanished from the scene and research on particles became the norm.

The difficulty associated with the second use of *theory* (the mention of specific propositions) is the same as that associated with the notion of explanation, namely, p-predicaments. In fact, theories in this second sense turn out to be simply propositions that fall short of being explanations because they are not known to be true.

"Why-questions" is on a problem that I deliberately set aside as subsidiary in "An Approach to Explanation", namely: what conditions must correct answers to why-questions fulfill?

As I pointed out above, many contemporary philosophers of science see that as the real problem raised by the demand for explanation. There are good reasons for this. To begin with, many typical explanations turn out to be also answers to why-questions. More interestingly, why-questions, as a type of question, create issues for positivism that are reminiscent of those raised by the notion of explanation.

To see this, note that any true factual statement is easily construed as expressing the answer to some what-question. Any such statement can be mechanically transformed into a what-question and then read as an answer. So, for instance, in English (similar examples are forthcoming in other languages) *Sugar dissolves in water* can be mechanically transformed into *What does sugar dissolve in?* or into *What dissolves in water?* or into *What happens to sugar in water?* and then read as the right answer to any one of them. Thus being true is all that is required for being (or expressing) a correct answer to some what-question. And, by parity of reasoning, being well-confirmed, being probable, being plausible, is all that is required for being a well-confirmed, probable, plausible answer to some what-question. (More is, of course, required for being the correct, well-confirmed, probable, or plausible answer to this or that specific what-question: *Sugar dissolves in water* does not express any such answer to *What dissolves in alcohol?*, but that is irrelevant here.)

By contrast every true factual statement is not so easily construed as expressing the answer to some why-question. There is, for instance, no similar mechanical way of converting *Sugar dissolves in water* into a why-question whose answer is *Because sugar dissolves in water*. Being true is therefore not sufficient for being the answer to some why-question. Some additional conditions have to be met. Similar comments apply to being a well-confirmed, probable, plausible answer to a why-question. (More yet is required, of course, for being the correct, well-confirmed, probable, or plausible answer to this or that specific why-question, but that too is irrelevant here, though it is discussed at great length in "Why-questions".)

Insofar as science purports to provide factual answers to why-questions it therefore purports to be able to come up with statements that satisfy these further conditions. But what are these conditions? And, more important, are they compatible with the basic demands of empirical evidence, inductive justification, consistency, etc.? That problem is clearly akin to the problem raised in connection with the notion of explanation. So akin, as a matter of fact, that the two are easily confused.

I had a further reason for believing that an analysis of why-questions was needed. The so-called covering law model that I mentioned in connection with "An Approach to Explanation" and which was the accepted view in many circles, fails not only as an analysis of the notion of explanation, it also fails as an account of conditions on answers to why-questions. So it had to be replaced and the source of its failure (as well as its initial plausibility) had to be understood.

I became persuaded of this through a series of counterexamples which demonstrated that the covering-law model did not provide a set of sufficient conditions on answers to why-questions. The counterexamples are described in the paper itself and will not be reproduced here. The problem they create has come to be known as "the flagpole problem" because it can be illustrated with the example of a flagpole and its shadow. I am often credited with that example, and "Why-questions" is usually cited as its original source. Ironically, though I did think of the example, it appears nowhere in "Why-questions." In fact it appears in none of my published papers! It is described in papers by Hempel in which he generously recalls that I once presented him with the difficulty. "Why-questions" has obviously not been read by many people who refer to it.

The account in "Why-questions" was written with the "flagpole" and other such problems in mind. It does not represent as drastic a departure from the covering-law model as the account in "An Approach to Explanation," which is compatible with its being on a different topic. So, for instance, it entails that the covering-law model contains necessary conditions on correct answers. It basically modifies these necessary conditions so that they become sufficient ones. (The original modifications required slight further ones to meet ingenious counterexamples produced by Paul Teller and Holly Smith. The relevant places are noted in the text.) But beyond that it also identifies the premises in the covering-law model that enter into the answer, in other words, that are expressed by what follows the "because" in English.

Since why-questions include some of the clearest examples of questions that give rise to p-predicaments, their analysis falls clearly within the overall agenda of this collection. P-predicaments rank high on the difficulties that creative intelligence must overcome. The specific forms they can assume for why-questions can be particularly challenging. The paper should cast some light on why this is so.

"Questions" is not, like the previous papers, about possible conflicts between the aspirations of scientific curiosity and the constraints mandated by empiricism, but is about a possible conflict between these aspirations and the constraints imposed by language. If questions influence in a crucial way the development and assessment of scientific doctrines, then so must the interrogative **sentences**, i.e., linguistic representations, that express them. Scientific doctrines are, after all, available only through texts and can be reviewed only through words. But interrogative sentences belong to specific languages, each with its own lexicon and grammar. How can "scientific questions", that is, questions that motivate and structure scientific activities, be expressible in languages with lexicons and grammars as radically different as Japanese, English, Russian, French, modern Hebrew, etc.?

In the paper I list conditions that interrogative sentences from distinct languages must satisfy to express questions with the same scientific import. These conditions are not easily met, even by languages whose lexical structures and grammar are as similar as those of French and English!

My argument admittedly appeals to some doctrines on the syntax of interrogative questions that have become outdated. However its essential assumptions can be reformulated in current terms. I won't show how. That would take us too far afield, and any reformulation would, in any case, be soon outdated again: grammatical theory on interrogative sentences is fluid and still controversial. Furthermore, the argument assumes only that the underlying structures of wh-interrogative sentences (interrogative sentences expressed in English with *what, when, who, where,* though not necessarily *why*) mirror the underlying structure of the sentences that express their direct answers, and that assumption will probably survive in some form all changes in grammatical doctrine. And its conclusion is confirmed by the familiar observation that many fairly simple questions expressible in some language turn out not to be expressible in others.

I do not solve the conundrum in the paper. I only raise it. My intention at the time was simply to draw the attention of some erotetic logicians to it.

But I could not have offered a solution in any case. I did not know of any. And I still don't. But I now have an inkling of what is going on. Concentrating on how interrogative sentences behave in natural languages may have been a mistake. The vocabularies and grammars of natural languages (and hence the device for formulating questions in those languages) have special features responsible for the fact that such vocabularies and grammars can be acquired through mere exposure and without special pedagogic intervention. The notational devices in which scientific computations, reasoning, question raising, question answering, and communication are couched are very different. This becomes obvious when one looks at the more advanced sciences, where such devices are essentially ideographic in nature, are often not pronounceable, and are seldom tied to the phonology of any particular language. These devices almost never fit the demands of acquisition through exposure or even the requirements of spoken conversation. Nor can they be mastered without a prior natural language. They are deliberately constructed to fit the requirements of theoretical analysis, reckoning, and problem (question) setting. Unlike ordinary expressions they can survive unchanged across multiple translations of the texts in which they occur. So the conundrum may be based on an illusion. The interrogative expressions that scientists with different mother tongues use when they practice their trade are essentially the same expressions pronounced, like Church Latin perhaps, with somewhat different accents, but otherwise sharing the same syntax and semantics.

Though the problem in "Questions" may vanish on close inspection, the paper still fits my general agenda. It too relates to a type difficulty that creative scientific intelligence must overcome. Scientific reasoning and problem solving are badly served by the natural grammars and natural lexicons that constitute our native linguistic endowment. This is so, not, as some philosophers have asserted, because natural grammars and lexicons suffer from vagueness, ambiguities, lack of reference, obscurity, unclear observational grounding, etc. That is true of the most effective scientific notations as well. The trouble lies much deeper. They are not articulated to serve the needs of theorizing! And science must overcome this shortcoming. It does so by creating its own notational systems, custom-made for the tasks at hand. How it does this is best left to the study of formal systems. That it does this, however, should not be forgotten by philosophers who reach conclusions about natural languages by examining the terminology of special sciences.

"Science and the Forms of Ignorance" was written as a Thalheimer lecture for a general university audience at Johns Hopkins University. It takes up many of the ideas in "An Approach to Explanation" and of "A Theory about the Theory of Theory and about the Theory of Theories" but applies them explicitly to what I call there "the appreciation problem," i.e., the problem of elucidating the criteria that guide—or ought to guide—our acceptance and rejection of alleged scientific contributions. The paper introduces modified analyses of the notions of p-predicament, explanation, theory, and of theories, that connect these notions more directly to the ways we evaluate scientific contributions. Readers should perhaps look at that paper before turning to the previous ones. It is probably easier to read, it forgoes appeals to ordinary language, it describes explicitly the agenda served by these other papers, and it gives curiosity its due from the very outset. I need not discuss how it fits the overall agenda since it already contains a sketch of that agenda.

"Rational Ignorance", like "Questions" is not about a problem created by possible conflicts between the aspirations of curiosity and the constraints of empiricism, but between those aspirations and other constraints. The constraint that provoked this paper affects our choice of questions. No individual, and no group of individuals, can at any time undertake to find the answer to each and every possible question. That is impossible, for both practical and a priori reasons. One must confine one's curiosity to some relatively narrow range. That is life! At most one can try to select questions rationally. But how? That is the main topic of the paper.

Philosophers have given much attention to the role of rationality in the acceptance of answers (or at least of propositions that express answers) but, with some notable exceptions, they have given little thought to its role in the choice of questions. The problem may seem unreal to those who find, as I do, that happenstance beyond our control usually decides these choices for us. But when one thinks of the plethora of unanswered questions that defy us at any given moment, it becomes clear that some selection has to take place, and there is no immediate reason to think that it could not be made rationally. The problem is real, though, as I will suggest in a moment, it may have no solution.

Some questions are automatically eliminated without the need for any choice by anyone. Questions to which the answer is already known, for instance, questions whose presuppositions are known to be false, inexpressible questions, and so on. The relevant factors are detailed in the paper. These factors eliminate uncountably many questions, including some excellent ones, but also leave infinitely many.

So choices have to be made, and if these choices are to be rational, values must come into play. But what values? Prospective values of answers. The paper discusses those values, and in particular how some values are a function of the instruments and theory available at the time.

The paper raises a conundrum that I do not know how to solve. I suspect that it cannot be solved and that in actual practice rationality can at best play a limited role. One cannot choose rationally among available questions without devoting time and effort on questions about the prospective value and cost of those available questions, i.e., on second order questions. But is the time and effort required by such second order questions more rationally spent than time and effort spent on some first order questions? It is hard to see how it could be, given that the very high number of first order questions imposes a very high cost on solving the pertinent second order ones. But if it is not, rationality is apparently in conflict with itself!

So we end with one more difficulty that creative intelligence must overcome. It cannot afford to figure out how to use its resources most rationally , and yet it should use those resources most rationally.

"What We Don't Know When We Don't Know Why" returns

to the topic of why-questions, but with issues raised in "Rational Ignorance" in the forefront. The object is to see how why-questions fare under the demands for rational choosing of questions. The conclusion is that many why-questions should be shunned!

There is a old school of thought according to which hard-headed researchers should concentrate on the what and how of phenomena and avoid why-questions as obscure and ill-defined. This paper, in a qualified way, vindicates that school, but not because of general skepticism about the possible value or reliability of answers to why-questions. On the contrary! If I am right, true answers to why-questions should be prized! The trouble lies not with the answers, but with the questions. Why-questions, unlike other wh-questions, can be obscure to the point of placing one "in the very non-plussing predicament of knowing that he does not know the answer to some why-question, yet not knowing what he must find out in order to know whether there is anything to know at all!" Note that the obscurity is not simply the obscurity of not knowing the answer, nor the obscurity of being in a p-predicament, nor even the obscurity of not knowing whether the question has an answer at all! It is much deeper. It is the obscurity of not knowing what, if anything, controls whether it has an answer at all. I don't know the answer to "How many angels are dancing right now on the head of this pin?" I don't even know whether it has an answer. But at least I know what I must find out to determine whether it has an answer: whether or not there are any angels dancing on the head of this pin right now. I don't know why there are only nine large planets. I don't know whether there is an answer to that why-question. But I am even worse off than that, for I don't even know (except in the vaguest and most useless way) what stands in the way of my knowing whether it has an answer. That ignorance, by the way, can be described more picturesquely: I don't know whether there being only nine planets isn't simply a brute fact.

The paper includes a grammatical explanation of why why-questions as a class threaten us with this predicament. The account rests on a conjecture about the logical form of why-questions based on empirical evidence. Since the evidence is empirical, it is not conclusive. It rests, for instance, on a certain view about traces that could be overturned by further evidence. It also needs to be enlarged to cover languages other than English. (I have discussed the case of

French and Japanese with some colleagues and, so far, they confirm the account.) But the conclusion of the paper, in any case, does not rest on the explanation. The fact that we have experienced the predicament suffices, and we don't need a grammatical explanation to become aware of that fact.

The bearing of all this on creative intelligence is obvious: creative intelligence can, and frequently does manage to overcome the predicament. It is a mark of such intelligence (but, unfortunately, also of some forms of stupidity) not to rest satisfied with alleged brute facts. And to expose an alleged brute fact as, for instance, really the consequence of something else is surely to do much more than simply collecting another observation.

I should point out that I came to the grammatical explanation in this paper while weighing Van Fraassen's criticisms of my "Why-questions" in his *Scientific Image*. In that book Van Fraassen claims that the analysis in my "Why-questions" cannot do justice to the fact that e.g., *Why did Adam eat the apple?* can call for different answers depending on where the focus is placed. This criticism was clearly based on too hasty a reading of "Why-questions". The account there is not only fully compatible with the fact that any why-sentence can call for and countenance very different answers, it predicts that most will. However Van Fraassen also made what turns out to be a more interesting mistake by failing to note that the location of focus is a function of where stress is placed, i.e., on whether it is placed on *Adam*, *eat*, or *apple*. He assumed, probably because English orthography does not encode stress, that the inscription *Why did Adam eat the apple?* can only stand for a single grammatical object. But different placements of stress, like the topicalization of different elements, creates different grammatical objects with different semantic features. His example was not, as he thought, an example of a sentence whose form underspecifies the questions it can express, but was an example of an orthographic structure that underspecifies which sentence it encodes. His mistake led him to assign a greater role to pragmatics than the facts warrant. It led me to wonder why different placement of stress has different consequences for when-questions than for why-questions. That turns out to be the key to what is going on.

"Types and Tokens in Linguistics" unlike the previous papers is about a particular natural science, linguistics. More specifically, it is about the fact that, when taken at face value, most contributions to linguistic theory are about abstract entities (of a sort called "types") such as sentences, phrases, words, morphemes, syllables. These entities are presumably neither in space nor in time, yet can nevertheless be instantiated in space and time by perceptible things (called "tokens"). How can this be true?

Take the relation of instantiation. How does it allow inferences from facts about tokens to conclusions about types? Since linguistics is an empirical science whose evidential base consists mainly of tokens, linguists should be able to perform such peculiar inferences if their conclusions do indeed reach to types.

Or take the types themselves. Do we have any good reason to believe that there are such things? Is the notion even coherent?

Similar questions may, of course, arise in other sciences. Physics, biology, and chemistry, for instance, are often expounded as if they were about types of objects and events rather than about actual objects and events. But that is generally seen (perhaps mistakenly) as unproblematic, as an illusion caused by the need to expound at a certain level of generality. No such way out seems expected in linguistics. Types are generally considered as real and as the ultimate referents of grammatical terms. A plausible case can even be made (it is stated in the paper) that tokens could not be the referent of the categorial labels used in linguistics. But if types are not, what is left? In any case, no comfort can be gained from the fact that other sciences also seem to mention types. That by itself does not solve anything.

In the paper I offer an analysis of the notion of type, built on an analogy with the notion of chemical substances. That analysis should demystify types. Types turn out to be rather innocuous things to which only the most unimaginative nominalists should object. They are not even sets, or sequences, or mereological sums of tokens. The analysis entails that linguistics is not just about types and tokens but is also inescapably about minds. That conclusion may not be so innocuous. It will be familiar to readers of Noam Chomsky's work, but the arguments given in the paper may not be.

So far I have described "Types and Tokens in Linguistics" as if it were unrelated to the previous papers, and as if it were irrelevant to the idea that links them. It is actually closely related to these previous papers. The analytic devices on which it relies all originate in these other papers. It can thus be read as an application of these devices and, insofar as it is successful, as a vindication. It adds to the general theme by describing in specific detail the nature, variety, and interplay of intellectual devices, including taxonomies, that the practitioners of a discipline must produce to give curiosity its due.

"The Ontology of Phonology" is a paper that Morris Halle and I wrote together. Since it is a paper that I would not and could not have written by myself, it may not belong in a book that is advertised as a compendium of papers by a single author. However it supplements "Types and Tokens in Linguistics" too importantly to be kept out. Like "Types and Tokens in Linguistics" it seeks to throw light on the ultimate character of the entities that linguistics studies, but it concentrates on those mentioned in phonology, a branch of linguistics that philosophers of science and philosophers of language have so far neglected. (As we argue in a long footnote, they do so at some cost.) One view about these entities, practically taken for granted in some circles, is that they are simply those studied by articulatory and acoustical phonetics, i.e., entities individuated by articulatory or acoustical properties. That view appeals particularly to people who hold that only disciplines that use measuring instruments can be scientific. It also appeals to wielders of Occam's razor. We argue that it is false. Another view, also practically taken for granted but not necessarily in the same circles, is that these entities are abstract types. That view seems to owe its wide acceptance to its apparent indispensability. We argue that it is dispensable. Our own view is that phonology, being neither about noises, nor gymnastics, nor Platonic ideas, is about a class of occurrent intentions and occurrent mental states.

If I were to rewrite these papers, I would rewrite them very differently, particularly the early ones. I would remove redundancies and smooth out changes of mind. I would also discuss criticisms to which they have been subjected and review pertinent developments. I would, however, not change the basic theses that they advocate. But I shall not rewrite these papers. My interests have shifted away from the topics discussed in many of them, and I would rather try to break new ground during the time still left to me.

Many people mentioned in the acknowledgments that accompany the papers generously commented on early drafts and helped in other ways to improve these papers. I will not repeat their names here, but I do wish to reiterate that their help was invaluable and that I am still grateful for it. Robert Stainton gave me perceptive comments on a previous draft of this introduction. Many people also helped me at various times in less direct ways through their friendship and by sharing their knowledge. Among those I should like to mention in particular Ned Block, George Boolos, Nancy Cartwright, Richard Cartwright, Jerry Fodor, Deirdre Wilson, Ken Hale, Peter Hempel, Jaakko Hintikka, Paul Horwich, Jim Higginbotham, Jay Keyser, Howard Lasnik, David Israel, Jerrold Katz, Paul Kiparsky, Alec Marantz, Michel Meyer, Julius Moravcsik, John Perry, Bill Poser, Hilary Putnam, Susan Rothstein, Jack Smart. James Thomson and Paul Grice belong high on this list but, unfortunately, can no longer receive my thanks. I am forced to leave many names out. Having Noam Chomsky, Thomas Kuhn, and Morris Halle as close friends has been a very special blessing.

This collection was edited, proofread, and checked for mechanical errors by Nancy Bromberger. That my admiration for her professional skills is surpassed only by my love may sound like a cliché, but it is nevertheless true. I also thank Tom Burke for his skillful handling of the manuscript, and Dikran Karagueuzian, director of CSLI Publications, for his support and patience.

Aristides de Sousa Mendes, to whom I dedicate this book, was Portuguese consul in Bordeaux in June 1940. As Hitler's troops were about to occupy the city, he issued visas to hundreds of Jewish refugees, defying edicts from the Salazar government which expressly forbade issuing visas to Jews. After being removed from Bordeaux by Salazar agents, he managed to get more visas issued to a crowd of frightened refugees huddled in the rain in front of the Portuguese consulate in Bayonne. My parents, my two brothers, and I were in that crowd. Back in Portugal, Aristides de Sousa Mendes was harshly punished and, as a consequence, died in poverty. His valor in saving hundreds of lives through his defiance of vicious orders was eventually acknowledged and officially commemorated by the Portuguese government in 1986 after a long campaign by his children. That is how I became aware of what he had done for me. I never saw him, he never saw me. May this dedication help, even if only in a small way, to perpetuate the memory of his name and of his saintly deeds.

1

An Approach to Explanation

The word explanation occurs so continuously and has so important a place in philosophy, that a little time spent in fixing the meaning of it will be profitably employed. J. S. Mill

1

Philosophers of science should be able to state the truth-conditions that govern the occurrences of 'to explain' when that verb functions as in, for example,

(1)   The kinetic theory of gases explains why the state equation of vapors near condensation differs markedly from that of an ideal gas.

These truth-conditions determine what must be true of any doctrine or proposition rightly said to explain something. Thus they constitute standards that play a crucial part in the critical analysis of any alleged piece of information or theory, and their explicit formulation is needed by anyone who wishes to know in general when and how specific scientific contributions meet these standards.

What are these truth-conditions? Most answers proposed up to now strike me as missing the heart of the matter, or as being at best about quasi-technical homonyms of 'to explain'. In this essay I shall propose an answer of my own. It too has weaknesses: it is unfinished and it raises a number of problems whose solution is not available at present. I think, however, that it sets matters in the right perspective and that it provides foundations for further inquiries.

'To explain' does not always function as in (1). Consider the following two statements:

18

(2)   Someone explained to somebody how World War II might have been avoided.

(3)   Newton explained a long time ago the variations of the tides.

Statement (2), unlike (1), can generate the questions 'where?', 'when?', 'using what words?', that is, (2), unlike (1), implies the occurrence of some datable and placeable exchange of utterances. (3), on the other hand, can give rise to 'when?' but not to 'using what words?'

The truth-conditions of statements in which 'to explain' functions as in (2) or as in (3) must obviously be different from those in which it functions as in (1). They are also of less direct concern to philosophers of science. In what follows I shall nevertheless give them a good deal of attention. I shall, in fact, begin with a long discussion of statements like (2). Nothing very deep lies behind this. It happens to be a convenient way of introducing certain notions that are at the heart of my approach.

Toward the end of this essay I shall turn to 'explanation', and explain what an explanation is.

A word of caution. The verb 'to explain' and the phrase 'explanation of' are often followed by the oratio obliqua of certain questions and these questions fall naturally into groups: one can explain why, or how, and have explanations of what really happens whenever such and such, or of what causes what, and so on. Many writings ostensibly about explanation are best understood as not about explanation at all but as about what is called for by the questions belonging to one or the other of these groups. That should not be true of this paper. It is *not* about causality, or reality, or why, or how; it is about explaining and explanation and only about that.

2

Let us begin by asking what it is for someone to explain something to someone, where the "something" can be specified by means of an indirect question.[1] In other words, what are the truth-conditions common to such statements as 'John is explaining to Rosalie how

---

[1] "INDIRECT QUESTION is the grammarian's name for a modification of what was originally a question, such that it does not stand by itself as a sentence, but is treated as a noun serving, for instance, as subject or object to a verb outside of it. Thus the direct question *who are you?* indirect question, *I asked who he*

ozone differs from ordinary oxygen', 'Rudolph explained to Susan what "functor" means', 'He will explain to you what you should do'? More formally, what are the truth-conditions governing statements of the form 'A E to B W', where A and B indicate positions occupied by expressions through which a person or persons are mentioned (that is, proper names, singular descriptions of specific people or groups of people, personal pronouns, 'somebody', 'someone', etc.) where W indicates a position occupied by an indirect question, and E indicates a position taken up by a tensed form of 'to explain'.

Two things may be noted immediately: (a) Many kinds of indirect questions can occupy the position indicated by W, and they may open with a variety of interrogatives—'Why', 'How', 'Whence', 'Whither', 'What'—but not every indirect question is at home there; some would be out of place, awkward, reminiscent of Eisenhower prose, for example, 'what the distance in miles between London and Paris is' or 'whether it will rain tomorrow' or 'what time it is' or 'which sister Sam married'. A good analysis should show why some indirect questions do not sit well in these contexts.

(b) In these statements, 'to explain' functions as an accomplishment term. 'Accomplishment term' is used here in the sense given to it by Vendler (1957).[2] It indicates a place within a fourfold classification: activity terms, accomplishment terms, state terms, achievement terms. What follows is a brief account of this classification.

---

was ..." (Fowler 1954, p. 268). I shall use 'indirect question' and 'question in oratio obliqua form' interchangeably.

[2] I believe that I have reproduced the distinctions that Vendler must have had in mind when he wrote his paper, but I do not rely on his criteria. He writes "... if I say of a person that he is running a mile or of someone else that he is drawing a circle, then I do claim that the first one will keep running till he has covered the mile and that the second will keep drawing till he has drawn the circle. If they do not complete their activities, my statement will turn out to be false." This is a mistake: if either the runner or the drawer should be interrupted before finishing, the statement will not "turn out" to be false. I have tried to avoid such objections by attending to the use of the simple past. But Vendler saw what had to be seen.

Note that the rest of the discussion does not require that the classification be exhaustive. Nor does it require that a given verb or verbal phrase occur as a member of the same class in every context. 'To explain', as we shall see, does not always function as an accomplishment term. The principle at work here is analogous to that in virtue of which some verbs can be transitive in some types of contexts but intransitive in others.

The first two classes, activity terms and accomplishment terms, include all those verbs that have a continuous (progressive) present or, more exactly, those whose continuous present makes sense as the main verb in answer to 'what is x doing?', for example, 'to run', 'to eat', 'to talk', 'to lunch', 'to speak'. They are used to describe episodes that require and occupy stretches of time, stretches at any moment of which the continuous present applies. The last two classes exclude these.

The difference between activity terms and accomplishment terms is readily seen when we compare their simple past tense (perfective). Both have a simple past tense that implies that the continuous present was applicable at some moments in the past. The simple past tense of an activity term is applicable as soon as such moments have passed, and implies only the existence of such moments in the past. Aristotle walked. This implies that at some moments in the past Aristotle was walking. It does not tell us whether or not Aristotle is through walking. The simple past tense of accomplishment terms implies more. It implies that relevant activities took place in the past, but furthermore that they have come to an end. And not to a mere stop, but to a conclusion. In other words, the simple past tense of accomplishment verbs entails that something has been finished, completed, something that might, in principle, have been left unfinished, incomplete, that might have been stopped before coming to its logical end. Typical accomplishment verbs are 'to fill', 'to draw a circle', 'to write a letter', 'to die'. During the appropriate sorts of goings on, it is true that Jane is filling a pillow, Zachary is drawing a circle, Rachel is writing a letter, Socrates is dying. But to say that Jane filled the pillow, that Zachary drew a circle, that Rachel wrote a letter, that Socrates died, is to imply that all the stuffing is in, that all the points of the perimeter have been joined, that the final salutation is on paper, that he is dead. Otherwise, all that may be said is that she was filling a pillow, that he was drawing a circle, that she was writing a letter, that he was dying.

Thus accomplishment terms differ from activity terms in being associated with distinctions between what constitutes completion and what constitutes mere stopping, mere interruption. As Vendler points out, activity terms lend themselves to such questions as 'How long did so and so do such and such?', for example, 'How long did Aristotle walk?', but accomplishment terms call instead for 'How long did it take so and so to do such and such?', for example, 'How long did it take Jane to fill the pillow?'[3]

The difference between state terms and achievement terms is of less immediate relevance. Briefly, state terms (for example, 'to know', 'to love', 'to want', in their nonepisodic senses) have present indicatives that apply throughout intervals of time, and that are true of something at more than one moment even if true of it only once; achievement terms (for example, 'to win', 'to hit', 'to join', in their nonepisodic sense) have present indicatives that are true of something at one particular moment only, unless they are true of that thing more than once.

It should be clear that in 'A E to B W' contexts, 'to explain' functions as an accomplishment term: it can appear there in the continuous present; episodes filling intervals during which a continuous present applies need not but may be followed by moments at which truth demands the substitution of the simple past; finally, the use of the simple past does imply that the agent mentioned as subject of the sentence completed something.

A good analysis should therefore make explicit the nature of the completion implied by statements in 'A E to B W' form in which 'to explain' occurs in the *simple past tense;* it should bring out what must be the case for a statement in 'A explained to B W' form to be true.

Let us now turn to such an analysis. To expedite the discussion, I shall refer to episodes whose completion can be conveyed by a statement of the form 'A explain*ed* to B W' as *explaining episodes.* I shall also refer in a general way to whatever person or persons would be mentioned at A as the *tutor,* and to whatever person or persons would be mentioned at B as the *tutee* in the episode; when I speak of 'the question', I shall mean the question whose oratio obliqua form would appear at W as the complement of 'explained'.

In what follows I shall examine—and reject—a series of hypotheses. Each offers a tentative and tempting analysis. My purpose in following this procedure is twofold: to bring out negative truths that are of intrinsic interest, and to discover the conditions that an ac-

---

[3]Verbs that in isolation function as activity terms may, of course, be constituents of verbal phrases that function as accomplishment terms, for instance, 'to write', as in 'to write a letter', 'to walk' as in 'to walk to the store'.

ceptable doctrine must satisfy. Each demonstrable defect of these tentative analyses will correspond to such a negative truth and to such a condition. Confidence in the last hypothesis will have to rest to a great extent on the fact that it has none of the defects of its predecessors and that it apparently has none of its own. Some fatal flaw may of course have escaped my attention. But I can think of no procedure that will yield conclusive results here. This one has a certain advantage: If defects of the last hypothesis do eventually come to light, they will show that I stopped too soon, but they will not vitiate the negative conclusions nor invalidate the negative conditions already established.

First hypothesis: A statement of the form 'A explained to B W' is true if and only if an episode has occurred

(a) at the beginning of which the tutee did not know the right answer to the question;

(b) in the course of which the tutor presents to the tutee all the facts that he, the tutee, must know to know the right answer to the question;

(c) at the end of which the tutor has presented all the facts mentioned in (b);

(d) at the end of which the tutee knows the right answer to the question.

The hypothesis avoids the implication that in every explaining episode someone actually asks the question. This is as it should be. The truth of 'Salviati explained to Sagredo what the grounds are for saying that similar solids are to each other in the sesquilateral ratio of their surfaces' does not imply that Sagredo asked the question, though we can discover by reading the dialogue that he did.

The hypothesis nevertheless still contains unnecessary conditions. Initial ignorance on the part of the tutee is not necessary, is not implied: we all know of the father who explained to his son how babies come into the world only to be told "I knew all that; I thought that you were going to tell me something about birds and bees!" Nor is ultimate knowledge on the part of the tutee necessary: "Max explained to Alonzo what the difference is between using and mentioning a term" does not entail that Alonzo now knew, that he was convinced, or that he even paid any attention.

Eliminating (a) and (d) and rephrasing (b) and (c) as

(b′) in the course of the episode, the tutor presents the facts that
      one must know to know the right answer to the question;

(c′) at the end of the episode, the tutor has presented all the facts
      mentioned in (b′);

would avoid these unwanted implications, but it would not take care
of another objection—that the hypothesis (or its revised version)
does not provide a set of *sufficient* conditions. At twelve o'clock
yesterday, I did not know the height of the Empire State Building; I
met Henrietta, who knew and who told me "1,250 feet." Now I also
knew. This episode meets all the requirements of the first hypothesis,
but it does not rate the description 'Henrietta explained to me what
the height of the Empire State Building is'.

Of course, no episode can rate the description, 'Henrietta explained to me what the height of the Empire State Building is'.
This may suggest that the sentence is perhaps not well formed, that
it is grammatically rather than semantically deviant. The point is
not without interest since we want to know why some questions do
not function properly as direct objects of 'to explain'. However the
following two illustrations bring out that more than syntax is at
play here; they show that the same string of words is a proper direct
object of 'to explain' in some circumstances but not in others.

First illustration: maximum security prison, walls that can't be
scaled, guards in every hall, dogs, and so on. A prisoner manages
to escape by digging a tunnel. The tunnel has been found, but no
one can figure out how the dirt from the excavations was disposed
of; all the possibilities that occur to anyone have to be rejected for
one reason or another. The prisoner is now recaptured. He is made
to describe his escape. He is clearly aware of the fact that his jailers
are baffled, and in the course of his description, he reveals how he
disposed of the dirt from his tunneling.

I take it that there can be no objection to saying that the prisoner
explained to his jailers (in the course of his account) how he disposed
of the dirt from his tunneling.

Second illustration: similar jail, similar escape, but in this case
it is easy to see how the prisoner may have disposed of the dirt; he
may have dropped it into the moat under his window, or he may
also have carried it out in his pocket to a garden where he was not

closely watched. But still, the jailers do not *know* how the prisoner disposed of the dirt, whether he used the moat or his pockets. The prisoner is recaptured, made to describe his escape, and he reveals how he disposed of the dirt (the moat) from his tunneling.

Here, as in the previous example, the conditions of the first hypothesis are satisfied, but I take it that 'The prisoner explained to his jailers how he disposed of the dirt from his tunneling' is out of place, distorts things, smacks of exaggeration, is at best a near truth.

It would not do, of course, to say simply that the prisoner did not explain to his jailers how he disposed of the dirt from his tunnel, and to let it go at that. This would suggest that he refused to explain, or failed to explain, or prevaricated, or perhaps did not address himself to the question at all. Normally some such thing is conveyed by the explicit denial that someone explained something on some specific occasion. Thus in the present instance that sort of denial would be misleading. The description does not apply, but neither does its denial. Not an unusual situation; one does not want to say simply that the Empire State Building is not happy, for this would suggest that it is melancholy. But one can't say that it is happy either.

Admittedly, the statement that in the second illustration the prisoner explained how he disposed of the dirt from his tunneling ceases to be glaringly odd when one limits one's mental picturing to the scene in which the prisoner describes his escape; more of the epistemic background must be kept in mind, that is, that what was said, though informative, merely settled for the audience *which* of the means of which it was already aware had actually been used, and that the prisoner realized this.

It should not come as a surprise that the first hypothesis is inadequate. A correct perspective on the nature of explaining episodes would reveal the difference between what is conveyed by statements of the form 'A explained to B W' and statements of the form 'A told B W'. The first hypothesis would obliterate that difference.

The first hypothesis requires that what the tutor tells the tutee be true. However, there is such a thing as explaining incorrectly, and a report that little Suzy explained to her brother what little girls are made of does not imply that what she said is true. Seen in this light, the requirement may seem uncalled for, but this would be an illusion. Statements of the form 'A explained to B W' *do* imply that the tutee was given correct information. The addition of 'incorrectly' does not add a detail that could have been left unspecified without affecting the truth of the statement; it *qualifies* the whole statement, and has the force of a partial denial: to have explained incorrectly is *not* to have explained, but to have been engaged in something akin to it. The same effect can be achieved through ironic, or sarcastic, or condescending, intonation.

Admittedly, statements of the form 'A explained to B W' are open to strict and to loose usage. Strictly, they imply that the tutor uttered verities. But one does not have to know that he did, to use such a statement; it is enough to assume that he did, and a loose usage even allows the tutor's views about the truth of what he said to prevail over those of the user. It does not rule out such statements even when the latter believes that what the tutor told the tutee was false. Such usage, however, is apt to mislead when one's listener does not know better.

The hypothesis also entails that the question itself must be sound, that is, must have a correct answer. Here too there is a strict and a loose usage. The former rules out questions that are based on false presuppositions, the latter countenances them. 'Max explained to Alonzo why the Gödel Incompleteness Theorem is of no epistemological significance' would normally commit the user of the sentence to the view that the Gödel Theorem is of no epistemological significance: the statement, unless qualified, implies this. Implications of this kind are stillborn whenever speaker and listener agree, and know that they agree, that the question is unsound.[4]

P-predicament

The statement of the second hypothesis must be postponed until the term 'p-predicament',[5] needed for its formulation, has been introduced.

Consider the following two questions:

---

[4]The discussion from here on will be limited to the strict usage. The looser usage is best handled after the analysis of the strict usage, but I will ignore it altogether as of little interest.

[5]The p of 'p-predicament' may be thought of as standing for 'puzzled' or 'perplexed', but mnemonically only. As will become obvious, one need not be either puzzled or perplexed to be in a p-predicament. (In more current terms, statements of the form 'A explained to B W' entail that the tutor held W to be sound and his answer to be true; they implicate, in Grice's sense, that the user agrees.)

(4)   What is the height of Mt. Kilimanjaro?

(5)   Why do tea kettles emit a humming noise just before the water begins to boil?

I know the answer to neither. However I am not equally ignorant with regard to both. This is brought out to some extent by the fact that I am prepared to say that *I do not understand* why tea kettles emit a humming noise just before the water begins to boil, whereas I am not prepared to say anything of the sort about what the height of Mt. Kilimanjaro is. We will say that I am in a p-predicament with regard to (5) but not with regard to (4).

What is the difference?

I take (4) to be a sound question, that is, to admit of a right answer,[6] to rest on no mistaken assumptions or false presuppositions; there is such a thing as Mt. Kilimanjaro, and it is the sort of thing that has a height. I also believe the following about the answer: (a) it can be put as a number followed by a unit of length; (b) if given in feet, the number must lie between 100 and 30,000; (c) if not in feet, then the number must be such that conversion into an equivalent number of feet would yield a number between 100 and 30,000; and (d) the number could be obtained through certain measuring operations that need not be described here. These conditions on the answer, even when combined with my other beliefs, do not uniquely determine an answer to (4); acceptance of them does not settle the question for me. But acceptance of them does require that I consider a number of expressions as not possibly being formulations of the right answer. These make up a varied lot: '12 feet', 'I don't know', 'Look it up in the encyclopedia', 'Morton White', '19,321 lbs', and so on.[7] Still, I can think of many expressions which do not

---

[6]Throughout this discussion, 'right answer' must be understood somewhat narrowly. I am using 'right answer to Q' (where Q is a question) to cover a possible reply to Q if and only if a statement of the form 'A told B W' (where W must be thought of as replaced by the oratio obliqua of Q, and A and B by expressions through which two persons are mentioned) would be true of any episode in which the reply had been given by the person mentioned at A in response to the asking of Q by the person mentioned at B. This excludes such possibly "correct" answers as 'I don't know.' Certain questions do not admit of a right answer, such as, 'Who is the present king of France?'

[7]Significant distinctions exist among the expressions that I must reject. The first three would, under most circumstances, count as replies when uttered in response to an utterance of (4), but very special circumstances are called for in

belong in that lot, such as, '15,000 feet', '8,000 feet', '3 kilometers', and others.

I also take (5) to be a sound question: tea kettles do emit a humming noise just before the water in them begins to boil. I have views about its answer too: (a) it must be statable in the form of a sentence or conjunction of sentences preceded by the word 'because'; (b) this sentence or conjunction of sentences must include—perhaps among other things—a description of something that actually happens when water is about to begin boiling; and (c) this description must entail that on each such occasion something causes air to vibrate with an amplitude, frequency, and overtones corresponding to the loudness, pitch, and quality of the noise in question. As before, the conditions do not add up to an answer, even when supplemented with my other beliefs. Acceptance of them again requires that I reject a number of expressions as incapable of being formulations of the right answer. These too make up a varied lot: 'Because Cleopatra had a short nose', 'I don't know', 'Look it up in the encyclopedia', 'Ruth Otto', '19,321 feet'. But this time I am unable to conceive of any others—I can think of nothing, I can imagine nothing, I can conjure up nothing, I can invent nothing, I can remember nothing, that can survive confrontation with what I take to be conditions on the right answer. And this is clearly a consequence not only of the character of those conditions but also of the limits of my intellectual repertoire.

To recapitulate: (i) I take both (4) and (5) to be sound questions, to admit of a right answer.

(ii) I know, or believe I know, enough about each answer to be able to eliminate a number of possible utterances, that is, of expressions, as not being formulations of the answer.

(iii) In the case of (4), I can think of some possible utterances that I cannot eliminate in this way.

(iv) In the case of (5), I can think of no expression[8] that I cannot eliminate in this way.

---

the case of the last two. Furthermore, as a reply to (4) the first must convey a falsehood, the second may convey a truth, the third can convey neither a truth nor a falsehood. These distinctions are not relevant to our present purpose.

   [8] "Can think of no expression" and "can think of no answer" (as short for "can imagine nothing, conjure up nothing, invent nothing, remember nothing, conceive nothing …") do not cover the familiar states of momentary amnesia during which one has the answer "on the tip of one's tongue" but cannot utter it.

Let us say of anyone who stands with regard to any question Q in the relation in which I stand to (5) that he (she, they) is (are) in a p-predicament with regard to the question Q. In other words, *A is in a p-predicament with regard to Q if and only if, on A's views, Q admits of a right answer, but A can think of no answer to which, on A's views, there are no decisive objections.*

'A is in a p-predicament with regard to Q' is a neologism, but the meaning of each statement of that form is intimately related to the meaning of some statement of the form 'A does not understand q', with q replaced by the oratio obliqua form of the question mentioned at Q. Any statement of the form 'I am in a p-predicament with regard to Q' implies and is implied by the corresponding 'I do not understand q'. In other words, the two kinds of statements are interchangeable when the person speaking is the person spoken about. The relation is a little more complicated when the speaker is not the person spoken about. In those cases 'A is in a p-predicament with regard to Q' should convey what would be conveyed by an 'I do not understand q' uttered by the person mentioned at A—with one difference to be specified in a moment—but need not convey what would be conveyed by the corresponding 'A does not understand q'. This is a consequence of the following:

(a) Any 'A does not understand q' implies that the question alluded to at q is sound. Thus its use by anyone conveys (pragmatically implies) that the user believes the question to be sound. Its cognate 'A is in a p-predicament with regard to Q' does not imply that the question is sound, but only that it is sound on the views of the person mentioned at A; its use by anyone should therefore not convey that the user takes the question to be sound (except for a first-person A). In other words, the meaning of 'A does not understand q' requires that the opinion of the user concerning the soundness of the question be dominant, but the meaning of 'A is in a p-predicament with regard to Q' requires that the views of the person mentioned, about matters relevant to the soundness of the question, be dominant.

(b) An 'A does not understand q' statement may be used to report or describe situations in which *either* (1) none of the answers that the person mentioned at A can conceive is an answer that that person can accept—and this includes situations in which the person spoken about can conceive of the right answer, but cannot accept it in the

light of his or her other beliefs—*or* (2) none of the answers that the
person mentioned at A can conceive is the right answer—and this
includes situations in which that person can conceive of one or more
answers that he or she can consistently accept. These statements
are thus marked by an ambiguity, and demand contextual clues that
indicate whose conditions on the answer are at play, the speaker's
or those of the person spoken about. 'A is in a p-predicament with
regard to Q' suffers from no such ambiguity; it refers only to the
sort of situations described under (1) above, that is, the meaning is
such as to require that the relevant beliefs of the person mentioned
at A be dominant. Here too the difference vanishes when the person
spoken about is the person speaking.

An illustration will fix these two points. Neither Sam nor Rebecca know or think they know the answer to 'How did God make
Eve, a whole human being, from just one bone?' Rebecca, a pure
but simple soul, knows of no reason for dismissing the view that He
first broke Adam's rib in as many pieces as He needed parts for her
body, that He then stretched and shaped each of these into one of
these parts, that He next assembled them into the well-known con-
figuration, and that He finally blew life into the whole. Sam cannot
accept this answer. He knows about the principle of conservation
of matter, about the differences in chemical composition of muscles,
hair, bones, skin, nerves, stomach, appendix. But he cannot think
of anything that he would find acceptable. Max the atheist would
reject the whole question. Sam would be right in saying that he
himself is in a p-predicament with regard to the above question, and
it would make sense for Max (or anyone else) to say that Sam is
in a p-predicament with regard to the question, even though Max
could not rightly say that Sam does not understand how God created
Eve. But Sam, or Max, or Rebecca (or anyone else for that matter)
would be mistaken in saying that Rebecca is in a p-predicament with
regard to the question, since she can think of at least one possibility that she need not reject. Nevertheless, Sam would be correct
in saying that she does not understand how God created Eve. No
one should say that Max is in a p-predicament with regard to the
question.

There is one respect in which an 'A is in a p-predicament with
regard to Q' statement not made by the person mentioned at A
conveys less than its cognate 'I do not understand q' when uttered

by that person. The latter statement conveys that that person knows or believes that he or she does not understand q, but the former does not entail that the subject knows or believes that he or she is in a p-predicament with regard to Q, and could not convey it.

Being in a p-predicament with regard to a question may sound like greater ignorance than merely not knowing the answer. It isn't. Being in a p-predicament usually calls for more learning than does mere ignorance. Sam would not be in a p-predicament with regard to 'How did God make Eve?' had he not studied chemistry. It was once suggested to me that the noise emitted by tea kettles just before the water begins to boil might come from surface vibrations set off by air bubbles released before vapor bubbles begin to form. For a while thereafter I was not in a p-predicament with regard to 'Why do tea kettles emit a humming noise just before the water begins to boil?' Since then I have had occasion to observe the phenomenon a little more closely, and I have satisfied myself that these air bubbles are too small and too few to account for the noise in question. I would not be in a p-predicament today had I not learned these facts. Or again, I am not in a p-predicament with regard to 'What is the relation between the Debye temperature θ and the temperature at which the atomic heat of a solid element is equal to 3R/2?' I hardly know enough to understand the question; the only condition I associate with it is that the answer must be statable as a mathematical function of θ, but I can construct indefinitely many of those![9]

Second hypothesis: A statement of the form 'A explained to B W' is true if and only if an episode has occurred

---

[9] All my examples have been homespun cases. To lend dignity and significance to this discussion it would no doubt be better to use illustrations taken from the history of science. I have not done this because the analysis required to show that some scientist was in a p-predicament with regard to some question at some time would be very long and very complex: it would demand an examination of theoretical background, available evidence, implicit assumptions, and the like. But it is obvious that there have been times in the history of science when scientists were in a p-predicament with regard to some question, for example, when a maximum height to which water can be pumped was known but the concept of atmospheric pressure had not yet been discovered; when the mathematical representation of energy distribution for black body radiators was known but the quantum hypothesis had not been thought of or admitted; when the Michelson and Morley results were known but the Special Theory of Relativity had not been advanced, and so on.

(a) at the time of which the tutor knows the right answer to the question;[10]

(b) at the beginning of which the tutee was in a p-predicament with regard to the question;

(c) at the beginning of which the tutee thought of himself as in a p-predicament with regard to the question;

(d) during which the tutor knows, or believes, or at least assumes that, at the beginning of the episode, the tutee was in a p-predicament with regard to the question;[11]

(e) in the course of which the tutor presents the facts that in his opinion the tutee must learn to know the right answer to the question;

(f) at the end of which all the facts mentioned in (e) have been presented to the tutee by the tutor;

(g) at the end of which the tutee knows the right answer, and knows it as a result of, and in virtue of what he has been told by the tutor in the course of the episode.

Some of these clauses obviously do not stand for necessary conditions. (b) and (g) would require initial ignorance and ultimate knowledge of the right answer by the tutee. This is uncalled for, as we saw in the comments to the first hypothesis. But (c) and (d) are not necessary either. (c) too implies initial ignorance of the right answer. (d) (and incidentally (c)) would imply that the following correct account is incorrect. Until the age of five I was convinced that babies grew in cabbages. My older brother knew this about me, and on my fifth birthday, as a present, he told me the facts of life; on that day he *explained* to me how babies come into the world. At the age of four, I was not, nor did I think myself to be,

---

[10]This implies of course that the question must have a right answer.

[11]'Assumes' throughout this discussion must carry a heavy load. To assume may simply be to take for granted. It may be something else. When I give an examination to my students, I always tell them to assume that they are writing for someone who knows nothing about the subject; but I do not want them to take for granted that I know nothing about the subject. I always assume that they know very little philosophy when I prepare a lecture for them, though I often have no strong convictions on this. 'To assume' is thus sometimes 'to go on the assumption that'. It can also be 'to take for granted' *and* 'to go on the assumption that'. In stating these hypotheses, I have assumed that 'to assume' may do the job of a disjunction of all these possibilities.

in a p-predicament with regard to 'How do babies come into the world?' since I had an answer, though admittedly a false one. My brother knew this about me, and the statement that he explained to me how babies come into the world does not imply the contrary, that is, it does not imply that he thought or assumed that I would not have been able to come up with an answer compatible with my total set of beliefs. This is in general true of statements of the form 'A explained to B W'. They do not imply that the tutor (or tutee) believed or assumed that the tutee would have been or should have been puzzled (in a p-predicament way) by the question before the explaining episode.

If we eliminate all these conditions, however, we are left with (a), (e)—'learn' being perhaps replaced by 'learn or know'—and (f), a set enough like the revised first hypothesis to be recognized immediately as not sufficient.

On the other hand, this hypothesis in its original form, unlike the first one, does seem to provide a set of sufficient conditions. I don't know how one can prove this. My own conviction on the matter rests on the fact that I am unable to construct any illustration that meets these seven clauses yet is not an explaining episode. It helps, in this connection, to look at the counterexamples showing the insufficiency of the previous hypothesis.

The first counterexample, it will be recalled, consisted of an episode in which I was told the height of the Empire State Building, something I had not known before, but knew thereafter. But 'What is the height of the Empire State Building?' is not a question with regard to which I was or could have been believed to be in a p-predicament (the same, by the way, is true of 'What is the height of Mt. Kilimanjaro?').

The second example was an episode in which a prisoner told how he had disposed of the tunneled dirt, and, in effect, settled in the mind of his audience which of a number of obvious methods he had actually used. Here again the tutee, that is, his audience, was neither known nor thought to be in a p-predicament with regard to the question. This illustration was contrasted at the time with another one, in many respects similar, but which was clearly recognizable as an explaining episode, that is, as properly describable by an 'A explained to B W' statement. The latter episode, notice, does satisfy the present hypothesis.

The present hypothesis has a minor virtue that may strengthen
its prima facie plausibility as a set of sufficient conditions. The
etymology of a word, we have frequently been told, often provides
the key to the analysis of its meaning. The origins of 'to explain'
and of its French cousin *expliquer* go back to expressions used to
speak of making smooth by removing folds and wrinkles. But what
were these ancestral folds and wrinkles? The literature contains a
number of suggestions. In *La Théorie Physique*, Pierre Duhem offers
the following one: "To explain [expliquer], *explicare*, is to strip reality
of the appearances in which it is wrapped as in veils, in order to see
this reality naked and face to face." There is a more Lockean[12] and
more plausible possibility compatible with a more modest reality.
The second hypothesis would support it. People who contemplate
a question with regard to which they are in a p-predicament are
prone to frounce their foreheads, to screw up their faces, to knit
their brows, and they usually shed most of these folds and wrinkles
and present a smoother countenance upon being told the answer.
We know that one who remedies a p-predicament often explains in
this sense which, if original, is now obsolete. Is this account correct?
Perhaps not. (And yet ... the first quotation under 'to explain' in
the O.E.D. is: "He must caulm and explain his forehead," 1569; and
the second reads "Their faces are explained and flattered by art,"
1650.) For our purpose, that does not really matter. It is enough if
the account reminds us that sentences of the form 'A explained W to
B' are aptly chosen to report episodes in which a tutor turns someone
who could truly have said 'I don't understand W' into someone in
a position to assert 'I know W', and if it provides the occasion for
seeing that the hypothesis does justice to this fact.

All this suggests that the clauses making up the second hypothesis should perhaps be divided into three classes: first, some that are
necessary conditions, (a), (e), and (f); second, some that are totally
dispensable, (b), (c), and (g); and third, one that is not necessary by

---

[12] "It may also lead us a little towards the original of all our notions and
knowledge, if we remark how great a dependence our words have on common
sensible ideas: and how those which are made use of to stand for actions and
notions quite removed from sense, have their rise from thence, and from obvious
sensible ideas are transferred to more abstruse significations, and made to stand
for ideas that come not under the cognizance of our senses; ..." John Locke,
Essay Concerning Human Understanding, Book III, chap. 1, sec. 5.

itself but is a member of a set of conditions whose *disjunction is* a necessary condition, (d).

At the beginning of this discussion I pointed out that a good analysis of explaining episodes should show why some indirect questions are out of place as direct objects of 'to explain'. An account could be built on the second hypothesis. That account would not rest on any of the "totally dispensible" clauses listed above, and may therefore be part of the truth. To the extent to which it strikes one as such, it will confirm my suggestion that the present hypothesis is a disjunct of the truth that we are after. I will therefore give a rough sketch of that account.

Indirect questions beginning with 'whether'. These represent questions whose right answers must be either 'yes' or 'no'. But no tutee can be thought to be in a p-predicament with regard to such a question. If the views held by him require that he reject both 'yes' and 'no' as each violating some belief or assumption of his, then he cannot take the question to be sound, to admit of a right answer. But then he cannot be in a p-predicament with regard to the question either, since one can only be in a p-predicament with regard to questions that one can consistently think of as having a right answer. On the other hand, if he is not compelled to reject both 'yes' and 'no', he cannot be in a p-predicament either. Could a tutee be in a situation in which he can think of 'yes' (and have to reject it) but not of 'no', or vice versa? Perhaps, but then the question is one that he does not understand, and indefinitely many answers will be open to him. In the case of these indirect questions, then, nothing corresponds to the sort of knowledge or belief or assumption called for in (d) and the conditions of the hypothesis cannot be satisfied.

Indirect questions beginning with, for example, 'What is the height of ... ?', 'What is the weight of ... ?', 'What is the distance between ... ?', that is, questions calling for an answer expressible in the form of a number and a unit of measurement. A tutee who knows or thinks he knows the form of the answer and who knows or thinks he knows appropriate units of measurement must either reject every number, in which case he cannot take the question to be sound, or there is some number that he does not have to reject. But how could he be in a p-predicament in the latter case? To be able to conjure up further answers he need only be able to generate numbers. One *can* imagine situations in which a tutor believes that he is dealing with a partly educated tutee unable to count, yet able to reject the possibilities that would occur to him. But in those cases, if the conditions of the hypothesis are satisfied, an 'A explained to B what ...' would be true. And in the others (d) could not be satisfied. In the remaining cases, where the tutee does not think that he knows the form of the answer, he is in a situation analogous to the one that I described as mine with regard to the question about the Debye temperature, and thus not in a p-predicament because in no position to reject possibilities apt to occur to him. If the tutor believes that this is the situation, (d) is not satisfied. One can also imagine cases where the tutee is thought of as in a position to reject every kind of unit of which he is aware but as not aware of the right kind of unit. In those cases, however, 'A explained to B W' statements will be true, if the conditions of the hypothesis are all satisfied.

Indirect questions beginning with 'which'. These represent interrogatives that open with the word 'which'. An interrogative sentence beginning with the word 'which' is not the formulation of a question unless and until it becomes associated with a specific set of alternatives that include the right answer, if any. Anyone thought to be in a position to have views on the soundness of the question must also be thought to know the members of that set. But then (d) cannot be satisfied. The tutor must either believe that the tutee should reject every member of the relevant set and ipso facto should reject the question itself as without correct answer, or the tutor must believe that one alternative at least is an open possibility on the views of the tutee. Either belief rules out thinking that the tutee is in a p-predicament with regard to that question.

B-predicament

The third hypothesis too requires the introduction of a new phrase, 'being in a b-predicament with regard to a question'. A statement of the form 'A is in a b-predicament with regard to Q' (in which A must be replaced by an expression referring to some person or persons, and Q by one referring to some question) is true if and only if the question mentioned in it admits of a right answer, but that answer is beyond what the person mentioned can conceive, can think of, can imagine, that is, is something that that person cannot remember, cannot excogitate, cannot compose.

My position with regard to 'Why do tea kettles emit a humming noise just before the water begins to boil?' can be used to bring out the difference between a p-predicament and a b-predicament. I am in a p-predicament with regard to that question. I am also in a b-predicament with regard to it, since I am unable to think of the right answer. However there was a time when I was in a b-predicament with regard to the question *without* being at the same time in a p-predicament with regard to it, when I was able to entertain 'because the surface of the water is made to vibrate by escaping air bubbles that form before vapor bubbles do' as possibly the correct answer. Note that it is also possible to be in a p-predicament with regard to a question *without* at the same time being in a b-predicament with regard to it. This is the case when someone is in a p-predicament with regard to a question that in fact admits of no right answer. It is also the case when someone rejects the correct answer to a question with regard to which he is in a p-predicament. Such would be my situation if the air-bubble theory were correct. Such was Kepler's situation with regard to 'What is the shape of planetary orbits?' while he refused to admit the possibility of elliptical paths.[13]

Third hypothesis: A statement of the form 'A explained to B W' is true if and only if an episode has occurred

(a) at the time of which the tutor knows the right answer to the question;

(b) during which the tutor knows, or believes, or at least assumes that at the beginning of the episode, the tutee was in a b-predicament;

(c) in the course of which the tutor presents the facts that, in his opinion, the tutee must learn to know the right answer to the question;

(d) at the end of which all the facts mentioned in (c) have been presented to the tutee by the tutor.

---

[13]'A is in a b-predicament with regard to Q' is in some respects closer to 'A does not understand W' than is 'A is in a p-predicament with regard to Q'. It requires a sound question. Its truth is independent of the opinions held by the person mentioned concerning the soundness of the question or concerning the conditions that the right answer must satisfy. Notice, however, that 'A is not in a b-predicament with regard to Q' unlike 'A understands W' does not require that the question be sound.

This hypothesis includes or implies none of the clauses shown so far to stand for conditions that are not necessary conditions. It does not require initial ignorance or ultimate knowledge of the answer by the tutee, and it does not require that the tutor think the tutee to have been in a p-predicament at the beginning of the episode.[14]

Like the second hypothesis, the third seems to be a set of sufficient conditions. Again, I can't prove this, but again I am unable to construct a case that meets the requirements of the hypothesis but is not an explaining episode. Those that brought out insufficiency before won't do so here. I was not nor could I have been believed to be in a b-predicament with regard to 'What is the height of the Empire State Building?' Our prisoner while the protagonist in a nonexplaining episode was addressing an audience that was not, and was not thought to be, in a b-predicament with regard to the question. But his audience was believed to be in a b-predicament (as well as a p-predicament) in the explaining episode. Furthermore, the illustration showing that (d) of the second hypothesis is not a necessary condition, satisfies the conditions of the present hypothesis: my brother knew that I was in a b-predicament with regard to 'How do babies come into the world?'

Speculative etymology may stir the relevant intuitions here too. The prototypic folds should now be brought to mind by the story of the excitable Frenchman who, when shown an oldfashioned telephone requiring the earpiece to be held in one hand and the mouthpiece in the other, protested: "Mais alors, comment s'explique-t-on?" Words often seem too weak to cure a b-predicament, gestures seem called for, unfoldings of arms, openings of hands. These may have been the original topic of 'A E to B W' descriptions! The O.E.D. fails us at this point, but not completely; under 'To explicate' we find "When he intendeth his business to purpose, then he standeth upon his feet, explicateth and displayeth his limbs" (1620).

This hypothesis, too, will support an account of why some indirect questions are out of place as direct object of 'to explain'. Its

---

[14]Someone in a b-predicament with regard to a question cannot know the answer to that question, but (b) is phrased to allow for explaining episodes at the beginning of which tutees do know the answer. (c) and (d) furthermore are phrased to allow for explaining episodes in which tutors exert themselves in vain, are not understood, are not listened to attentively, etc., that is, explaining episodes at the end of which the tutee still does not know the answer.

outlines are readily drawn; the details would get us into the arid territory of erotetic logic.

Indirect questions beginning with 'whether'. To believe that someone is in a b-predicament with regard to a question whose right answer must be either 'yes' or 'no' is to believe that someone is incapable of thinking of either 'yes' or 'no'. This is not merely to believe or to assume that the person is unable to accept, or to conceive of himself as accepting either 'yes' or 'no' as the correct answer; it is in effect to impute to that person the inability to come up with the thought of 'yes' or 'no' as even the wrong answer. On the present hypothesis, an 'A E to B whether ...' statement cannot be true unless some tutor (i) believed or assumed some tutee to be that colossally dull and yet (ii) undertook to convey information to that tutee. But (i) and (ii) are pragmatically incompatible: the occurrence of (ii) would establish the falsehood of (i). Thus the conditions of the hypothesis cannot be met in these cases.

Indirect questions like 'What is the height of ... ?' 'What is the weight of ... ?', that is, indirect questions calling for a number followed by a unit of measurement. The cases involving units of measurement familiar to practically everyone can be dealt with in the same way as indirect questions beginning with 'whether'. The fact that a tutor undertakes to inform a tutee is prima facie evidence that he does not believe or assume that one specific combination of a number and an obvious unit of measurement surpasses what the tutee can conceive. Normally the conditions of the hypothesis are not fulfilled.

The cases involving less familiar dimensions and less familiar units are a little more complicated. Indirect questions standing for questions of that sort *can* serve as direct object of 'to explain'. Their aptness in that role depends, however, on how much the tutor tells the tutee. Thus

(6)   Picard explained to Mme. Rouge what the difference of potential between the poles of his car battery is.

is not warranted if Picard merely said to Mme. Rouge, "The difference of potential between the two poles of my battery is six volts." But then that would be prima facie evidence that (b), (c), and (d) are not satisfied. But (6) is *not* unwarranted if Picard presented Mme. Rouge with a lengthier exposition, one designed to convey not only the sound of the answer, but its meaning as well, that is, designed to put her in possession of notions not previously in her intellectual repertoire. This too is compatible with the hypothesis.

Indirect questions beginning with 'which'. To hold that a tutee is in a b-predicament with regard to a question beginning with 'which' a tutor would have to assume that the tutee associates with it the same set of alternatives that he does: these alternatives are part of the very identity of the question. The tutor would also have to assume that one of those alternatives is the right answer. It is therefore impossible for a tutor to believe or to assume that some tutee is in a b-predicament with regard to such a question.

Even so, the third hypothesis cannot be a set of necessary conditions. Consider the following example:

I am the Dr. Watson to some Sherlock Holmes. Yesterday morning we were called to investigate a crime. The body was found in a room with a fireplace, two windows, one door. According to irrefutable evidence, the doors and the windows were locked from the inside, by the victim, before he was killed, and were not touched again until investigators entered the room. The chimney is too narrow to allow the passage of a grown man. Walls, floor, and ceiling have been checked; there are no secret doors, no hidden outlets. The victim did not commit suicide: he was killed by a bullet in the head, was not wearing gloves, and the fingerprints on the gun do not match his.

How did the assassin leave the room?

All day yesterday I was in a p-predicament with regard to that question. The only answers that occurred to me were ones that I was forced to reject: through the door, the north window, the south window, the chimney, the floor, the ceiling, the walls.

At dinner time, my Sherlock Holmes, who knew my condition, explained to me how the assassin had left the room: through the chimney. He was a midget, small enough and slender enough to get through it.

This counterexample does not come as a surprise. The third hypothesis cannot be a set of necessary conditions if the second hypothesis is a set of sufficient ones, since these two hypotheses can be independently satisfied. The midget case is merely an explaining episode that accords with the second but not with the third. But it confirms the hunch that the final doctrine must contain a disjunctive clause.

Fourth and Last Hypothesis: The essential characteristics of explaining episodes are the following:

(a) the question is sound, that is, admits of a right answer;

(b) the tutor is rational and knows the right answer to the question at the time of the episode;

(c) during the episode the tutor knows, or believes, or at least assumes that at the beginning of the episode the tutee was in a p-predicament with regard to the question, or that at the beginning of the episode the tutee was in a b-predicament with regard to the question, or that at the beginning of the episode the tutee was in either a p-predicament or b-predicament with regard to the question;

(d) in the course of the episode the tutor presents the facts that in his opinion the tutee must learn to know the right answer to the question;

(e) in the course of the episode the tutor also provides the tutee with such instruction as he (the tutor) thinks necessary to remove the basis of whichever of the states mentioned in (c) he deems the tutee to be in;

(f) at the end of the episode all the facts mentioned in (d) and (e) have been presented to the tutee by the tutor.

I have expressed this hypothesis in the material mode, and have included three clauses, that is, (a) and (c) and (f), that are superfluous since (a) is implied by (b), and (c) and (f) by (d) and (e). I have chosen the material mode because the hypothesis concerns more than our understanding of an English verb.[15] The superfluous clauses are apt to be overlooked and deserve an explicit statement.

A word about (e). It excludes from the class of explaining

---

[15]There is another reason for using the material mode. Put in the formal mode, this hypothesis provides only truth-conditions for statements in the form 'A explained to B W', that is, with 'to explain' in the simple past tense. But we are interested in all 'A E to B W' statements, regardless of the tense of the verb. Extending the above conditions to include cases with other tenses would require the discussion and resolution of difficult problems about the relationship among truth-conditions of statements in every respect alike but for the tense of the verb. The use of the material mode should enable us to visualize the relevant points in a way that is adequate for present purposes; for example, the continuous present is applicable while an explaining episode is going on, the past tenses if it took place in the past, the future tenses if it is to take place, and so on.

episodes those episodes in which the tutor provides no more information than might have been put in the form 'The answer to Q is …', for instance, 'The answer to "How did the assassin leave the room?" is "through the chimney".' In one sense, such statements, if true, contain all that one has to learn to know the answer to the question. But they cannot make up the total substance of explaining episodes.

It is easier to indicate what (e) excludes than to indicate what it is designed to include. A fully adequate treatment of what is involved would take us far afield. I shall evoke the relevant facts through illustrations.

Picard, in a previous example, it will be recalled, knew or believed, or at least assumed, that Mme. Rouge was in a b-predicament with regard to the question 'What is the potential difference between the two poles of Picard's car battery?' How could he know, or believe, or assume this? He knew that the answer has to be expressed in volts. He also knew that 'volt' is what some have called a 'theory laden term', that is, he knew that before one can understand the term 'volt' one must become aware of certain phenomena and of principles, concepts, ideas, and facts used to represent, to reason about, and to record these phenomena. He furthermore knew or believed, or at least assumed that Mme. Rouge did not possess the background just alluded to, that she had never acquired the modicum of factual and theoretical knowledge required to understand 'volt'. He assumed that she could not have conjured up the answer because he assumed that she literally did not have the concepts that she would have had to have. The basis of her alleged b-predicament with regard to the question presumably went deeper than mere ignorance of the words needed to formulate the answer; to remove it Picard had to enlarge her conceptual repertoire, that is, he had to teach her some elements of electricity.

Removal of the basis of a b-predicament or p-predicament with regard to a question will in general require instructions about matters not covered by a mere statement of the answer, but the above example ought not to mislead us into thinking that it always requires *theoretical* instruction. Remember how my brother, on my fifth birthday, removed the basis of my b-predicament. Even less theory will often do. Picard does not know who the author of *De Fabrica* was. He is in no position to think of the answer because he has never heard of Vesalius. To remove the basis of his b-predicament with regard to 'Who was the author of *De Fabrica?*' one must do more than give him the name of the author; to explain to him who the author of *De Fabrica* was one must tell him who Vesalius was. But this demands no abstract principles or theoretical notions. Or consider the case of someone assumed to be in a p-predicament but *not* in a b-predicament with regard to some question. I was in a p-predicament with regard to 'How did the assassin leave the room?' because I took it for granted that the culprit was a full-sized, normal human being. The correct answer was ruled out for me by a false assumption. In all such cases removal of the basis of the p-predicament requires instructions that lead one to *revise* one's views. (Einstein had to do something of the sort when he explained why no interference pattern had been observed by Michelson and Morley. In his episode theory had to be expounded, but not so in that of Holmes.) Holmes would not have explained how the assassin had left the room had he merely said 'through the chimney', but the additional information was short and pedestrian.

What is to be said in behalf of this fourth hypothesis?

If the second hypothesis (with its "totally dispensible" clauses removed) and the third hypothesis are each a set of sufficient conditions, then this one must also be a set of sufficient conditions. This hypothesis does not contain any of the conditions, either explicitly or implicitly, that we have had occasion to reject as not being necessary ones. It includes all the conditions that we have had occasion to recognize as necessary ones. It lends itself to an account of why some indirect questions are out of place as direct objects of 'to explain'. (The account is readily constructed by combining those suggested by the second and third hypotheses.) It even lends itself to the speculative etymology to which the second and third ones lend themselves. I, for one, cannot think of an episode that fits all the clauses in this hypothesis and that is not correctly described by an 'A explained to B W' sentence, nor can I imagine an episode that is so describable but that does not fit all the clauses of this hypothesis.

There is one possible objection that ought to be considered. We speak on occasion of someone's having tried to explain something to someone without having succeeded, and we often imply thereby that at the end of the episode the tutee did not know the answer. This may suggest that ultimate knowledge is necessary after all, since to have tried to explain something to someone without succeeding is no more to have explained something than to have tried to scale Mt. Everest without succeeding is to have scaled it.

But the fourth hypothesis accommodates these utterances in a natural way. Statements of the form 'A tried to explain to B W but failed' cover unfinished explaining episodes, that is, episodes in which (f) is not satisfied, and which therefore do not meet the truth-conditions proposed here. They cover episodes in which a tutor comes to realize that he is not being listened to and gives up; they cover episodes in which he is prevented from finishing; they also cover episodes in which he withholds nothing yet realizes that there are some things, things that have not occurred to him, that the tutee must be told to become properly informed under (e). Notice that they do *not* cover episodes in which all the conditions of our hypothesis have been satisfied, but at the end of which the tutee is still ignorant because of *his* failure to attend properly.

All this does not amount to a proof of the fourth hypothesis, but it goes a long way toward establishing a presumption in its favor.

3

I now turn to statements of the form 'A E X to B' and 'A E to B X' where A and B indicate positions occupied by expressions through which some person or persons are mentioned, where E indicates a position occupied by a tensed version of 'to explain', but where X is *not* replaced by an indirect question.

Statements of that form also describe, or report, or record the occurrence of explaining episodes. 'To explain' in each functions as an accomplishment term, and their truth entails that the truth-conditions of some 'A E to B W' statement (with identical replace-ments for A, B and E) are satisfied. Their own truth-conditions should therefore be readily obtainable from those of 'A E to B W' through some appropriate modifications.

Where X is replaced by 'something' (for example, 'Sam explained something to Rebecca') the question is simply left unspecified, and we can adapt the fourth hypothesis by substituting for (a),

(a₁) There is a sound question, that is, one that admits of a right answer.

The remaining cases fall under two headings, those in which X is replaced by a noun phrase (for example, 'Hector's behavior', 'the laws of electrostatics') and those in which it is replaced by a statement in oratio obliqua form (for example, 'that bones contain no dextrose').

First, those in which a noun phrase occurs. In 'A E to B W' statements the question is specified by an indirect question. However, questions can be specified in other ways and some noun phrases in some contexts can fulfill that function and can serve as surrogates of indirect questions. Thus 'Hector's behavior' will stand for 'why Hector behaves (or behaved) in the way he does (or did)' and 'the origins of the word "explain"' will stand for what the origins of the word 'explain' are. The precise description of the relevant transformations is something that we must leave to grammarians. The fourth hypothesis will cover statements with such noun phrases if we amend the definition of 'the question' on page 22 to read "the question whose oratio obliqua form or a surrogate for whose oratio obliqua form would appear at the position indicated by W or X."

Some occurrences of noun phrases do not convey enough information to be considered as surrogates of indirect questions. Mere knowledge of English is not sufficient to produce the question in an episode described by 'Mme. Rouge explained the third chapter of *Moby Dick* to Picard'; one must be acquainted with the third chapter of *Moby Dick* and know something of the questions to which it gives rise. The vagueness characteristic of such statements must be preserved in an adequate formulation of their truth-conditions. But this is easy to achieve. Simply replace (a) of the fourth hypothesis by

(a_2) There is a question about the topic mentioned at the X position that is sound, that is, that admits of a right answer.

Notice that though such noun phrases are vague, they are nevertheless indispensable. For instance, the third chapter of *Moby Dick* gives rise to a cluster of questions. It can happen that a tutee is not in a p-predicament with regard to any one of these questions taken in isolation, and that he is able to admit each as sound, but that he is nevertheless not in a position to think of a *set* of answers (to that set of questions) that he can consistently admit as possibly correct. This will happen when every nonobjectionable answer that he can think of to one isolated question would require him to reject

every nonobjectionable answer that he can think of to another isolated question. Even more complicated situations arise. A question
with regard to which a given tutee is in a p-predicament may itself
rest on a presupposition that the tutee trusts simply because it is
the only nonobjectionable answer that he can think of to some other
question. Giving him the correct answer to the latter may teach him
that the former has *no* right answer, and may thus "cure" him of
his p-predicament. In all such situations "the question" is complex
and is made up of disjunctions and conjunctions of more elementary
ones. In each case it can no doubt be put in oratio obliqua form but
the result must be unwieldy and awkward within an 'A E to B W'
statement.[16]

This point is worth remembering. Often the question in an explaining episode cannot be told from an 'A E X to B' description of
that episode. This may lead us to overlook the essential connection
that links explaining to questions.

Now, briefly, the cases in which the direct object of 'to explain'
is a statement in oratio obliqua. The nature of these statements is
obvious enough: they reproduce, if not the words, at least the gist of
what the tutee was told. To pass from a description containing such
a statement to a description containing a question in oratio obliqua
one merely has to phrase the question calling for the statement. This
is sometimes easy. But not always. A given statement may convey
the answer to more than one question. Moreover, the alluded-to
words may have conveyed not the content of the answer but part of
the background. Some explaining episodes, as we know, require that
the tutee be corrected about some assumption, and others that he be
informed of matters that will put the answer within his intellectual
grasp. To know the role played by something that the tutor told
the tutee one must know more than what he said. This will be
reflected in a statement of truth-conditions obtained by substituting
(a_1) again for (a). "There is a sound question, that is, one that
admits of a right answer"; and by supplementing (f) to read "At
the end of the episode all the facts mentioned in (d) and (e) have

---

[16]To simplify the discussion I have written as if the actual cognitive state of
the tutee were essential rather than what the tutor believes or assumes about
that state, and I have ignored b-predicaments altogether. The necessary adjustments are obvious enough, and do not merit the further circumlocution that their
exposition would require.

been presented to the tutee by the tutor, and these include the facts described by the statement at the direct object position."

4

I pass now to statements in which 'to explain' does not function as an accomplishment term. First, those of the form 'A explained W' in which A still indicates a position occupied by an expression through which a person is mentioned. When one says that Newton explained why there are tides, one need not mean that some explaining episode took place in which Newton was the tutor. One may mean that Newton solved the problem, found the answer to the question. Similarly 'Sherlock Holmes explained how the assassin left the room' may convey that Holmes solved the riddle. Here 'to explain' functions as an achievement term, not as an accomplishment term.

The fourth hypothesis does not require but is compatible with the occurrence of explaining episodes at the beginning of which the tutee is really in either a p-predicament or b-predicament with regard to the question, and by the end of which he actually has learned the answer and has had the grounds of his predicament corrected. I shall call explaining episodes of that sort *proper explaining episodes.*

A proper explaining episode involves a change in the tutee: at the beginning he does not know the answer to the question; in the course of the episode he learns certain facts, or (vel) he gains certain ideas and concepts, or (vel) he becomes aware of certain principles; at the end of the episode, he knows the answer, and he is competent to act as tutor in explaining episodes whose tutees are in a p-predicament or b-predicament with regard to the same question—they do not know some or all of the facts, ideas, concepts, or principles that our initial tutee has acquired in our initial episode. In other words, he is changed into someone who can explain the matter.

The kind of transformation just described can be brought about without benefit of tutor and without the occurrence of an explaining episode: research, reexamination of beliefs and assumptions, conceptual inventions, explorations, prodding for inspiration, exploitation of good luck, or grace may enable one to transform himself by himself into somebody able to explain something. To have succeeded in this sort of endeavor is to have explained something in the sense of 'to explain' to which we are now attending.

The connection, then, between the truth-conditions of 'A E W' and 'A E to B W'—put in the material mode—is that to have explained something in the sense now under consideration is to have become able to explain something in the sense discussed in the fourth hypothesis, as a result of one's own endeavors and ingenuity.[17]

5

Now finally the statements of the form 'T explains W' in which T is *not* a position occupied by an expression through which persons are mentioned. For instance, 'The Special Theory of Relativity explains why no interference pattern was observed by Michelson and Morley', 'Lumumba's prison record explains why he hated everything Belgian', 'The fact that the assassin was a midget explains how he was able to leave the room without touching door or window'. In such statements 'to explain' functions as a state term.

One might expect a characterization of the truth-conditions of these statements to require a list of the kinds of references that may be made at T. But this would draw us into a veritable philosophic Sargasso Sea: theories, facts, events, propositions, items of information, discoveries, principles.... The list seems to have no end, and each of its entries may ensnare and choke us. Fortunately, no such list is needed.

The transformation of someone into one who can explain something does not always include an explaining episode. We noted in the previous section that one can achieve this by oneself. The change can often be initiated by informing the tutee of things that will put him in a position to work out the answer and to correct by himself the deficiencies responsible for his predicament. About any question W with regard to which someone might be in either a p-predicament or a b-predicament, one may ask: *What must someone who is in a p-predicament or a b-predicament with regard to that question learn,*

---

[17]As an achievement term 'to explain' is also often used to credit people with certain scientific discoveries. 'Newton explained why the tides vary with the phases of the moon' may serve to mark the fact that Newton was the one who solved the riddle, who found the answer to a question with regard to which everybody had been in either a p-predicament or a b-predicament. To have explained something in this sense is to be one of the first to have explained it in the sense just analyzed in section 4, that is, to be one of the first to have been in a position to explain (in the sense of section 2) it to a tutee.

or of what must he be made aware to become able to explain W? Any noun phrase that is the right answer to *that* question may appear as the subject of a statement of the form 'T explains W'. Furthermore, *such a statement is true if and only if the subject at T is related to the question represented at W in the way that a right answer to a 'What must someone in a p-predicament or a b-predicament with regard to W learn, and of what must he be made aware to become able to explain W?' question is related to the question at W.*[18]

This question-using way of putting things is clearly a question-begging one. What is the relation referred to in the above biconditional? Under what conditions does it hold? One wants here a set of standards, a set of criteria, and an explicit general procedure that determine whether something that purports to explain something does indeed do so. This I cannot give for the present. Getting what is wanted here must wait for developments in at least two areas: (*a*) erotetic logic, and (*b*) the theory of p- and b-predicaments. Notice, by the way, that the latter is not to be thought of as the concern of psychology. Situations in which people are, or are not, in a p- or a b-predicament with regard to some questions depend on logical factors first, and on psychological ones only incidentally. For instance, some theories generate questions that, according to other theories, rest on unsound presuppositions. That this is so, is in each case, a matter of logic. It follows, however, that one who subscribes to one of the former theories can be in a p-predicament with regard to questions with regard to which someone who subscribes to one of the latter theories will not be in a p-predicament. Or again, two systems of assumptions and of concepts may differ in that only one is capable of generating answers to questions to which both provide presuppositions. This again must be a matter of logic. But it follows that one who relies on a specific system of assumptions may necessarily be in a p-predicament or b-predicament with regard to a question to which someone else, aware of different systems, will be able to envisage answers, perhaps even correct answers. The object of a theory of p- and b-predicaments must be to provide a general and systematic treatment of all such possibilities and of their grounds.

---

[18]The use of the past tense of 'to explain' here is worth noticing. It implies that the conditions for the above relation do *not* hold though they were once thought to hold.

One last point before we leave 'to explain'. Everyone in a p-predicament or b-predicament with regard to a specific question does not always need the same instruction. A may be in a p-predicament with regard to the question as a consequence of one set of objections to the right answer; B may not share those particular objections but may have some of his own; C may not be in a p-predicament at all but only in a b-predicament; D may be in both. Though the question is the same, in each case a proper explaining episode may have to correct different shortcomings and inform on different points. Therefore the truth of statements of the form 'T E W' is relative to something left unmentioned by them, that is, the basis of the p-predicament or b-predicament with regard to the question. Such statements taken out of context may thus suffer from a peculiar ambiguity: they are true when viewed against such and such nescience, but not when viewed against some other.

6

What is an explanation? An explanation may be something about which it makes sense to ask: How long did it take? Was it interrupted at any point? Who gave it? When? Where? What were the exact words used? For whose benefit was it given?

It may also be something about which none of these questions make sense, but about which it makes sense to ask: Does anyone know it? Who thought of it first? Is it very complicated?

We are not dealing here with two kinds of explanation, but with two senses of the word 'explanation', one that refers to a certain type of didactic performance, and instances of it, the other that refers to something more abstract, to something that constitutes the cognitive substance of such performances. I will therefore speak of a *performance sense* of 'explanation' and of a *text sense* of 'explanation'.

Each instance of *the* explanation (in the performance sense) of something coincides with an explaining episode; the two form necessarily coextensive classes. Thus the explanation of something by someone is merely the performance by someone of the role of tutor in an explaining episode.

Instances of *an* explanation (in the performance sense) of something form a wider class. They cover not only genuine explaining episodes, but also episodes corresponding to what I have called a

looser use of 'to explain', that is, episodes in which the tutor *thought*
that he was explaining something, but was mistaken and did not
know the answer to the question, or did not give it.

The text sense of 'explanation' is more elusive. Ontological snares
cover the genus within which its reference subsists, and should discourage a straightforward extensional explication. Something is *the*
explanation (in the text sense) of something if and only if it is the
right answer to a question formed from:

(7)   What must one tell someone in a p-predicament or a b-predic-
        ament or either a p-predicament or b-predicament with regard
        to Q in order to explain (in the accomplishment sense) W to
        him?

by putting a question at the position indicated by Q and the oratio
obliqua form of that question at the position indicated by W, the resulting question being understood as calling for an actual utterance
of what must be said to the tutee, not a description of what must
be said.

Anything that is *the* explanation (in the text sense) of something
is obviously an explanation of something. But everything that is *an*
explanation (in the text sense) is not necessarily the explanation of
anything. *An* explanation (in the text sense) of something is simply
an answer to a question formed from (7) in the above way. Thus an
explanation, like an answer to a question formed from (7), may be
right or wrong, clear or unclear, confirmed or disconfirmed, complete
or incomplete. Like an answer to such a question, its rightness or
wrongness is relative not only to the question that would be cited at
the place indicated by Q, but also to the known or assumed basis of
a known or assumed predicament.

The remarks made earlier should be repeated here. The account
of the nature of explanation just given falls short of what is eventually
wanted: it fails to provide the sort of insight that can be translated
into explicit standards and into a pattern of analysis applicable to
all explanations and capable of deciding their correctness; it fails
to make explicit the criteria that make correct explanations *correct*
explanations. But as I remarked before, an adequate account that
tells us all we want to know about explanations in general must wait
until prior problems have been solved. This discussion merely brings
us to the problems, and merely suggests an approach.

2

A Theory about the Theory of Theory and about the Theory of Theories

In this essay I shall present two abstract notions of theory that depart radically from the traditional view, that is, the view according to which a theory is an interpreted calculus or is something that can in principle be cast as such a calculus. My reasons for abandoning this traditional view are the same as those that motivate other philosophers who are developing new ways of conceptualizing scientific knowledge. The hypothetico-deductive conception of theories has been nurtured by some of the soundest, most intelligent, most informed, and most dedicated philosophers of recent times, and yet it has contributed very little to our critical understanding of the science of scientists. It has generated many problems that are of little relevance to that science and solved few that are. It once seemed to promise an explicit formulation of the principles that govern or that ought to govern the acceptance, rejection, and replacement of scientific doctrines, but it has not lived up to that promise. Its main virtues were a deliberate commitment to empiricism—albeit a tenuous version of empiricism—and a proneness to build on developments in logic. This is hardly enough to claim our allegiance while alternatives are conceivable that have the same virtues and that may have others as well.

The title of this essay is "A Theory about the Theory of Theory and about the Theory of Theories." Let me explain briefly what this title should suggest.

The theory of theories—if there can be such a thing—must provide a set of abstract concepts that are exemplified in all theories.

52

In the light of these concepts, any theory should come to be seen as mirroring features found in every theory. Furthermore, these concepts should enable us to formulate principles and to raise questions that pertain to any and to all theories.

Similarly, *the theory of theory* must provide a set of abstract concepts that are exemplified in the theory of any field of investigation that has a theory. In the light of these concepts the theory of any field of investigation should come to be seen as reflecting features found in the theory of any field of investigation. These concepts should enable us to formulate principles and to raise questions that pertain to the theory of any and all fields of investigation for which there is a theory.

I propose to sketch a theory. My theory presupposes the possibility of both the theory of theories and the theory of theory. It is a tentative sketch of the concepts basic to each.

Now let me indicate how I shall proceed.

I have here before me copies of three scientific texts: the first, the *Handbook of Chemistry and Physics;* the second, a copy of Page's *Introduction to Theoretical Physics*; and the third, a passage from John Dalton's *A New System of Chemical Philosophy.* I shall take up each of these texts in turn and outline how what can be learned from each might be described without being divulged.

Let me illustrate. Suppose that I had told you that one can learn from the *Handbook of Chemistry and Physics* that the boiling point of nitrogen under pressure of one atmosphere is −195°C. I would then have described one item of information obtainable from the handbook, and I would also have divulged that information to you, that is, I would have divulged that the boiling point of nitrogen under pressure of one atmosphere is −195°C. Suppose now that I had told you instead that one can learn from the *Handbook* what the boiling point of nitrogen under pressure of one atmosphere is but had not gone on to tell you the boiling point. I would again have described that item of information, but this time I would not have divulged it. It is the latter sort of description that will concern us. I shall refer to such descriptions as "didactic promises" to which texts lend themselves, or fail to lend themselves. I propose then to characterize the kind of didactic promise to which each of the texts now before me lends itself.

Notice that I say *the kind* of didactic promise to which each of these texts lends itself. I shall thus not seek to state actual didactic promises—except by way of examples—but I shall try to give general characterizations. You can no doubt guess my reasoning. I look upon each of these texts as an instance of a type, and I think of the type as identified by the kind of didactic promises to which its instances lend themselves.

Any text can lend itself to more than one didactic promise. Some didactic promises, however, illuminate the character of a text more revealingly than others. How is this possible? Again let me begin with an illustration. Suppose that the author or publisher or some other authorized sponsor of some handbook had said that one can learn from that handbook what the exact population of the Volta Republic is. Suppose now that the answer to "What is the exact population of the Volta Republic?" is nowhere to be found in the book, or that an answer can be found but is one known to be incorrect, or again that an answer can be found, but that no census of the Volta Republic has ever been taken and that therefore no one, least of all the author, is in a position to inform anyone else about the size of its population. Something would then be amiss with the book. This would not be so had we not been given the right to expect that the size of the population of the Volta Republic could be learned from it. Thus a didactic promise can be thought of as something that should be sayable in behalf of a text; and once it is thought of in this way, it ipso facto determines conditions of adequacy and of acceptability that the text must meet. In what follows, when I speak of didactic promises, let us think of them in this way, that is, as entailing standards. The more illuminating didactic promises for our purpose will be those that bring out most clearly the character of the critical tests that the texts to which they apply must be able to pass.

Didactic promises have been the subject of philosophic speculation and of philosophic controversy (though not under that name). The dispute between Cardinal Bellarmino and Galileo, for instance, was essentially a dispute concerning the validity of Andreas Osiander's didactic promise in his preface to Copernicus's *De Revolutionibus.* "There is no need for these hypotheses to be true, or even to be at all like the truth; rather one thing is sufficient for them—that they should yield a calculus which agrees with the observations."[1] The

---

[1] Translation from Popper 1956.

issue was whether one could learn from the text—or from Galileo's—
the actual configurations of the solar system, or only how to compute
positions of of certain observable spots in the sky.

You will perhaps object that the dispute was not about a text,
but was about a doctrine or a theory. We need not disagree. What
I say in this essay about texts—actual or possible—has obvious and
immediate implications for the things of which texts are expositions.
There is no convenient way of referring to these things, and I have
chosen to point to them by speaking of the texts in which they are
or could be set forth.

I began by announcing a theory, but I have been talking about
didactic promises and about types of didactic promises. Let me
now show you the connection and let me also bring out why I have
been talking about "the theory of theory" and about "the theory
of theories," and not simply about "the theory of theory" or simply
about "the theory of theories."

When we use the English word 'theory' we may be talking about
one of at least two entirely different sorts of things. Consider, for
instance, the following two lists:

List I   The theory of heat
            The theory of systems in stable equilibrium
            The theory of games
            The theory of communication
            Input-output theory
            Electrostatic theory

List II   The kinetic theory of heat
            The electromagnetic theory of light
            The heliocentric theory
            The sense datum theory
            The theory of evolution
            The phlogiston theory

It may be difficult to state the principles that govern admission
to one or the other list, but we know them well enough to see that,
for example, "the atomic theory of matter" belongs on the second
list, whereas "atomic theory" belongs on the first. Let us dwell on
this for a moment.

Every item on these lists is represented by an expression that
includes the word 'theory'. Each is something that can be studied,

taught, mastered, that can conceivably be improved, that could possibly be set up in axiomatic form. These similarities, however, are pale when compared with the differences. The entries on List II are things that can be accepted, rejected, believed, remembered, stated, granted, confirmed, refuted, have authors, be entailed by and entail propositions. In short, they are propositions. Not so the items on List I. None of these can be accepted, rejected, believed, remembered, stated, granted, confirmed, refuted, have authors, be entailed by or entail propositions. (This is not to deny that they may encompass things that can.) But they can include contributions from many sources; they have founders and perhaps foundations; they are academic subjects; they can be and they have subdivisions that also belong on the list.

The second list is a list of theories, that is, of things that can be *called* theories; not so the first list. (The theory of heat is not a theory.) Thus 'rational mechanics', 'geometric optics', 'thermodynamics' fit naturally in the first list—though they do not contain the word 'theory'—but they do not belong on the second list.

It is easy to envisage how one would pass from any segment of List II to a display of the actual items listed in that segment. The display might take the following form:

This is the kinetic theory of heat: Material bodies are made up of molecules in a state of thermal agitation and the heat contained in any body is the total energy within its system of molecules. This is the electromagnetic theory of light: Light waves are electromagnetic waves. This is the heliocentric theory: The earth and the planets, and the stars travel along closed paths that surround the sun. . . .

Each entry of List II refers to a proposition. Clearly, we cannot pass in a similar way from the segments of List I to a display of the things listed in that segment.

Note, by the way, that though List I is a sequence of category terms, that sequence is not made up of terms that refer to aggregates, classes, or complexes of some sort made up of items belonging on List II. Lagrange's equations of motion, Euler's equations for ideal fluids, the mirror image method for solving electrostatic problems all are part of things that belong on List I, but they do not belong under items on List II.

Let us then provide ourselves with two words, 'theory$_1$' corresponding to 'theory' as it occurs in List 1, and 'theory$_2$' corresponding to 'theory' as it occurs in List II. Having *two* words here may be helpful. Failure to attend to the theory$_1$–theory$_2$ distinction has often resulted in confusions that this bit of jargon should help us avoid.

The theory of theory as I conceive it, and as I think others must have conceived it, is the theory of theory$_1$. It concerns itself with the features peculiar to the texts subsumable under one of the category terms that make up List I.

To recognize these features we must remind ourselves of one important role played by such subsumptions.

Any individual's quest for knowledge and wisdom and know-how and ideas consists not only in original observations, personal witnessing of events or things, cogitations, reflections, and reckonings. It includes the picking of brains, that is, reading and listening and thus learning from others what others already know or have already thought of. I know the height of Mt. Everest, I know how to prove that the sum of the squares of the adjacent sides of a rectangular triangle is equal to the square of the hypotenuse, I know that laziness in children can be viewed as a form of rebellion, but others took the measurements, sweated the sweat, frustrated themselves into the insights: I merely read the appropriate books and registered for the relevant courses.

None of us wants to or can read every book, take every course, master every paper, listen to every lecture. The abundance of instrumentalities through which something can be learned thus creates the need for devices that reveal the cognitive gains available through this or that didactic instrumentality, and that do this without requiring actual mastery; devices, in other words, that reveal the didactic promise to which the instrumentality lends itself.

Many words can be used for that purpose. Think of 'History,' 'Geography,' 'Science,' 'Biology,' etc. To say that a book is a history book, that a course is a biology course, that a paper is about geography, is to indicate the kind of didactic promise to which the book, the course, the paper lends itself. It is to indicate it in a rough way, but fine enough for many purposes. Other phrases can do the job more precisely.

The category terms on List I can be used for the same purpose. To say that a course is a course in the theory of heat is to indicate something about what can be learned from it; to put a monograph under the heading of "theory of systems in unstable equilibrium" in a catalogue is to indicate *grosso mode* the sort of problems that have been worked out for the reader, and so on.

It seems, therefore, reasonable to assume that there is a type of didactic promise to which every text subsumable under one of the categories of List I must lend itself. To establish that type, if it exists, must be one of the primary tasks of the theory of theory$_1$.

I said "reasonable" above. Whether the assumption is true or not cannot be established by examining only our use of the word 'theory.' The appropriate procedure is to make explicit the type of didactic promise implicit in our use, and then to check against actual scientific literature to see whether the latter conforms to the presuppositions of the former. If it does, our assumption will have been vindicated. The matter is well worth our attention, however. If such a defining type of didactic promise does exist, then there must also exist conditions of acceptability and of adequacy essential to all texts subsumable under a theory$_1$ category. It is the first duty of the philosophy of science to find and to judge such conditions. A general didactic promise would be a priceless guide.

What has been said about theory$_1$ can be repeated with minor changes for theory$_2$. To say that a book or a paper sets forth a theory is to reveal a part of the didactic promises to which the text lends itself. It is also to imply something about the proper way to assess its content. It is to point then to features that are the concern of the theory of theories$_2$.

Let us then turn to the *Handbook of Chemistry and Physics.* It is not the sort of text with which we are primarily concerned, but, for reasons that will become clear, it is a convenient starting point. To expedite matters somewhat, let us ignore those parts of the book that do not provide information in tabular form, those that contain definitions, those that contain conversion rules for units, those that contain first-aid instructions, and—but this only temporarily—those that contain formulae. Even so, there will be some distortions of the remainder of the text in what I shall say, but none that will matter very much for present purposes.

Our question then is: To what sort of didactic promise does this text lend itself? We need some definitions.

1. By a *question matrix* I mean an incomplete expression that can be used to ask a question when completed in accordance with certain specifications. For example,

> What ... ?
> What is the volume of ... ?
> What is the volume (in cubic feet) of ... ?
> Why ... ?
> What occurred at ... on ... ?
> Is ... ?

2. By a *question schema* I mean an ordered pair consisting of a question matrix and of the stipulations of how it is to be completed. For example,

> What is the distance (in meters) between ... and ... ? (Each blank must be filled with an expression used to specify a point in space.)
>
> What is the distance (in meters) between ... and ... ? (The first blank must be filled with an expression specifying a city; the second blank must be filled with an expression specifying a city different from that referred to in the first blank.)

These are two distinct schemata that share the same matrix.

The notion of a question schema is thus the analogue with regard to questions of the logician's notion of a statement schema, that is, of an incomplete expression that can be used to make a statement when completed in accordance with certain specifiable instructions.

In the examples that follow I shall record question schemata by indicating how the blanks must be filled, in the blanks themselves. This is a somewhat casual procedure, but it will do for now, and it has the virtue of shortening things and of yielding expressions that, to the ear if not the eye, come close to expressions in the vernacular. For example,

> What is the distance (in meters) between ... [a point] ... and ... [a different point] ... ?
> Why did ... [an event] ... take place?

3. By a *substitution instance of a given question schema S,* I mean a question that one would be asking by uttering (by way of asking a

question) a completed version of S's matrix, completed in accordance
with the stipulations peculiar to S. For example, the question asked
by asking

> What is the distance (in meters) between the position occupied
> by the center of the earth at 6:13 A.M. on July 7th, 1924 and
> that occupied by the center of gravity of the moon at the same
> instant?"

would be a substitution instance of the first question schema above.

We can now describe the *form* of a didactic promise to which the
bulk of the *Handbook* lends itself. It would consist of a list of question
schemata and a statement that the answer to all the substitution
instances of these schemata that have known answers can be obtained
from the text. One need not adopt this form in actually specifying
the didactic promise, but one must adopt a statement that implies
a didactic promise in that form. The table of contents as provided
by the publisher is often such a statement. Thus it is made up
of such entries as "Physical constants of organic compounds," and
this amounts to saying that we can find the answer to substitution
instances of the following sort of schemata:

> What is the formula of ... [an organic compound]?
> What is the boiling point of ... [an organic compound]?
> What is the melting point of ... [an organic compound]?

In judging the adequacy of this kind of didactic promise, we must
ask ourselves whether the book would fail to be what it purports to
be if it did not give the answers to substitution instances of such
a list of schemata, if it gave incorrect answers, if it gave unreliable
answers; that is, if it were not a device that can put its readers in the
same position with regard to a set of questions as that of the men
who carried out successfully the original search for the answer; or,
alternatively, we must ask ourselves whether a critical examination
of the text, conducted by philosophers or by scientists, must not seek
to determine whether the text does indeed lend itself to the sort of
didactic promise outlined above.

Notice, by the way, that in general a handbook is a handbook
only if it lends itself to a didactic promise in the form that I have
described above.

Let us now turn to the sections of the *Handbook* in which formulae of various sorts are put forth. These sections, too, lend themselves to a didactic promise in the form of a list of question schemata followed by a statement to the effect that the sections provide the answers to substitution instances of these schemata. But looking at the matter in this way blurs important distinctions between the contents of the sections and between the conditions that they must satisfy. It also hides the fact that formulae call for their own sort of critique.

So, we need more definitions!

4. By a *datum* I mean an ordered pair consisting of a question and its right answer (or answers, if the question has more than one right answer).

5. By a *problem* I mean an ordered pair of sets, whose first member consists of data (as defined above) and whose second member consists of questions. By the *data questions* of a problem, let us understand the set of questions each of which is a member of a datum of the problem, and by the *queries* of a problem, let us understand the questions that appear alone in the problem. For example,

> What is the length of the simple pendulum in Frick 42? 20 cm.
> What is the value of free-fall acceleration in the vicinity of Frick 42, in cm per sec^2? 980 cm per sec^2.
> What is the period of the pendulum in Frick 42 (in sec)?

constitute a problem. Its data questions are:

> What is the length of the simple pendulum in Frick 42?
> What is the value of free-fall acceleration in the vicinity of Frick 42 in cm per sec^2?

Its query question is:

> What is the period of the pendulum in Frick 42 (in sec)?

6. By a *problem schema* I mean an ordered list of question schemata divided into two nonoverlapping sublists. One sublist is referred to as *data questions schemata*, the other as *query schemata*. For example, data question schemata:

> What is the length (in cm) of ... [a simple pendulum] ... ?
> What is the value of free-fall acceleration (in cm per sec^2) at ... [the vicinity of the last-mentioned simple pendulum] ... ?

Query schema:

> What is the period (in secs) of ... [the last-mentioned simple pendulum] ... ?[2]

7. By a *substitution instance of a given problem schema P*, I mean a problem (*a*) whose data questions are substitution instances of the data question schemata in P, and standing in one-to-one correspondence with them; and (*b*) whose query questions are substitution instances of the query schemata of P, and standing in one-to-one correspondence with them. For example,

> The problem serving as illustration of (5) above is a substitution instance of the problem schema serving as an illustration of (6) above.

8. A *problem type corresponding to a problem schema P* is the set made up of all the substitution instances of P.

9. A problem type is said to be *solved* when, and only when, a procedure is known through which the right answers to *any* query of *any* of its members can be computed using only the information in the statement of the problem and of the procedure.

10. Such a procedure will be called a *valid formula*. A valid formula of a problem schema is a procedure through which the correct answers to *any* query of *any* of its substitution instances can be determined with only the information in the procedure and in those substitution instances (i.e., the data). For example,

> Properly interpreted, '$T = 2\pi\sqrt{l/g}$' is the statement of a formula of the problem schema previously defined. The interpretation is obvious: Divide the answer to the first data question by that to the second; find the square root of the quotient; multiply by twice pi.[3]

---

[2]The example is a plausible example only on the assumption that 'last mentioned' can be cashed in for something that requires no allusion to the order in which substitution instances of the various question schemata—and other utterances as well—would actually be put. In a fuller and more refined treatment this could no doubt be achieved, but the additional complications would take us far afield and not be warranted by my present objective; a sketch is all I am after.

[3]The expression '$T = 2\pi\sqrt{l/g}$' is a shorthand way of indicating a procedure for solving every problem of the type we have been using as illustration. But it can have, and very often does have, other roles as well. It can be used to express

Numerical formulae of physics most likely spring to mind, but it is important to realize that, in the sense in which 'formula' is being used here, these are not the only formulae. Not all formulae stipulate arithmetical operations on numbers in answers to data questions. Think, for instance, of the "left-hand rule" for determining the direction of the magnetic field about a wire in which current is flowing; or of the "formulae" of chemistry as bases for procedures by which the *qualitative* result of certain chemical combinations can be determined; or of Gresham's law, as it is (or was) used in the solution of problems of a type whose query was 'Will the number of [a type of coin] being hoarded increase or decrease?' or even, for that matter, the procedure associated with the simple pendulum formula, to solve a problem whose data indicates that the length will be increased, and whose query was whether the period will increase or decrease.

11. By a *formula of a problem schema S*, I mean a procedure by which an answer (not necessarily the right answer) to any query of any of its substitution instances can be obtained, with only the information contained in the statement of the procedure and in that substitution instance.

12. A formula will be said to be *reliable* when there are grounds for deeming it to be valid, and there are none for deeming it not to be valid.

We can now describe a form of didactic promise appropriate to the sections of the *Handbook* that make up a "formulaire." It would consist of a list of problem schemata and a statement that the sec-

---

the relation that holds between periods, lengths, etc., of all simple pendulums and thus serve as a *general description* of a feature common to all simple pendulums; it can also serve as the statement of a *law* governing the behavior of all simple pendulums. Nothing said above should be interpreted as meaning that it and similar expressions are in any sense *really* only formulations of procedures for solving problems of a certain type. All these roles are no doubt intimately related, so intimately related none can probably be fulfilled unless all can, but this provides no ground for ascribing to any *one* of these cosmological priority. See in this connection particularly Hanson 1959, chap. 3.

We know, of course, that the formula is not valid as it stands. It is valid only when the only force on the pendulum is the force of gravity. What this means, in effect, is that the question schemata should actually have been so expressed as to allow only substitution instances referring not just to simple pendulums, but to simple pendulums under the influence of no forces other than gravity.

tion makes available reliable formulae for these schemata. (Perhaps it would be more correct to say "a statement that the text makes available expressions that the initiated will know how to translate into formulae as defined above.") In practice, of course, the didactic formula need not be given in that form; less formal devices will do. But whatever form is used, it must entail that the text lends itself to a didactic promise in the above canonical form, and—more important—it must entail that the text is subject to the requirements implicit in that form.

We now have two forms of didactic promises, each characterizing its own recognizable body of texts, but we still do not have the form of didactic promise peculiar to texts subsumable under one of the theory₁ categories. We are getting close, however. All we need are a few definitions!

13. I say that a formula is *testable* when the problem type it covers includes members with data questions and query questions whose correct answer can be obtained without the formula. In other words, let F be a formula, let S be the problem schema for which F is the formula, let S_i be a substitution instance of S, let D_i be the data questions of S_i, let Q_i be the query questions of S_i. If the answers to D_i and Q_i can be obtained without using the formula, then F is testable. (If there is more than one such S_i so much the better.) The formula for the simple pendulum, for instance, is a testable formula, since we know how to construct a simple pendulum, measure its length, measure g, and measure its period, all this without ever using the formula.

14. By the *test* of a testable formula I mean a comparison between, on the one hand, an answer obtained by the formula and, on the other hand, the right answer when the right answer has been obtained without the help of the formula. Such a test has been *passed* when the two answers coincide.

15. A formula is an *empirical* formula when (*a*) it is reliable and (*b*) the grounds of its reliability are that it has been tested and has passed the test each time. Obviously all empirical formulae must be testable, but the converse need not be true. A formula may be both testable and reliable, and nevertheless not be an empirical formula.

16. The reliability of a formula may rest on different sorts of grounds.

There are formulae that are *derivatively* reliable. A formula is derivatively reliable if it has been derived from principles and in accordance with principles from which (*a*) testable formulae have been derived in the past, (*b*) some of these have actually been tested, (*c*) all those that have been tested qualify as empirical formulae. Let us call such formulae *derived formulae*.

An empirical formula can obviously be a derived formula, and vice versa. For example,

> The formula embodied in '$T = 2\pi\sqrt{l/g}$' is *testable*. To test it one merely has to build a simple pendulum and to take measurements giving its length, the value of free-fall acceleration in its vicinity, and the period, then to compute the period on the basis of the formula, and to compare the two values. It is an *empirical* formula, since the above test has been carried out and (I assume) passed. It is also a *derived* formula, since it can be derived from the principles of mechanics and procedures for the solution of differential equations, and for the decomposition of forces, a combination that has yielded tested formulae which qualify as empirical.

17. A *field of investigation* is simply a set of question schemata.

18. The *formulae of a field of investigation* is the set of reliable formulae (if any) for problem schemata whose query schemata are question schemata in the field of investigation.[4]

19. The *theory₁* of a field of investigation is a set consisting of all the derived formulae of that field of investigation, together with their actual derivation from and in accordance with principles satisfying (*a*) and (*b*) of 16. 'Theory₁ of ... [a field of investigation] ...' is thus itself a schema (not a question schema) for collective names which refer to the theory₁ of the field of investigation mentioned in the name.

Let us look again at List I: To each entry there corresponds a field of investigation. That field is suggested by the words surrounding 'theory₁', though it is not fully revealed by them. (For example, in

---

[4]The reason for not requiring that the data questions belong to the field should be clear: Many of the formulae of the theory of heat, for instance, pertain to problems whose data questions are thought of as belonging properly to mechanics or electricity.

the case of 'the theory of heat': 'What is the temperature of ... [a body of matter] ... ?', 'What is the amount of heat absorbed in ... [the occurrence of a process] ... ?', 'What is the rate of change of temperature during ... [an episode] ... ?', etc.) It is always a field of investigation of a special sort, that is, a field of investigation with which there is associated a body of deduced *formulae*, and a set of principles on which the derivations of these formulae are based and from which they derive their reliability.

There are question schemata that group themselves into "systematic" fields of investigation in that (*a*) each is the query question schema of solved problem schemata; (*b*) the formulae that constitute the corresponding solutions can all be derived from and in accordance with the same set of principles. Let us call such fields of investigations *"new-sciences,"* in honor of Galileo. Some "new-sciences" are very old, though most are not. The fact that men can discover new sciences is what is meant when it is written that God created man after his own image.

Let us at last turn to Page's *Introduction to Theoretical Physics*. To each section there corresponds a "new-science." To each section there corresponds a didactic promise which consists of a characterization of the question schemata that constitute the field of investigation and a statement that the text makes available the principles of the "new-science" and gives instructions for the derivation of formulae from and in accordance with these principles.

The gist of what I have said can be put a little more concretely.

It is *sometimes* possible to obtain the answer to a question through the following sequence of steps: (*A*) The question is construed as the query of a problem to whose data questions one knows the answer. (*B*) The problem is next construed as the substitution instance of a problem schema. (*C*) A formula for the problem schema is then derived from principles and according with principles that generate reliable formulae. (*D*) The answer to the question is finally reckoned through the use of that formula.

The advantages of being able to establish the answer to a question in this way are obvious; reckoning is often the more economical and simplest way available; it is often also the only one.

To be able to do this, one must learn the principles from which reliable formulae can be deduced, and one must learn the principles in accordance with which reliable formulae must be deduced. Each of the headings entered on List I is a category label under which expositions of such principles, and grounds for deeming them reliable, are presented. But mastering the relevant reliable principles is not always enough. The discovery of the route from principles to formula is a matter that often requires more ingenuity and luck and even genius than many of us possess. However, once discovered by one person it can be opened to all. Under the headings on List I, one will also find expositions in which formulae are actually derived.[5]

When a number of reliable formulae are available in a field, it is often possible to present their deductions in a systematic order that expedites the exposition and that affords mnemonic economy. Such systematic compendia, such general treatises also belong under each heading. Hence the plausibility of a Machian conception of theory.

These then are the considerations that govern subsumption under one of the labels on List I. Each is a category corresponding to a branch of learning and to a field of investigation. The texts under each are designed to teach one how to reckon the answers to substitution instances of the question schemata of the field, when such answers can be reckoned.[6]

It follows from what I have said that we can't expect a single revealing didactic promise form to fit every text subsumable under one of the theory categories. The form appropriate to each text must reveal what gap it will help cross. Problem solving is covered with dissimilar gaps. There is one common feature that all the di-

---

[5]It is somewhat misleading to suggest that the only cognitive gain in studying the deduction of a formula is knowledge of how to derive the formula and of the nature and grounds of its reliability. The study of deductions teaches how to construct deductions through examples, sources of suggestions, and opportunities for flexing one's deductive muscles.

[6]This, of course, does not mean that the significance of what is in these texts is due solely to their function in the sort of tasks described above. As noted before, the reliability of a formula may be taken to reflect the existence of certain laws of nature; similarly, the fact that reliable formulae are derivable from a certain principle is itself a revelation of something about *reality*, namely, that it is probably so constituted as to make formulae derived from those principles valid. The study of texts subsumed under one of those headings should, therefore, not be thought of as yielding merely instrumental knowledge. It yields facts or presumed facts. But the *exposition* of such facts belongs under the headings, however, *in virtue* of their connection to the solving of problems.

dactic promises concerned with theory must share, however. Each must imply that the text is to be assessed as a contribution to problem solving.

I would like to investigate with you consequences of this implication, and in particular to show how it accounts for the fact that so many philosophers have thought of theories as interpreted calculi and as "merely" intellectual instruments. However, we still have to consider theory$_2$. I fear, furthermore, that you may not be completely at home with the jargon that I have been inflicting on you and that any discussion in which it is used in large draughts may no longer be very edifying. I must therefore refer you for further details to my posthumous works, where all of this is worked out in great detail. On, then, to theory$_2$.

Chapter 2 of John Dalton's A *New System of Chemical Philosophy* contains the following passage:

There are three distinctions in the kinds of bodies, or three states, which have more especially claimed the attention of philosophical chemists; namely, those which are marked by the terms *elastic fluids, liquids,* and *solids.* A very familiar instance is exhibited to us in water, or a body, which, in certain circumstances, is capable of assuming all the three states. In steam we recognize a perfectly elastic fluid, in water, a perfect liquid, and in ice a complete solid. These observations have tacitly led to the conclusion which seems universally adopted, that all bodies of sensible magnitude, whether liquid or solid, are constituted of a vast number of extremely small particles, or atoms of matter bound together by a force of attraction, which is more or less powerful according to circumstances, and which as it endeavors to prevent their separation, is very properly called in that view, *attraction of cohesion*; but as it collects them from a dispersed state (as from steam into water) it is called *attraction of aggregation* ...

This passage sets forth a theory$_2$, namely, that "all bodies ... are constituted of a vast number of extremely small particles ... bound together by a force of attraction which is more or less powerful according to circumstances." Details of the theory$_2$ that are not cited are readily guessed, for example, that the forces among the particles of a body in solid state are greater than the forces among the particles of the same body in liquid state, and so on. This theory$_2$ is connected to the observation that samples of certain substances can exist in three states, and more specifically to the fact that a sample of ice can turn into a sample of water (liquid). What is the connection? How do the facts "tacitly" lead to the conclusion?

Consider first the connection between the theory$_2$ and the fact that samples of ice turn, under certain circumstances, into samples of water. The fact gives rise to the question 'What happens when a sample of ice turns into a sample of water?'—gives rise in at least the minimal sense that the question presupposes the fact (that is, it would be logically impossible to tell anyone what happens when a sample of ice turns into a sample of water, were that not a fact). The theory$_2$, on the other hand, provides an answer to the question (that ice is made up of particles held together by forces of a certain magnitude; when a sample of ice turns into a sample of water the forces among the particles are weakened). This answer, furthermore, is compatible with other known facts (for example, that ice and water are alike in some respects and different in others) and accepted doctrine, and is incompatible with no known fact or accepted doctrine (let us assume Dalton's position for the moment). These known facts and accepted doctrines constitute conditions on the question, in that no answer to it could be deemed correct if it were known to be in conflict with them.

Consider now the question 'What happens when a sample of ice turns into a sample of water?' It differs in one very important respect from many other questions: There is no systematic way of generating answers to it. All questions are not like that. We can generate all possible answers to, for example, 'Is the present king of France bald?' The answer must be either yes, or no, or the question must rest on a false presupposition and have no correct answer. Or again, 'What is the mass of a hydrogen molecule?' Either there is no correct answer or the answer must be expressible as a number followed by a unit of mass, and belongs in a set that can be generated as the numbers are. Imagine now a situation in which every answer *that we can think of* to our question fails to meet the conditions on the question. We would be in the following odd predicament: We would consider the question to be sound, that is, to rest on no false presupposition, and to have a correct answer; we would know or believe that we know conditions that the answer must satisfy, but we would not be able to think of any answer that we would not also be forced to rule out. Elsewhere I have called being in this sort of predicament with regard to a question "being in a p-predicament ('p' for 'puzzled' or 'perplexed') with regard to the question."[7]

There is a puzzled man who has established to his satisfaction that the birth rate and mortality rate have been approximately the same for males and females over the last few decades in a certain country in Africa. He is also certain that there has been no large influx of women into that country. Yet he knows that each adult male there has at least five wives. That man was in a p-predicament with regard to the question 'Where do all the wives come from?'

Now let us go back to that theory$_2$ alluded to by Dalton. At the time, it provided an answer to the question about ice and water, and that answer was the only one known at the time, that did not have to be ruled out in the light of available facts and accepted doctrines. This did not show that the answer was correct, but it did create a presumption in its favor. In general, where Q is a question with regard to which it is in principle possible to be in a p-predicament, and A is the only known answer not ruled out, a presumption exists in favor of A. A quasi-disjunctive syllogism supports such As: Either you accept them, or you accept answers known to be false, or you freeze in a p-predicament. But of course it is always possible that the correct answer has not been thought of.

In "An Approach to Explanation," I tried to show that what we call "explanations" are or contain correct answers to questions with regard to which it is in principle possible to be in a p-predicament. This should be qualified but need not detain us now. I mention it only to point out that there are connections between what we are talking about here and the concept of explanation.

Questions with regard to which it is in principle possible to be in a p-predicament, and whose correct answers we do not know, create logical situations that deserve the attention of any philosopher interested in the logic of confirmation. Thus, let Q be such a question, but let there be no known answer not ruled out, and let S be a contrary of some presupposition of Q. Let S also be compatible with the facts and with accepted doctrine. Then there exists a presumption in behalf of S. Such indeed was the initial presumption in favor of the Special Theory of Relativity, Q in that case being

---

[7]See "An Approach to Explanation," this volume.

'Why weren't Michelson and Morley able to detect the motion of the earth relative to the aether?' Or again, let Q be a question with regard to which it is in principle possible to be in a p-predicament. Let $A_1, A_2, A_3, \cdots, A_n$ be a finite set of mutually exclusive answers, none of which is known to be true, but none of which is ruled out by what is known. In such a case there exists a presumption in favor of the disjunction of the set, but there also exists a presumption in favor of each member, though one that is weaker when the set contains more than one element.

I am now ready to tell you what I think a theory$_2$ is. Let Q be any question with regard to which it is in principle possible to be in a p-predicament; if A is a known proposition not known to be true, and not known to be false, but that contains an answer to Q, then A is a theory$_2$. If each of $A_1, A_2, \cdots A_n$ is a known proposition that contains an answer to Q, and each excludes the other, and each in the absence of the others would contain the only answer to Q not ruled out by what is known, and each is neither known to be true nor known to be false, then each is a theory$_2$. If X is a proposition that is the contrary of some presupposition of Q, and X is not known to be true, and is not known to be false, then X is a theory$_2$. Nothing else is a theory$_2$. Thus a theory$_2$ is a hypothetical explanation, if my understanding of the nature of explanations is correct.

The theory$_2$ to which Dalton alludes in the quoted passage satisfies the above characterization. The theory$_2$ that he himself developed was more complicated; it contained an answer to a more complex question, subject to more demanding conditions. These differences are not relevant here.

The above characterization of 'theory$_2$' assigns to that term a meaning that departs from our ordinary term 'theory' in one important respect. According to it, a proposition may be a theory$_2$ at one time, and then cease to be one, as new facts are uncovered that rule it out. To avoid the need for more definitions, let us think of the above passage as specifying the meaning of 'acceptable theory$_2$' only. From here on, whenever I say "theory$_2$" please understand that I mean "acceptable theory$_2$."

A canonical form for didactic promises peculiar to texts setting forth a theory$_2$ is now readily set up: It would consist of a question with regard to which it is in principle possible to be in a p-predicament, and a statement to the effect that the text provides a proposition that stands to that question in the manner described in my characterization of theory$_2$.[8]

If I were interested in philosophic theories only, I would stop here. Scientific theories, however, are subject to further constraints that should be reflected in the didactic promise we assign to them, namely, they must not themselves give rise to questions that are *demonstrably* unanswerable.

Let me explain. As I have already pointed out, a proposition P can give rise to a question Q only if it is a presupposition of Q, and it is a presupposition of Q only if A's having a correct answer would entail that P is true. But this is not enough. 'What is the median mass of oxygen atoms?' presupposes that there are atoms, but 'There are atoms' by itself does not give rise to the question. What else is required? I can't tell you in detail. Very roughly, P must be a conjunction of all the presuppositions or must entail such a conjunction. Thus the proposition that gives rise to the above question runs somewhat like this: There are oxygen atoms, and these have inertia. Logic does not exclude the possibility that some true propositions give rise to questions whose answers can never be discovered, for instance, 'What was the population on July 7, 1924 of that part of Africa now called the Volta Republic?' The question is sound, but the answer is probably forever beyond our reach. However, it is not *demonstrably* beyond our reach. No scientific theory$_2$ is acceptable if it gives rise to questions reliable answers to which are *demonstrably* beyond anyone's reach.[9]

The general form for didactic promises peculiar to theories$_2$ is

---

[8]Books and papers setting forth theories usually contain much more than is required by the sort of didactic promise just outlined. They usually contain expositions of the facts that give rise to the question calling for a theory$_2$, expositions of the question itself, expositions of alternative answers and of reasons for rejecting these, as well as the theory$_2$ itself.

[9]Whether a specific proposition suffers from that particular defect can be a very ticklish matter. Duhem and the energeticists believed that atomic theories should be rejected on such grounds. Their naive empiricism led them to think that the invisibility of atoms made reliable answers to questions about them impossible. Such epistemological qualms were forgotten, of course, as soon as answers did become available, that is, as soon as experiments were made that turned these questions into substitution instances of problems belonging to solved types, and for which data could be obtained.

readily adjusted to reflect this requirement on scientific theories. The promise takes the form of a question with regard to which it is in principle possible to be in a p-predicament, accompanied by a statement to the effect that the text provides a proposition that stands to the question in the manner described in my characterization of theory$_2$, and a statement to the effect that the proposition does not give rise to any questions that are demonstrably unanswerable.

I have made a distinction between theory$_1$ and theory$_2$, and I have tried to fix it by specifying two canonical forms of didactic promises. I have followed this course because I am interested in exploring bases for the critique of contributions to theoretical knowledge. I could have drawn the distinction in a different way, however; I could have pointed out that the distinction between theory$_1$ and theory$_2$ corresponds to a distinction between two sorts of scientific commitments or two species of acceptance. One has accepted a contribution to the theory$_1$ of a field of investigation when one is prepared to accept the formulae derived in accordance with it, and when one is prepared to trust answers obtained from such formulae and reliable data. But to accept a theory$_2$ is to accept as sound the *questions* to which it gives rise. For the layman this may mean adjustment to new degrees of ignorance; for the scientist this may mean heeding the call of new frontiers; and for the empiricist this may mean revising once more the conception of what constitutes experience.

Philosophers of science, on the whole, have tended to ignore the distinction between theory$_1$ and theory$_2$. The reason for this neglect cannot be the simple linguistic accident that in most Western European languages one word must do the job of my two. The reason, of course, is that theory$_1$ and theory$_2$ are often intimately connected. Let me mention just two such situations.

First, propositions to the effect that certain principles constitute an adequate basis for the theory$_1$ of a given field of investigation are themselves often theories$_2$. Thus the overthrow of classical mechanics was the overthrow not only of the basis of a theory$_1$ but also of a theory$_2$. The acceptance of the new mechanics was the acceptance not only of new ways of solving problems, it was the acceptance of a theory$_2$.

And second, a theory$_2$ often generates a field of investigation whose theory$_1$ must then be created. It can do so by supplying presuppositions for all the substitution instances of the members of the field. This is illustrated by the interplay between the kinetic-molecular theory$_2$ and statistical mechanics.

The moral supported by such intimacies is not that the difference should be ignored but only that the details of the theory of theory cannot be developed independently of the details of the theory of theories.

3

Why-Questions

1

In this paper we seek to pin down the conditions that define correct answers to why-questions. The problem can be stated more precisely. We will mean by a *why-question* a question that can be put in English in the form of an interrogative sentence of which the following is true: (1) the sentence begins with the word *why*; (2) the remainder of the sentence has the (surface) structure of an interrogative sentence designed to ask a whether-question—that is, a question whose right answer in English, if any, must be either "yes" or "no"; (3) the sentence contains no parenthetical verbs, in Urmson's sense (1956, p. 192).[1] A why-question put as an English sentence that satisfies (1), (2), and (3) will be said to be in *normal form*. By the *inner question* of a why-question we will mean the question alluded to in (2) above—that is, the question reached by putting the why-question in normal form, then deleting the initial 'why' and uttering the remaining string as a question. By the *presupposition* of a why-question we

*This work was supported in part by the Joint Services Electronics Program under Contract DA36–039-AMC-03200(E); in part by the National Science Foundation (Grant GP-2495), the National Institutes of Health (Grant MH-04737-5), the National Aeronautics and Space Administration (Grant NsG-496), and the U.S. Air Force (ESD Contract AF19(628)-2487). This essay is dedicated to Carl G. Hempel and to Peter Hempel as a token of gratitude for the tough-mindedness of the one and the gentle-mindedness of the other.

[1]Clause (3) eliminates from our discussion questions designed to ask for an opinion rather than a fact. Thus, it eliminates, e.g., 'Why do you think that nail biting is a symptom of anxiety neurosis?' in the sense of 'Why, in your opinion, is nail biting a symptom of anxiety neurosis?' although not in the sense of 'Why do you hold the belief that nail biting is a symptom of anxiety neurosis?'

will mean that which one would be saying is the case if, upon being asked the inner question of the why-question through an affirmative interrogative sentence, one were to reply "yes," or what one would be saying is the case if, upon being asked the inner question through a negative sentence, one were to reply "no." Thus, 'Why does copper turn green when exposed to air?' is a why-question in normal form; its inner question is 'Does copper turn green when exposed to air?'; and its presupposition is that copper turns green when exposed to air. The presupposition of 'Why doesn't iron turn green when exposed to air?' is that iron does not turn green when exposed to air.[2]

We will not be concerned with every sort of why-question. We will ignore why-questions whose normal forms are not in the indicative. We will ignore why-questions whose presupposition refers to human acts or intentions or mental states. Finally, we will ignore why-questions whose correct answer cannot be put in the form 'because p', where p indicates a position reserved for declarative sentences. Notice that this last stipulation affects not only why-questions whose correct answer must be put in some such form as 'in order to ...' or 'to ...',[3] but also why-questions that one might wish to say have no correct answer, and in particular why-questions

---

[2] A little care is needed in using the notion introduced here. A given why-question can often be put in more than one normal form, some of which will be ambiguous. This is particularly true of those that may be put in interrogative sentences with token reflexive expressions (e.g., 'Why is your temperature above normal?' as put to Henry and 'Why is Henry's temperature above normal?' as put to his doctor). Whenever this is the case, the inner question can also be ambiguous. We must therefore always think of the inner question as put under circumstances that give ambiguous expressions the same disambiguation given to them in the mother question.

We could have introduced the notion of presupposition by availing ourselves of some grammatical devices, e.g., the presupposition is what one would be saying is the case by asserting the sentence whose underlying structure preceded by a 'why' morpheme yields the why-question (or at least the interrogative sentence) when subjected to the Question Transformation. But we wish to avoid complicating the exposition beyond necessity or involving ourselves in grammatical issues that are still in flux. See in this connection particularly section 4.2.4 of Katz and Postal 1964. Note that what we call the presupposition of a why-question does not turn out to be what they call the presupposition of a why-question.

[3] It is not clear whether there are such questions—that is, whether, for example, answers of the form 'in order to ...' cannot always be replaced without loss of meaning by answers of the form 'because (subject) wished to ...', and similarly

with false presupposition and why-questions whose inner question itself has no answer—e.g., 'Why doesn't iron form any compounds with oxygen?' and 'Why does phlogiston combine with calx?' More may be ruled out, and we shall return to this point in section 6.

To simplify matters, we will disregard the fact that correct answers to the why-questions that do concern us can often be put in some other form than 'because p' with a declarative sentence at the p. Furthermore, we will reserve the term *answer* to refer to what is conveyed by the sentence at p abstracted from the 'because ...' environment. Thus, if 'Because the temperature is rising' is the correct answer to some why-question we will speak of 'the temperature is rising' as expressing the answer.

We can now put our problem very simply. Let a and b be any two true propositions; what necessary and sufficient conditions must they jointly satisfy if b is to be a correct answer to a why-question whose presupposition is a?[4]

2

So far we have relied on a characterization of why-questions in which features peculiar to the English lexicon and to English grammar play an essential role. We have carefully avoided identifying why-questions as a class of English interrogative sentences, but we have nevertheless defined them as questions that must be expressible in a certain way in English.

This may seem to detract from the interest of the problem. Philosophers of science in particular may feel wary of a typology of questions that rests squarely on the availability of certain forms in a specific natural language. There are good grounds for such suspicion. After all, scientific questions are for the most part only accidentally expressible in English. They can also be put in French, German,

---

for the other types of answer. The issues involved here are extremely interesting but not central for this paper.

[4]As should be clear by now, 'correct answer' must be understood in a narrow sense. 'Correct answer to Q' (where Q is a question) covers a possible reply to Q if and only if a statement of the form 'A told B W' (where W indicates a position occupied by the oratio obliqua form of Q, and A and B indicate positions occupied by expressions through which persons are mentioned) would be true of any episode in which that reply had been given by A to B in response to Q. 'Correct answer', therefore, does not cover such possibly warranted replies as 'I don't know' or 'The question involves a false presupposition'.

Russian, Japanese, etc., not to mention artificial languages. Furthermore, some of these questions may not be expressible in English at all, especially so if by 'English' we mean contemporary, "ordinary" English. 'Why is the emf induced in a coiled conductor a function of the rate of change of magnetic flux through it and of the resistance of the coil?' could probably not have been asked in seventeenth-century English and a similar situation may hold for questions that have not yet arisen.

One could try to meet such reservations by providing at the outset a language-independent definition of why-questions, or rather of *Why*-questions, a class of questions that would include all why-questions but that would not be limited to questions expressible in English. However, it is not clear how one is to be guided in setting up such a definition. We propose to deal with the matter somewhat differently. We will set as one condition on the solution of our problem that it abstract completely from the peculiarities of English—that is, that it be stated in terms that transcend linguistic idiosyncrasies and are applicable to expressions in any relevantly rich language. Having done this we should be able to give a definition of Why-questions that preserves whatever warrants an interest in the nature of why-questions on the part of philosophers of science.

3

What we have just said commits us to two hypotheses. The first of these hypotheses is that the relation between presupposition and (correct) answer to a why-question can be analyzed in language-independent terms. This hypothesis may be false, in which case we will not be able to solve our problem within the restrictions that we have adopted. However, it should be clear that the hypothesis cannot prevent us from accepting as relevant intuitions about the presence or absence of the relation in specific cases available to us as speakers of English. When we say that the relation is language independent, we do *not* mean that it hinges only on extra-linguistic facts. We mean that insofar as it hinges on linguistic features it hinges only on syntactic and semantic properties that expressions from every language share. Thus, the properties of being true and of being mutually implied are properties that expressions may have whether they belong to English or Chinese or Beulemans. The property of being the result of a do-transformation (the transformation that inserts 'do' in, e.g., 'He did not eat' or in 'Didn't he eat?' but not in 'He will not eat' or in 'Hasn't he eaten?') is a property shared only by English expressions. Our hypothesis is therefore compatible with the tenet that any speaker of English has the faculty to perceive whether the semantic and syntactic properties of two given English sentences meet (or fail to meet) the conditions that would make one of these sentences express the answer of a why-question whose presupposition is expressed by the other. He must, of course, understand the sentences, and he must also have certain relevant beliefs. On the other hand, to say that he has the faculty to perceive whether this sort of condition is satisfied in specific instances is not to say that he can describe them or analyze them. Nor is it to say that he will never or ought never to hesitate before pronouncing something to be a correct answer to a why-question. Hesitation is to be expected where the case at hand is complex and demands slow and careful scrutiny. It is also to be expected when the truth of the sentences or of the relevant beliefs are themselves objects of hesitation. But there are clear-cut cases and these constitute a corpus for which, as speakers of English, we must account.

4

The second hypothesis is that there are issues in the philosophy of science that warrant an interest in the nature of why-questions. The most obvious of these issues are whether science (or some branch of science or some specific scientific doctrine or some approach) ought to, can, or does provide answers to why-questions, and if so, to which ones. In other words, when appraising critically the state of scientific knowledge (or of some branch of science or some doctrine or some approach), how much weight should we give to unanswered why-questions? Should we consider that some why-questions are beyond the reach of scientific methodology or rules of evidence? Should we refrain from accepting as final any doctrine that raises why-questions to which no answers are forthcoming? We will have little to say about these very complex issues here, but since they provide much of the motivation for our inquiry, a few words of caution are called for.

These issues are usually discussed in English with the word 'explanation' used instead of 'why-question' or 'answer to why-

question'. Analogous substitutions occur in other languages. This
way of putting things can be innocuous and is possibly justified by
the awkwardness of using the more contrived locutions. But it is
ambiguous and may be a source of confusion. To become aware of
this we need but notice that 'explanation' may refer to the answers of
a huge variety of questions besides why-questions, the only requirement being that their oratio obliqua form fit as grammatical object
of the verb 'to explain' and its nominalization 'explanation of', e.g.,
how-questions, what-is-the-cause-of-questions, what-corresponds-at-
the-microscopic-level-questions, etc. Yet the issues raised by these
other types call for considerations peculiar to each type and different from those called for in the ones of why-questions. Confusion is
therefore likely to ensue and is apt to be further compounded if we
allow ourselves to forget that 'explanation' may also refer to things
not readily specified as answers to a specific class of questions. To remain aware of the range of issues covered by a given analysis we must
therefore keep sharp the differences among questions about (1) truth-
conditions of sentences generated from 'A explains B' and from 'A is
the explanation of B' by substituting any grammatically appropriate
phrase for B, (2) truth-conditions of sentences obtained by substituting for B only oratio obliqua forms of grammatically appropriate
questions, (3) truth-conditions of sentences obtained by substituting
for B the oratio obliqua form of some more narrowly defined class
of questions (e.g., why-questions, how-questions, what-corresponds-
at-the-microscopic-level-questions, etc.), (4) conditions that are satisfied by answers and presupposition of all questions whose oratio
obliqua form can be substituted for B, (5) conditions that are satisfied by answers and presupposition of some narrower class of questions whose oratio obliqua form can be substituted for B.[5] It should

---

[5]The literature abounds with discussions that are weakened by a failure to see
these possibilities. A classic example will be found in Part I of Pierre Duhem's
La Theorie Physique (1914) in which it is argued that the object of a physical
theory is not to explain a set of empirical laws. However, 'explain' is construed
in effect to mean giving the answers to questions of the form 'What fundamental
entities involved in what processes and governed by what laws underlie ...?' As
a consequence, Duhem did not examine a number of other types of explanations
that one might plausibly assign to theoretical physics.

The notion of presupposition used in this section is broader than that defined
earlier, since it also pertains to questions that are not why-questions. No analysis
of this broader notion is needed for this paper.

be clear that we will limit ourselves to a special case of (5) in this paper, the case of why-questions. In fact, our limits are even narrower since we have eliminated from consideration certain types of why-questions.

Offhand, it may seem that the (1) to (5) enumeration above is redundant and that we might have stopped after (3). Actually, subtle but important distinctions underlie the difference between 'Explanation of Q' and 'Answer to Q'. We have discussed these at some length elsewhere[6] and will say just a few words about them here to suggest the sort of further problems involved.

Let us describe someone as in a *p-predicament (p* can be thought of as standing for 'puzzled' or 'perplexed' but for *mnemonic* purposes only) with regard to some question Q, if and only if on that person's views, the question Q admits of a right answer, yet the person can think of no answer, can make up no answer, can generate from his mental repertoire no answer to which given that person's views, there are no decisive objections. For instance, a physicist committed to classical physics but aware of the photoelectric effect would be in a *p*-predicament with regard to the question 'Why does a photoelectric current appear without delay as soon as light of frequency above the threshold frequency impinges on the target, and this no matter how low the frequency of the impinging light?' Let us also describe someone as in a *b*-predicament with regard to a question Q if and only if the question admits of a right answer, no matter what the views of the person, but that answer is beyond what that person can think of, can state, can generate from his mental repertoire. Thus, someone unacquainted with the kinetic-molecular theory of matter would be in a *b*-predicament with regard to the question 'What is the mechanism by which water evaporates from uncovered dishes left in the open?' Let us say furthermore that a question Q is *unanswerable relative to a certain set of propositions and concepts C* if and only if anyone who subscribes to these propositions and limits himself to these concepts must be in either a *p*-predicament or *b*-predicament with regard to the question Q. The search for and discovery of scientific *explanations*, we think, is essentially the search for and

---

[6]Some of the ideas in this section have been discussed in greater detail in "An Approach to Explanation" and in "A Theory about the Theory of Theory and about the Theory of Theories."

discovery of answers to questions that are unanswerable relative to
prevailing beliefs and concepts. It is not, therefore, merely a quest
for evidence to settle which available answer is correct, it is a quest
for the unthought-of.

The difference between 'explanation' and 'answer' just sketched
transcends the distinction between why-questions and other questions. It should nevertheless be kept in mind when we deal with the
issues described at the beginning of this section. These need not be
resolved in the same way for why-questions that are unanswerable
relative to the set under consideration and for those that are merely
unanswered.

5

According to a very familiar theory, explaining a fact (an event, a
phenomenon, a natural law) consists in deducing a statement describing the fact from the statement of a true law and additional
true premises. Thus, according to this theory, the explanation of a
fact is a valid and sound (that is, all the premises are true) deduction, none of whose premises are superfluous, some of whose premises
are empirical laws, and whose conclusion is a description of the fact
explained. The premises of such a deduction are the *explanans* and
the conclusion is the *explanandum*. We will refer to such deductions
as *deductive nomological explanations* and to the theory itself, whose
most famous and competent exponent has been Carl Hempel, as the
Hempelian doctrine.[7]

As a general characterization of the notion of explanation, that
is, as a description of the truth-conditions of statements of the form
'A explains B' or 'A is a correct explanation of B', or their non-
English equivalents, the Hempelian doctrine obviously will not do,
a fact that its proponents have always recognized. The evidence for
this also shows that the doctrine does not describe necessary and
sufficient conditions on the answers to all the sound questions whose

---

[7] A complete bibliography on the subject probably appears in Hempel's *Aspects
of Scientific Explanation* (1965), which I have unfortunately not yet seen as
this essay is being written. Otherwise, consult, e.g., the bibliography at the
end of Hempel's magnificent "Deductive-Nomological vs. Statistical Explanation"
(1962); Part I of Scheffler's The Anatomy of Inquiry (1963); and Chapter 9 of
Grünbaum's *Philosophical Problems of Space and Time* (1963). For a more recent
bibliography see Salmon's *Four Decades of Scientific Explanation* (1989).

oratio obliqua form may be substituted for B. Answers to, or explanations of, how cloud chambers work, of what the nature of light is,
of what occurs at the molecular level when water freezes, etc. need
not be explanans (nor even a pragmatically selected component of
explanans). On the other hand, the doctrine no doubt does describe
necessary and sufficient conditions on answers to *some* questions
whose oratio obliqua form can be substituted for B. Thus, every
deductive nomological explanation is an explanation or at least a
sound answer to questions of the form 'How could anyone knowing
that ... (here put the conjunction of all the premises in a deductive
nomological explanans) ... but not that ... (here put the corresponding explanandum) ... have predicted that ... (here repeat the
explanandum) ... ?' and obviously the conjunction of the premises
also constitutes a correct answer to questions of the form 'From what
laws and antecedent conditions can the fact that ... (here put the
explanandum) ... be deduced?' But does the Hempelian doctrine
tell us what we want to know about why-questions? Is a proposition
p the correct answer of a why-question whose presupposition is q if
and only if p is the conjunction of premises (or of some pragmatically
selected subset of premises) of a deductive nomological explanation
whose conclusion is q? The following counterexamples (and they are
easily multiplied) strike us as settling the matter and this quite apart
from some technical difficulties connected with the relevant notions
of deducibility and law.

    1. There is a point on Fifth Avenue, M feet away from the
base of the Empire State Building, at which a ray of light coming
from the tip of the building makes an angle of θ degrees with a
line to the base of the building. From the laws of geometric optics,
together with the "antecedent" condition that the distance is M feet,
the angle θ degrees, it is possible to deduce that the Empire State
Building has a height of H feet. Any high-school student could set
up the deduction given actual numerical values. By doing so, he
would not, however, have *explained* why the Empire State Building
has a height of H feet, nor would he have *answered* the question
'Why does the Empire State Building have a height of H feet?' nor
would an exposition of the deduction be the explanation of or answer
to (either implicitly or explicitly) why the Empire State Building has
a height of H feet.

    2. From the Leavitt-Shapley Law, the inverse square law for light, the periods of Cepheid type variable stars in the Andromedan Galaxy, their apparent range of brightness, one can deduce that the Andromedan Galaxy is 1.5×10^6 light years away from the earth. The premises of the deduction, however, do not tell why or explain why the Andromedan Galaxy is 1.5×10^6 light years away from the earth.

3. Whenever the pointer of the water meter points to 5, and only the bathtub faucet is open water flows at a rate of five gallons per minute into the bathtub. The pointer has been on 5 for the last three minutes, and no faucet except the bathtub one is open. Therefore, fifteen gallons of water must have flowed into the bathtub. The deduction does not explain or tell or reveal *why* fifteen gallons of water flowed into the bathtub during the last three minutes.

4. All of Cassandra's predictions always come true. (Cassandra is a computer.) Yesterday Cassandra predicted that it would rain today. But obviously that is not why it is raining today.

5. Only men who are more than six feet tall leave footprints longer than fourteen inches. The footprints left by Gargantua on the beach are more than fourteen inches long. Therefore Gargantua is more than six feet tall.

Again the reasoning fails to mention *why* Gargantua is more than six feet tall.

These counterexamples are compatible with the thesis that answers and presuppositions of why-questions *must* be premises and conclusions of deductive nomological explanations. They do show, however, that this cannot be *sufficient.*

It has been suggested that these counterexamples and others like them are not really binding on philosophers of science, that they ultimately involve an appeal to ordinary usage and that such appeals are not appropriate when we deal with inquiries that are far removed from ordinary concerns. These objections can be construed in a number of ways.

1. They may mean that our refusal to call the explanans examples of *explanations,* or to look upon them as telling *why* something is the case, merely reflects allegiance to unscientific intellectual practices that scientists qua scientists have or should have abandoned. But this is hardly plausible. In 1885, Balmer devised a formula from which the frequencies represented in the spectrum of a sample of excited hydrogen could be deduced. But any scientist worthy of the name would have refused to accept such a deduction as the answer to why these particular frequencies were represented. The case is far from unique, and we owe the birth of quantum mechanics and of modern astronomy to that sort of refusal.

2. They may mean that the verb 'to explain' and its cognates have a technical meaning in scientific contexts, a status similar to that of 'work', 'action', 'model', etc. But this is false. 'To explain' does not belong to any technical jargon (except perhaps that of some philosophers), and anyhow the crucial words in our inquiry are 'why' and 'because'.

3. They may mean that, although we do not say of these inferences that they explain or tell why something is the case, we could, and that only an unscientific tradition prevents us from doing so. This would make sense if "ordinary use" merely demanded that we *refrain* from saying of the premises of the above inferences that they tell why something is the case, but words meaning what they do, we must also *deny* it. The deduction about Gargantua does *not* tell why Gargantua is more than six feet tall; 'because the footprints he left on the beach were more than fourteen inches long' is *not* the answer to 'why was Gargantua more than six feet tall?' My typewriter is neither blind nor not blind. That is a state of affairs for which "ordinary language" is partly responsible and a case might be made for extending the meaning of 'blind' so that my typewriter can be said to be blind. That horses are warm-blooded, however, is a fact about horses, not language. It would remain true even if 'warm-blooded' meant 'member of the Ku Klux Klan', although we would then have to put the matter differently. That the premises of the inference about Gargantua do not make up a correct answer to why Gargantua was so big is a fact about these premises. It would remain a fact even if 'why' were to become a request-marker for premises of deductive nomological explanations, although we would then have to put the matter differently.

4. The relation between the explanans and the explanandum of a deductive nomological explanation—let us call it the H-relation—can be defined in language-independent terms, that is, in terms applicable to the expressions of any language rich enough for science. On the basis of such a definition it is also possible to define, in *language-independent* terms, a class of questions very much like why-questions, whose answer and presupposition need only be H-related. Let us call them H-why-questions. Their definition is a little complicated, but anyone familiar with Hempel's doctrine will sense this possibility and will recognize it as one of the virtues of the doctrine. Those who reject the above counterexamples may simply doubt that why-questions can also be defined in language-independent terms and may believe that H-why-questions are the nearest possible language-dependent approximation. Accepting the counterexamples as binding would then mean giving up the principle that scientific questions are essentially language independent. However, such qualms are premature if, as we believe, why-questions *can* be defined in language-independent terms.

5. The objection may finally mean that by insisting on the relevance of these examples we must not only be insisting on the importance of why-questions (which have their own interrogative in English), but must be denying the importance of H-why-questions (which do not have an interrogative in English). We do not.

6

What is essential is not always easy to distinguish from what is accidental in the relation between why-questions and their answers. For instance, it is often assumed that besides being true, presuppositions of why-questions that have answers must also be something surprising, something that conflicts with what had been expected, or at least something unusual. Stated a little more precisely, the view amounts to this: We ask questions for all sorts of reasons and with many different purposes in mind—e.g., to test someone's knowledge, to offer someone the opportunity to show his erudition, to kill time, to attract attention; but questions have one basic function, the asking for information not already in our possession. On the view now considered, why-questions can fulfill that basic function only when asked by someone who finds the truth of the presupposition surprising and unexpected.

Why-questions no doubt are often asked by people to whom the presupposition comes as a surprise and the fact that they ask them is often related to their surprise. Furthermore, some why-questions whose presupposition is not surprising or unexpected seem to have no answer. Why does the earth have only one satellite? Why does every gram-molecular weight of matter contain 6×10^{23} molecules? Why can anything not move with a velocity greater than that of light? Why do bodies attract one another with a force that is directly proportional to their mass and inversely proportional to the square of their distance? Why is *chien* the French word for dog? Why has there never been a President of the United States whose first name was Clovis? Why does anything exist at all? Anyone will feel about at least one of these questions that he cannot provide a 'because ...' answer, although not because he does not know or has forgotten but simply because there is no answer. The view is even compatible with the use of 'why-should' questions that challenge one to show that a given why-question has an answer—e.g., 'Why should there have been a President with the first name Clovis?', 'Why shouldn't every gram-molecular weight contain 6×10^{23} molecules?'

If it were true that presuppositions of why-questions must be surprising, we would now have to seek out the relevant criteria for being surprising. Fortunately, it is not true. There is nothing unsound about the question 'Why is the train late today?' asked by the harassed New Haven commuter who would be more surprised if the train were on time; nor is there anything unsound about why-questions raised by scientists about very familiar everyday phenomena. The same sort of considerations show that presuppositions need not be departures from regularities.

The view that we have just described is close to another view that is equally tempting and equally false. According to this second view, why-questions have answers only when there exists a plausible argument in behalf of a contrary of their presupposition. This could account for all the things accounted for by the previous view and for further things as well. If true, it would require us to analyze the relevant notion of plausible argument. But it is not true. No such plausible argument is forthcoming in the case of 'Why has there never been any President of the United States with the first name Clovis?' and yet the question is sound and has an answer: 'Because no one by that name has ever been elected to the office or been the Vice-president when a President died in office.' The example is deliberately chosen from the list of questions cited previously as seeming to have no answer. It suggests that one's attitude toward the presupposition and other "pragmatic" considerations play no crucial role.

7

The solution that we are about to propose requires a few preliminary definitions. These definitions are stated with the help of predicate logic notation. The use of this notation introduces a number of theoretical problems that we will simply ignore. The problem of lawlikeness is but one of them. There are others that anyone familiar with the discussions of Hempelian doctrine will immediately detect.[8] We use the notation because it strikes us as providing the simplest way of exhibiting at present certain purely formal matters and we hope that our illustrations will bring out the intentions behind the schematisms. All these definitions must eventually be replaced by ones that make use of better representations. We think, however, that the heart of the analysis is essentially sound and that it may therefore be of some interest even in this temporary form. Each definition will be preceded by paradigms. This should make the formulae easier to read; it should, in fact, enable one to skip them altogether.

First Definition: General rule.

Paradigms: The level of a liquid in a cylindrical container on which a melting object is floating always rises. All French nouns form their plural by adding *s*. The velocity of an object never changes.

A general rule is a *lawlike* statement of the form

$$(\forall x)[(F_1 x \ \& \ F_2 x \ \& \ \dots \ \& \ F_j x) \rightarrow (S_1 x \ \& \ S_2 x \ \& \ \dots \ \& \ S_k x)]$$
$$(j \geq 1, k \geq 1)$$

Note that the definition does *not* require that a general rule be true or even plausible.

Second Definition: General abnormic law.

Paradigms: (1) The level of liquid in a cylindrical container on which a melting object is floating at room temperature will rise unless the object is made of a substance whose density in liquid form is the same or is greater than that of the original liquid at room temperature. If the density is the same, the level will remain the same; if the density is greater, the level will go down.

(2) The level of liquid in a cylindrical container on which a melting object is floating at room temperature will rise unless upon melt-

---

[8]See particularly Eberle, Kaplan, and Montague 1961; Kaplan 1961; and Kim 1963.

ing completely the floating object undergoes a decrease in volume equal to or greater than the volume originally above the surface of the water. In the former case, the level remains the same; in the latter case, the level goes down.

(3) All French nouns form their plural by adding *s* unless they end in *al* (except *bal*, *cal*, *carnival*, etc.) or in *eu*, or in *au*, or in *ou* (except *chou*, *genou*, etc.) or *x*, or *z*, or *s*. If and only if they end in *al* (except *bal*, etc.) they form the plural by dropping the last syllable and replacing it with *aux*; if and only if they end in *eu* or *ou* or *au* (except *chou*, etc.) they form their plural by adding *x*; if and only if they end in *x* or *z* or *s* they form their plural by adding nothing.

These are examples only if we are willing to assume that they are true as they stand.

A general abnormic law is a *true*, *lawlike* statement of the form

$$(\forall x)[(F_1x \ \& \ F_2x \ \& \dots \& \ F_jx) \rightarrow$$
$$[(\neg Ex \leftrightarrow (A_1x \lor A_2x \lor \dots \lor A_nx$$
$$\lor \ B_1x \lor \dots \lor B_mx \lor \dots \lor Rx))$$
$$\& \ (A_1x \lor A_2x \lor \dots \lor A_nx \leftrightarrow S_Ax)$$
$$\& \ (B_1x \lor B_2x \lor \dots \lor B_mx \leftrightarrow S_Bx)$$
$$\& \dots$$
$$\& \ (R_1x \lor R_2x \lor \dots \lor R_ex \leftrightarrow S_Rx)]]$$
$$(n \geq 2, j \geq 1)$$

of which the corresponding following statements are also true:

(a) $(\forall x)[(F_1x \ \& \ F_2x \ \& \dots \& \ F_Ix) \rightarrow$
$$(Ex \lor S_Ax \lor S_Bx \lor \dots \lor S_Rx)] \qquad (R \geq I)$$

(b) $(\forall x)([A_1x \rightarrow (\neg A_2x \ \& \ \neg A_2x \ \& \dots \& \ \neg A_nx$
$$\& \ \neg B_1x \ \& \dots \& \ \neg B_mx \ \& \dots \& \ \neg R_ex)]$$
$$\& \ [A_2x \rightarrow (\neg A_1x \ \& \ \neg A_2x \ \& \dots \& \ \neg A_nx$$
$$\& \ \neg B_1x \ \& \dots \& \ \neg B_mx \ \& \dots \& \ \neg R_ex)]$$
$$\& \dots$$
$$\& \ [R_ex \rightarrow (\neg A_1x \ \& \ \neg A_2x \ \& \dots \& \ \neg R_{e-1}x)]])$$

(c)   It (the statement) does not remain true and lawlike when any disjunction (in any of its internal biconditionals) is replaced by any expression that properly entails that disjunction, or when the conjunction in its antecedent is replaced by any expression prioperly entailed by that conjunction. By "properly" is simply meant that the converse entailment does not hold.[9] (These three conditions are redundant, but we are obviously not after elegance in this sketch.)

(d)   The closure of the main antecedent is not a logical truth or contradiction.

(e)   The closure of none of the internal disjunctions is a logical truth or contradiction.

(We construe the "unless" in the paradigms as exclusive disjunction.)

   Third Definition: Special abnormic law.

   Paradigms: (4) The velocity of an object does not change unless the net force on it is not equal to zero.

   (5) No sample of gas expands unless its temperature is kept constant but its pressure decreases, or its pressure is kept constant but its temperature increases, or its absolute temperature increases by a larger factor than its pressure, or its pressure decreases by a larger factor than its absolute temperature.

   Again we must assume that these are true.

   A special abnormic law is a true, lawlike statement of the form

$$(\forall x)[(F_1x \;\&\; F_2x \;\&\; \ldots \;\&\; F_jx) \rightarrow (\neg Ex \leftrightarrow A_1x \lor A_2x \lor \ldots \lor A_nx)]$$
$$(n \geq 2, j \geq 1)$$

that satisfies conditions (a) to (e) on general abnormic laws. (It is easy to show that every general abnormic law is equivalent to a conjunction of special abnormic laws but we will not make use of this fact.)[10]

   Fourth Definition: Antonymic predicates of an abnormic law.

   Paradigms: The antonymic predicates of (3) above are 'Forms the plural by adding s', 'Forms the plural by dropping the last syllable and replacing it with aux', 'Forms the plural by adding x', 'Forms the plural by adding nothing'. Those of (4) are 'Has a velocity that is changing', 'Does not have a changing velocity'.

   The antonymic predicates of a general abnormic law are the pred-

---

[9]This replaces the following in the original text: "It does not remain a true, lawlike statement when one or more disjuncts in any of the internal biconditionals is dropped or when one or more of the conjuncts in the initial antecedent is dropped." This slight modification will meet counterexamples in Teller 1974.

[10]Since every special abnormic law is also a general abnormic law, we could have dispensed with one of those two notions but not without complicating the exposition.

icates that appear in the consequent of (a). Those of a special abnormic law are the predicate substituted for E in the statement of that law, and the negation of that predicate.

Fifth Definition: Completion of a general rule by an abnormic law.

Paradigms: (1) and (2) are each a completion of the first paradigm of a general rule. (3) and (4) are the completion of the next two paradigms of a general rule.

An abnormic law is the completion of a general rule if and only if the general rule is false and is obtainable by dropping the "unless" qualifications—that is, by closing the statement before the first exclusive disjunction. (With our representation of the exclusive disjunction this requires negating the predicate substituted for E—or dropping the negation if it is already negated—deleting the biconditional connective, and making the obvious bracketing adjustments.)

We can now describe what we believe to be the relation between presuppositions and answers to why-questions. Before doing so, we will briefly present an example that points out the relevant features. The example and those to follow will only involve monadic predicates and will therefore fit the formulae in the definitions given above. But the predicates of presuppositions and answers of why-questions will not always be monadic and these definitions are thus too narrow as they stand. The shortcoming is readily remedied. We can either replace the references to the various formulae by references to the closure of the formulae obtainable by substitution from those given, or we can replace the formulae by more abstract schemata that allow for polyadic and for "zero-adic" predicates.[11] We shall assume that some such correction has in fact been adopted without actually carrying it out. Doing so would not solve the deeper problems alluded to in the introductory paragraph of this section, and the apparent gain in rigor would only be deceptive.

Why is the plural of the French noun *cheval chevaux*, that is, formed by dropping the last syllable and replacing it with *aux*? Answer: (Because) *cheval* ends in *al*.

---

[11] A "zero-adic" predicate will occur if, for instance, a position indicated in one of our schemata by a predicate letter and variable bound to an initial quantifier is replaced by a sentence with no free variables—that is, with no variable bound to the initial quantifier. Abnormic laws with occurrences of such internal closed sentences are required for why-questions whose presupposition or answer are expressed by closed sentences, as in the case of laws.

The answer together with abnormic law (3) and the further premise that *cheval* is a French noun form an explanans whose conclusion is the presupposition. The further premise that is not part of the answer together with the general rule completed by the abnormic law constitute a valid (but not sound) deduction whose conclusion is a *contrary* of the presupposition.

Here then is the relation: b is the correct answer to the why-question whose presupposition is a if and only if (1) there is an abnormic law L (general or special) and a is an instantiation of one of L's antonymic predicates; (2) b is a member of a set of premises that together with L constitute a deductive nomological explanation whose conclusion is a; (3) the remaining premises together with the general rule completed by L constitute a deduction in every respect like a deductive nomological explanation—except for a false lawlike premise and false conclusion, whose conclusion is a contrary of a; (4) the general rule completed by L cannot be completed into a true abnormic law when the conjunction in its antecedent is replaced by an expression properly entailed by that conjunction (i.e., not also entailing that conjunction).[12]

More examples may loosen up this jargon.

Why has there never been a president of the United States with the first name Clovis? We get the answer in the following way.

General rule: Every name is the name of some President of the United States.

Abnormic law that completes this general rule: Every name is the name of some President of the United States unless no one by that name has ever been elected to the Presidency and no one by that name has ever been Vice-President when a President died in office.

Premises that together with the law form a deductive nomological explanation whose conclusion is the presupposition: Clovis is a name; no one with the name Clovis has ever been elected to the Presidency of the United States, and no one by that name has ever been Vice-President when a President died in office.

---

[12]This replaces the following in the original text: "the general rule completed by L has the property that if one of the conjuncts in the antecedent is dropped the new general rule cannot be completed by an abnormic law." This slight modification of the original will meet counterexamples in Teller 1974 and others pointed out to me by Holly M. Smith.

Premises that together with the general rule lead to a contrary of the presupposition: Clovis is a name.

Remaining premise: the answer.

Next is an illustration of a why-question that has more than one correct answer. The case is adapted from Hempel 1958 (p. 272): "In a beaker filled to the brim with water at room temperature there floats a chunk of ice which partly extends above the surface. As the ice gradually melts, one might expect the water in the beaker to overflow. Actually, however, the water level remains unchanged. How is this to be explained?" We construe the last question as simply meaning, "Why did the level of water not rise?" Two relevant abnormic laws, (1) and (2) on page 88, are available and both are completions of the same general rule—that is, that given as our first example. The propositions that the content of the beaker is a liquid on which a melting object is floating, that the liquid is water, that the object is made of ice, that ice upon melting becomes water— that is, has the same density in liquid form as water, together with (1) form a deduction whose conclusion is the presupposition. One answer to the question is '(Because) ice upon melting has the same density as water'. The other premises together with the general rule lead to a contrary of the presupposition. We leave it to the reader to show that (2) leads in the same way to the answer '(Because) the ice undergoes a decrease in volume equal to the volume originally above the surface of the water'.

It is instructive to read what Hempel wrote about this example:

The key to an answer is provided by Archimedes's principle, according to which a solid body floating in a liquid displaces a volume of liquid which is the same weight as the body itself. Hence the chunk of ice has the same weight as the volume of water its submerged portion displaces. Now since melting does not affect the weights involved, the water into which the ice turns has the same weight as the ice itself, and hence, the same weight as the water initially displaced by the submerged portion of ice. Having the same weight, it also has the same volume as the displaced water; hence the melting ice yields a volume of water that suffices exactly to fill the space initially occupied by the submerged part of the ice. Therefore the water level remains unchanged.

Insofar as there is an answer conveyed in all this, it seems to be roughly equivalent to our second one.

Hempel was undoubtedly right in holding that the key to the explanation is provided by Archimedes's principle. However, if we look upon the question as a why-question, the principle is no more crucial than the principle that melting does not affect weight. It is the key in the sense that it provides a clue, also in the sense that anyone in a p-predicament or b-predicament with regard to the why-question must in all likelihood be told or be reminded of the principle; it is also an essential piece of knowledge for establishing that the answers are true, but it is not essential to establish that the answers, granted that they are true, are also correct answers to the why-question.

Our last illustration was a why-question that has more than one correct answer. Most why-questions are probably like that—that is, true presuppositions seldom if ever determine unique answers. According to our analysis, this is to be expected since more than one abnormic law is usually available from which a given presupposition can be derived. Our analysis, then, does not segregate good answers from poor ones, only correct ones from incorrect ones. We could, therefore, expect it even to account for the degenerate cases made famous by Molière: "Why does opium put people to sleep? Because it has dormitive power." One might as well have said, "Because it puts people to sleep." Such cases almost go through because of the availability of abnormic laws, like 'No substance puts people to sleep unless it puts people to sleep', which are instances of the valid formula '$(\forall x)[Fx \rightarrow (\neg Ex \lor Ex)]$' and of other schemata obtainable from '$p \rightarrow (q \leftrightarrow q)$' by substitution and generalization. However, these cases do not quite satisfy (2) on page 92, since the definition of 'deductive nomological explanation' requires that the abnormic law be *empirical*. Thus, we see how, on the one hand, one can assimilate such answers with correct answers and why, on the other hand, they ought to be rejected.

8

Our analysis accounts for some familiar facts about why-questions. In general, a question arises when one believes that it has an answer, but the answer is not known. This will happen for why-questions when one believes that the presupposition is true, views it as a departure from a general rule, and thinks that the conditions under which departures from the general rule occur can be generalized by an abnormic law. One may be mistaken about this. One may, for instance, be mistaken in thinking that the presupposition is true. In that case, no answer (as we have defined the term, that is, correct reply in the form of 'because ...') will be forthcoming. (There will be, of course, appropriate replies. A statement to the effect that the presupposition is false will provide the relevant information.)

One may also be mistaken in thinking that the presupposition represents a departure from a general rule. In that case, again, there will be no answer (although there will be other appropriate replies). "Why does this live oak keep its leaves during the winter?" "All live oaks do!" (Not however, "Because all live oaks do.") This sort of reply, like the previous one, has the force of a correction and entails that the question does not really arise.

One may, finally, be mistaken in thinking that the conditions under which departures from the general rule occur can be generalized. In such cases too no answer will be forthcoming: "Why is Johnny immune to poison ivy?" "Some people are and some people are not." However, an "answer" built from a degenerate abnormic law will also do, e.g., "No one is immune to poison ivy unless he is," and from that, "Because he is." (Note that this does not tell why Johnny is immune.)

These everyday situations should not be taken too lightly by philosophers of science. Why-questions must sometimes be countered with a general rule rather than with an answer. This should remind us of the fact that scientific investigations of why something is the case often end not with the discovery of a 'because ...' answer, but with the establishment of a new general rule. And this raises a problem: When is such a response merely a *begging* of the why-question? When does our ignorance demand that we not trade a why-question for a H-why-question but find the limits of a general rule? Why-questions even in science must sometimes be dealt with by denying that a departure from a general rule can be nontrivially generalized. This raises further problems: What sort of evidence warrants such denials? Can any fact ever be *shown* to be ultimate and unexplainable?

We mentioned in section 6 a view according to which why-questions can fulfill their basic function only if the presupposition is something surprising or if there is at least a plausible argument forthcoming in behalf of one of its contraries. It is easy to see how such a view might come to be accepted: many instances support it.

This is no accident. One often guides one's expectations by general rules, rules that are sometimes explicitly and sometimes only implicitly acknowledged. Reliance on such rules entails expectation that they work in most cases. But it also leads one to construe certain facts as departures from general rules, a prerequisite for a why-question to arise. This prerequisite thus is often satisfied under circumstances that surprise or that provide the grounds for a plausible argument for a contrary of a presupposition (the argument whose lawlike premise is the false general rule). As the counterexamples show, such circumstances, although frequent, are not essential, and they do not provide the key to the nature of why-questions. Here too, an interesting problem for philosophers of science arises. A clear mark of scientific genius is the ability to see certain well-known facts as departures from general rules that may have no actual instances, but that *could* have had some, and the germane ability to ask why-questions that occur to no one else. This way of looking at things sometimes yields important insights, but it is sometimes simply foolish. Is the difference grounded on logic, or is it fundamentally a matter of psychology or perhaps theology?

Another view frequently held about why-questions, particularly about why-questions with negative presuppositions, is that their answer must describe the absence of a necessary condition for a contrary of the presupposition. This is close to the truth in many cases to which these notions are easily applied, but it is an oversimplification, even in those cases. In the typical cases, the answer must describe the absence of (or at least something incompatible with) not merely *any* necessary condition for the contrary of the presupposition, but of a necessary condition belonging to a set (1) only one of whose members can be false, (2) each of whose members is necessary, and (3) all of whose members are jointly sufficient for that contrary. This follows from the nature of abnormic law. It is easily seen by looking at the propositional structure of instantiated special abnormic laws. A typical structure is

$$(1) \qquad Ya \rightarrow [Xa \equiv (Aa \lor Ba \lor Ca)]$$

where '$Ya \rightarrow \neg Xa$' is the propositional structure of the instantiated general rule, 'Xa' that of the presupposition, and the answer must be one of the disjuncts to the right of the biconditional. Typically, when (1) is true, so is

(2) $$Xa \equiv (Aa \lor Ba \lor Ca)$$

('Ya' being the true premise that together with the general rule leads to a contrary of the presupposition) and so then is

(3) $$\neg Xa \equiv (\neg Aa \ \& \ \neg Ba \ \& \ \neg Ca)$$

This shows that the answer ('Aa' or 'Ba' or 'Ca') describes the absence of a necessary condition ('$\neg Aa$' or '$\neg Ba$' or '$\neg Ca$') for the contrary of the presupposition. (Throughout we follow the practice of using 'contrary' to mean 'contrary or contradictory'.)

Condition (b) in the definition of an abnormic law requires that the disjuncts in (1) be mutually exclusive—that is, that if one of the conjuncts in (3) is false, the others must be true. (3) by itself requires that these conjuncts be jointly sufficient for '$\neg Xa$'.

We can test this consequence against an idealized, concrete instance. Two switches, A and B, are in series in a circuit so that current flows if and only if both switches are closed. Current is not flowing and both switches are open. Why is the current not flowing? Because both A and B are open. It would be misleading to say 'Because A is open', although it is true and although it mentions the absence of a necessary condition for the contrary of the presupposition, and similarly for 'Because B is open'. Either of these replies *in this context* would imply that the other switch is closed. The possible answers, then, are: *A is open although B is closed; B is open although A is closed; A and B are both open.* These are mutually exclusive. The negations are: *either A is closed or B is open; either B is closed or A is open; either A or B is closed.* But this is a set of conditions for the contrary of the presupposition (1) only one of whose members can be false, (2) each of whose members is necessary, (3) all of whose members are jointly sufficient.

We can now understand the function and form of the why-should questions mentioned in section 6. "Why is the current flowing?" "Why shouldn't it be flowing?" They are designed not only to bring out grounds for believing that the original why-question has an answer, but also to narrow down the area within which the answer is expected. They do this by asking what necessary conditions for the contrary of the presupposition *are satisfied*, what necessary conditions belong to a set of jointly sufficient conditions only one of which is presumably false.[13] The answer wanted for the original why-question is thereby defined since it must negate the one remaining condition. Why-should questions take on the force of a challenge when there is reason to doubt that only one condition is missing. On the other hand why-should questions have no answer when a necessary and sufficient condition for the presupposition of the why-question is forthcoming—that is, in cases where (1) has only one disjunct or (3) has only one conjunct.

We now turn to the examples cited in section 5 against the Hempelian doctrine. How do they fail as answers to why-questions? Let us look at a simple but typical member of the family. The telephone post at the corner of Elm Street is forty feet high. Its top is connected by a taut wire to a point thirty feet from its foot. The length of the wire is fifty feet. Why is the pole forty feet high? According to one interpretation of the Hempelian doctrine, an answer should be forthcoming that mentions the facts about the wire, since the height can be deduced from these facts and laws of physical geometry. There would be such an answer according to our analysis if it were a (abnormic) law that no pole is forty feet high unless a taut fifty-foot-long wire connects its top to a point thirty feet from its foot. But there is no such law. Fifty-foot-high poles may have no wires attached to them, or they may have wires attached to them of a different length and connect to a different point on the ground. If we extend the clause after 'unless' with disjunctions that include the cases with other wires and with no wires, we will still not end up with a true abnormic law; some of the disjuncts will not be mutually exclusive and, furthermore, the law will remain a law if all the disjuncts except that pertaining to the case of no wires are dropped.

There would also be an answer made up of the facts about the wire according to our analysis if it were a law that no pole is forty feet high unless, if there is a taut wire connecting the top to a point on the ground and the wire is fifty feet long, then the point on the ground is thirty feet from the foot. But there is no such law. If there were, it would entail that every pole to which no wire is attached must be forty feet high!

---

[13]Such a request obviously need not be met with an actual listing of conditions. The set can be indicated in many other ways—e.g., by pointing to other cases that seem in all relevant respects like those of the presupposition, but of which the predicate of the presupposition is not true.

However, the following is a law: No pole whose top is connected
to a point on the ground by a wire that is fifty feet long is itself forty
feet high unless that point on the ground is thirty feet from the foot
of the pole. Still, it does not meet the requirements of the analysis.
According to (4) on page 92, in the description of the relation, the
general rule completed by the abnormic law must not be such that
by dropping one or more of the conjuncts in the antecedent a new
general rule is obtained that can also be completed by an abnormic
law. But the above abnormic law violates that condition. We know
enough about poles to be confident that there is an abnormic law of
the form 'No pole is forty feet high unless ...'.

All the cases cited against the Hempelian doctrine will fail for
similar reasons. Just as we are confident that there are laws according to which poles will be forty feet high regardless of whether wires
are attached to them, so there must be laws according to which the
Empire State Building will have the height it has even in total dark-
ness, the distance to the Andromedan Galaxy would be what it is
even if no light traveled to us from it, the rate of flow of water into
the bathtub would be what it is whether or not measured, Gargantua would be more than six feet tall even if he had not gone to the
beach.[14]

---

[14]We can cope with these cases in a different way. Instead of individuating
why-questions by their presupposition, as we have done so far, we individuate
them by an ordered pair consisting of their presupposition and a false general rule.
Thus distinct why-questions can now share the same presupposition. We restate
the characteristic relation of why-questions as follows: b is the correct answer to a
why-question whose presupposition is a and whose general rule is g, if and only if
(1) there is an abnormic law L that is a completion of g, and a is an instantiation
of one of L's antonymic predicates; (2) b is a member of a set of premises that
together with L constitute a deductive nomological explanation whose conclusion
is a; (3) the remaining premises together with g constitute a deduction in every
respect like a deductive nomological explanation except for a false lawlike premise
and false conclusion, whose conclusion is a contrary of a. We eliminate (4) on
page 92. Instead of appealing to it in analyzing the failure of the counterexamples
to the Hempelian doctrine (when these examples are reconstructed to include true
abnormic laws), we construe the failure as that of not containing the answer to
the why-question most reasonably inferred from context and general background.
This is compatible with the possibility that the examples contain the answer to
some why-question with the given presupposition. The failure is nevertheless
fatal. Note that this approach still allows for why-questions—even under this
new individuation—that have more than one correct answer.

There is much to be said for this approach. It conforms to many of our

The very same sorts of considerations will account for certain asymmetries that have puzzled philosophers. From the laws of the simple pendulum, and the length of a piece of string at the end of which a bob is hanging and local free-fall acceleration, one can deduce the period with which that bob is oscillating. From the same law and data about local free-fall acceleration and the period with which the bob is oscillating, one can deduce its length. Yet a statement of the length is an answer to 'Why does the bob oscillate with such and such a period?', whereas a statement of the period of oscillation is not an answer to 'Why is the length of the string at the end of which the bob is hanging so many inches long?' The asymmetry is traceable, in a manner similar to the previous reasoning, to the fact that whereas the period would not have been what it is if the length had not been what it is, the length would have been what it is whether the bob had been oscillating or not.

Condition (4) may seem at first blush somewhat arbitrary. A little reflection will bring out, however, that it expresses a generally acknowledged and reasonable norm. It demands on the one hand that the answer be a consequence of the most general abnormic law[15] available, and it demands on the other hand that questions of the form 'Why is this A a C?' not be given answers that are really designed for 'Why is this AB a C?'

It may seem odd that abnormic laws should come provided with a special interrogative. But they are, after all, the form in which many common-sense generalizations that have been qualified through the ages are put. They are also a form of law appropriate to stages of exploratory theoretical developments when general rules are tried, then amended, until finally completely replaced. We are always at such a stage. We constantly discover exceptions to our general rules and inquire about their nature.

---

practices. It does justice to our intuition that why-questions are governed not only by presuppositions but also by presumptions. It avoids certain difficulties with the argument in the text. However, it introduces certain pragmatic issues that we prefer to delay as long as possible.

[15] For a discussion of a similar demand in connection with something the author calls "scientific understanding" (a notion whose relevance to the topic of why-questions is not clear to us), see p. 310 of Grünbaum's *Philosophical Problems of Space and Time* (1963).

4

Questions

A science, at any moment of its history, consists of a set of accepted (or at least seriously entertained) propositions, a set of unanswered questions to which these propositions give rise, and a set of principles or devices for establishing the answers to such questions. The evolution of a science is a sequence of related changes among these components. In particular, when new propositions are admitted, new questions must be allowed; when propositions are discarded, so are the questions to which they give rise; when questions are deemed answered, new propositions are automatically established; and, when questions are rejected as unanswerable, propositions also go. For most sciences, this process normally takes place in many languages at once; that is, it takes place through declarative sentences and interrogative sentences built by distinct grammars from distinct lexicons. In what follows I want to bring out some requirements that must be satisfied for this to be possible and some problems raised by these requirements. More specifically, I want to discuss some requirements that two languages L_1 and L_2 must jointly satisfy to be capable of serving simultaneously as the medium through which a given science can evolve. These requirements concern actually only those parts of the languages that are pertinent to the science. I do not know how to segregate these parts from the rest, and, to avoid circumlocutions, I shall not make this qualification where it

---

*A better account of the linguistic notions used in this paper will be found in *An Integrated Theory of Linguistic Descriptions* by Jerrold J. Katz and Paul M. Postal (1964), to which I owe a great debt. Ronald W. Langacker's "French Interrogatives: A Transformational Description" (1965) is also most pertinent. Some of my own notions will be found in "Why-Questions," this volume.

is needed, but will count on the reader to include it. The discussion will be crude in many other respects, and it will involve some enormous oversimplifications. It will, for instance, limit itself to *wh-questions* (those questions expressed in English through the interrogative 'what', 'which', 'where', 'how', 'why', 'when', and so on. This does not include 'whether' questions, that is, questions calling for a 'yes' or 'no' or their equivalent) and will disregard many of their subtleties. Any refinements or complications that I could bring to the discussion at this point would not, I believe, affect the main line.

1

The first requirement is that every interrogative sentence I of L_1 be mirrored by an equivalent interrogative sentence I' of L_2. What this means is fairly obvious. The English interrogative sentence 'What did Henry eat yesterday?' when uttered as a question will take as answers 'Henry ate some meat yesterday' (or its reduced form 'some meat'; we shall ignore these reduced forms in what follows) or 'Henry ate a huge meal cooked by his paternal grandmother', but it will not take 'Henry wrote a letter yesterday' or 'The Vietnamese war will forever blacken the record of the Johnson administration'. I will borrow the expression 'set of presented alternatives' from Belnap's magnificent *An Analysis of Questions* to refer to the set of declarative sentences that an interrogative sentence (uttered as a question) will take as (correct or incorrect) answers. I and I' are equivalent if the sets of alternatives they present can be put into a one-to-one correspondence that pairs declarative sentences with identical meaning. When Belnap introduced the expression 'set of presented alternatives' he had in mind situations in which an actual questioner presents a set of choices to an actual respondent rather than the more abstract situation in which a *sentence* is said to present the alternatives. Since a respondent must usually elicit the set by interpreting an interrogative sentence, we can disregard this difference.

2

The second requirement is that, if S is a declarative sentence of L_1 that entails the interrogative sentence I of L_1, then there must be in L_2 a declarative sentence S' that is synonymous with S and entails an interrogative sentence I' equivalent to I.

The relation of entailment concerned here is illustrated by the relation between the following:

(1)   Henry wrote something

(2)   What did Henry write?

If (1) is true, then (2) must have a correct answer, and, conversely, if (2) has a correct answer, then (1) must be true.

To see what is involved here, we must undertake some elementary linguistic analysis.

According to the most reasonable approach to language available nowadays, every sentence of English must be viewed as the product of two sorts of generative rules. A first set of rules, the "base rules" of the language, produces a structured (or parsed) string of "terminal elements." This is called the *underlying structure* of the sentence and serves as the basis for the semantic interpretation of the sentence. A second set of rules then deletes or combines or rearranges the elements of this underlying structure and produces another structured string, called the *surface structure* of the sentence, that provides the basis for the phonological interpretation of the sentence. Logical relations depend on underlying structures.

The underlying structure of (1) consists (roughly) of a subject noun phrase (Henry) followed by a verb phrase (wrote some thing); the verb phrase in turn consists of an auxiliary (the past tense), a verb (write) and an object noun phrase (some thing); this last noun phrase in turn consists of an indefinite determiner (some) and a pro-form (thing). A pro-form ('it', 'thing', 'one', and 'do' form a paradigmatic but by no means exhaustive group) is a sort of specialized blank provided by the grammar. Its function is to fill a position that—in accord with the base rules of the language—must be filled, but it does not have the semantic content carried by lexical elements in the same position. Its function is similar to that of free variables in systems that allow more than one kind of variable each of which may be replaced by only its own kind of constant.

The surface structure of (1) is obtained from the underlying structure through rules that combine the tense and the verb and that amalgamate the determiner with the pro-form.

The underlying structure of (2) is obtainable from the underlying structure of (1) by making two additions: (*a*) by prefacing the sentence with a symbol indicating that it stands as a question (linguists

usually represent this with 'Q', laymen with '?'); (*b*) by inserting
at the beginning of the object noun phrase a symbol 'wh' to indicate what pro-form is being questioned. (The need for this sort of
indication is seen in the difference between 'When did Henry write
something?' and 'What did Henry write sometime?')

   The surface structure of (2) is obtained from its underlying
structure through a series of transformations and morphophonemic
rules. The former will replace the 'Q', will move the constituent
(a constituent is a natural part of a sentence: the various phrases
mentioned above are all constituents; on the other hand the sequence 'Henry past' does not make up a constituent) made up by
'wh + some + thing' to the front of the sentence, will move the
auxiliary verb (if there is one—otherwise it first inserts 'do') and
tense next to this. The latter combine 'do + past' into 'did' and
'wh + some + thing' into 'what'. The details of these rules are of no
interest in this context. Different rules come into play with different
types of underlying structure.

   We can represent the underlying structure of (1) and (2) by
means of the labeled trees:

(3)

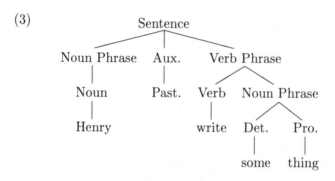

(4)

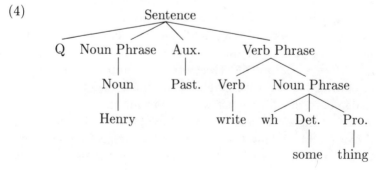

These trees show clearly the grounds for the entailment between (1) and (2): their underlying structures differ only by elements that neither add to nor subtract from the information about the subject matter of the sentences. Furthermore, the sentences in the set of alternatives presented by (2) are those whose underlying structure is obtainable from that of (2) by (*a*) removing the initial 'Q' and (*b*) replacing the constituent in which 'wh' and the pro-form appear (that is, the "questioned" constituent) by a constituent of appropriate semantic and syntactic character. The syntactic character is determined by the rules of the grammar. These rules bring into play the character of the pro-form and of the whole underlying structure. The semantic character, on the other hand, is determined by the truth-conditions of (1). The resulting sentences must have truth-conditions that include the truth-conditions of (1). Since (1) itself is always available as a sort of degenerate answer, the mutual entailment is assured.

We can generalize the relation between (1) and (2). A declarative sentence S entails an interrogative sentence I if and only if (*a*) the underlying structure of S contains a constituent in which a pro-form appears, (*b*) the underlying structure of I is obtainable from that of S by prefacing the latter with a 'Q' and attaching a 'wh' to the constituent that contains the pro-form. *The class of alternatives presented by* I is a subclass of the sentences that entail S; its members will have underlying structures identical with that of S except for the replacement of the pro-form-containing constituent by another constituent. The character of the pro-form determines what constituents may serve as replacements.

The importance of pro-forms must be emphasized. English has many pro-forms ('who' contains 'one', 'where' contains 'place', 'how' contains 'way', 'when' contains 'time', and so on), and yet it is easy to imagine new ones that could increase the number of available questions. For instance, English has only one verb-pro-form, 'do'. Furthermore, 'do' represents only a subclass of the class of verbs, namely that subclass whose members may cooccur with the progressive auxiliary(the auxiliary that appears in 'she is singing' but not in 'she sings'). Consequently, 'What does Henry do?' will present 'Henry works for General Electric' and 'Henry studies the Bible' but not 'Henry loves General Electric' or 'Henry believes the Bible'. Without a new pro-form there is no obvious way of forming a question that will present all four together with others like them, or that will present all the alternatives built around the verbs not represented by 'do'.

3

The third requirement is a generalized form of the second. If S is a declarative sentence of L_1 that entails and is entailed by a *cluster* of interrogative sentences $|I|$, then there must be in L_2 a declarative sentence S' synonymous with S and similarly related to an equivalent cluster.

(1) stands in a relation of mutual implication not only to (2) but also to 'When did Henry write?', 'Where did Henry write?', 'How did Henry write?', 'With what did Henry write?', and with multiple questions like 'What did Henry write when?', 'How did Henry write where?', 'When did Henry write what how?', and so on. These interrogative sentences express questions all or none of which have correct answers. Furthermore, most members of the set have answers that are related in the same way to a different but obviously connected set; 'Henry wrote yesterday' entails and is entailed by 'What did Henry write yesterday?', 'Where did Henry write yesterday?', and so on. This is the sort of set that I call a *cluster of questions*.

To account for the existence of this cluster we must improve our picture of the underlying structure of (1). The verb 'to write' is actually the verb 'to write some thing, in some where, at some time, some how, ...'; that is, the verb includes a number of adverbial and prepositional constituents that contain pro-forms. The selection of the verb introduces these *obligatorily* in the underlying structure. Further rules authorize their deletion or their replacement by constituents of appropriate semantic and syntactic character.

Each member of the cluster is obtained from the complete underlying structure of (1) by questioning one or more pro-form- containing constituent. The relations among them are easily accounted for by extending in a mechanical way the points made in the discussion of the second requirement.

4

I have introduced the second requirement as if it were not implicitly part of the third in order to distinguish it explicitly from the fourth:

if S is a declarative sentence of L_1 that *gives rise to* (but does not entail) an interrogative question I of L_1, then there must be a synonymous declarative sentence S' in L_2 that gives rise to (but does not entail) an interrogative sentence I' equivalent to I.

The cluster entailed by (1) does not include

(5)   To whom did Henry write?

Yet, knowing that (1) is true, one might wish to find the correct answer to (5) *if any*. An examination of only the relevant underlying structures will not reveal the grounds for this sort of relationship. We must look not only at the underlying structure and at the character of the various lexical items that occur in it, but also at the rules that generate it. The constituents introduced by the base rules of the grammar fall into two classes: obligatory constituents and optional constituents. Obligatory constituents may sometimes be deleted in a surface structure, but they must appear in the underlying structure. Optional constituents, on the other hand, need never be included, and their erasure yields an underlying structure that is still well formed. Consequently, a sentence without a certain optional constituent will usually have truth-conditions that may no longer be sufficient when the optional constituent is added. (5) entails and is entailed by

(6)   Henry wrote something to someone

The underlying structure of (6) contains the optional constituent 'to some one' in its verb phrase. This constituent does not appear in the underlying structure of (1); hence (1) does not entail (6) or (5). That it does not is evident from the fact that Henry may never have written to anyone, although he may have written a book.

In general, then, a declarative sentence S gives rise to (but does not entail) an interrogative sentence I if the underlying structure of I is obtainable from that of S by adding an optional pro-form-containing constituent, prefacing the resulting structure with 'Q,' and attaching a 'wh' to the optional constituent. When this is the case, the truth of S will not establish that I must have an answer: additional evidence is needed. Such evidence, however, is often available, as is attested by the fact that until recently there were very good reasons to believe that, if 'X has mass' is true, then 'What is the momentum of X at T?' and 'What is the position of X at T?' must each always have an answer.

5

The fifth requirement is more difficult to state precisely. If S is a declarative sentence of L_1 that entails (or gives rise to) an interrogative sentence I with regard to which it is possible to be in a *p-predicament*, then there must be in L_2 a declarative sentence S' that is synonymous with S and that entails (or gives rise to) an interrogative sentence I' with regard to which it is also possible to be in a p-predicament and which is equivalent to I.

A person is said to be in a p-predicament with regard to a question Q if, on that person's assumptions and knowledge, Q is sound and has a correct answer, yet that person can think of no answer, can conjure up no answer to which, on those assumptions, there are no decisive objections. For instance, theoretical linguists these days are in a p-predicament with regard to 'What are the characteristics of an organism that can acquire a language on the basis of a relatively small corpus of examples?'

I do not know how to account in general for the fact that some interrogative sentences can be the objects of p-predicaments. The trait seems to be associated with the fact that these sentences are usually construed as presenting a set of alternatives narrower than would be inferred from purely linguistic considerations. For instance,

(7)   Why does copper turn green when exposed to air?

has an underlying structure obtainable from that of

(8)   Copper turns green when exposed to air

by inserting a (optional) 'because of some thing' at an appropriate position, and questioning it. This alone should not exclude from the set of presented alternatives 'Copper turns green when exposed to air because Louis XIV was called Le Roi Soleil' or 'Copper turns green when exposed to air because it is easily confused with gold'. Yet these seem to be clearly excluded.

The case of why-questions deserves special attention. It is a little better understood than most of the others, and it represents a class that plays an important role in the sciences. Elsewhere I have tried to deal with this in some detail; here I will only sketch some essential lines. Let us call any sentence that stands to a why-question as (8) stands to (7) the *presupposition* of the why-question. By a *general rule* let us understand a false lawlike sentence of the form

'Every so and so is such and such'. By an *abnormic law* let us understand a true lawlike sentence of the form 'Every so and so is such and such unless A is true of it, or B is true of it, or C is true of it, ...'. The disjuncts after 'unless' are supposed to be mutually exclusive. Let us say of an abnormic law that it *completes* a given general rule when what precedes its 'unless' is identical with the general rule. A correct answer to a why-question is obtained when the constituent after 'because', the questioned constituent, is replaced by a *true* sentence S of which the following holds: (a) the presupposition is deducible from S together with other true premises, and these include an abnormic law; (b) a contrary of the presupposition is the conclusion of a deduction in every respect like the above, but in which S does not appear as a premise and in which the abnormic law has been replaced by the general rule it completes. The set of alternatives presented by a why-question is the set of all the declarative sentences that satisfy the conditions on a correct answer, but in which the sentence inserted after 'because' may be false. A person may be in a p-predicament with regard to a why-question by virtue of having evidence that an appropriate abnormic law holds but without knowing all the terms in the law: such a person may then be in a position to produce only alternatives that can be refuted.

The implications of this analysis for the fifth requirement are not trivial: it entails that the distinction between general rules and abnormic laws should be able to survive translations between, L_1 and L_2 and that the relation of completion should be preserved in the translation.

6

I now want to outline two artificial languages L_1 and L_2 which do not satisfy the above conditions. These languages have very similar grammars and very similar lexicons, and much that can be said in one can also be said in the other.

L_1 and L_2 have the following grammar:

1. Every declarative sentence may consist of three constituents: a 1st-phrase, a 2nd-phrase, a 3rd-phrase.

2. Nothing that can ever appear as an n-phrase can ever appear as an n'-phrase ($n = 1, 2, 3; n \neq n'$).

3. They each have two pro-forms. 'X_2' and 'X_3' are those of L_1;
   'Y_2' and 'Y_3' are those of L_2. Each "represents" the class of
   constituents corresponding to its subscript.

4. Each of these pro-forms can be questioned through the attach-
   ment of 'wh'.

5. In L_1, *but not in* L_2, the presence of a 3rd-phrase is always
   optional.

To show how semantic content is carried by expressions of the
language, I now describe a third language L.

6. The sentences of L include the following:

$$A\ B_1\ C_1\ D_1$$
$$A\ B_2\ C_2\ D_2$$
$$A\ B_3\ C_3\ D_3$$
$$A\ B_1\ C_4\ D_4$$

7. The synonymous sentences are:

in L_1	in L_2
$A'\ [B_1C_1]'\ D_1'$	$A''\ B_1''\ [C_1D_1]''$
$A'\ D_2'\ [B_2C_2]'$	$A''\ [B_2C_2]''\ D_2''$
$A'\ [B_3C_3]'\ D_3'$	$A''\ B_3''\ [C_3D_3]''$
$A'\ [B_1C_4]'\ D_4'$	$A''\ B_1''\ [C_4D_4]''$

The conventions I have used are obvious. The number of primes
on an expression indicates the language to which it belongs. Expressions between brackets are single constituents in L_1 or L_2 whose
semantic content is the same as that of the compound expression of
L between the brackets. Single letters that are primed correspond to
constituents that have the same semantic content as the expressions
represented in L by the same letters unprimed.

The following sentences are thus, also,

in L_1	in L_2
$A'\ X_2\ X_3$	$A''\ Y_2\ Y_3$
$A'\ X_2$	$A''\ Y_2\ D_2''$
$A'\ [B_3C_3]'\ X_3$	$A''\ B_3''\ Y_3$
$\cdots$	$\cdots$

(but not $A''\ Y_2$)

And so are the following interrogative sentences that cannot be translated between L_1 and L_2:

in L_1	in L_2
A' wh-X_2 wh-X_3	A'' wh-Y_2 wh-Y_3
A' wh-X_2	A'' wh-Y_2 D_2''
A' wh-X_2 D_1'	A'' B_3'' wh-Y_3
A' $[B_3C_3]'$ wh-X_3	

L_1 and L_2 are not natural languages. Their differences and similarities, however, are very much like the differences and similarities between vast portions of natural languages, even natural languages that are as closely related as English and French. The a priori probability that any two natural languages should satisfy the five conditions seems, therefore, practically nil. But the history of science provides very good evidence that many languages do to a large extent satisfy them. How come? What is the nature of the underlying logic that they all somehow reflect, and how do they reflect it? These are questions with regard to which I at least am in the deepest p-predicament. I offer them not only as illustrations but as topics that we who are interested in erotetic matters should begin to tackle.

5

Science and the Forms of Ignorance

1

I am a very ignorant person and I have long assiduously deplored this fact. Ignorance is an invitation to scorn; it presumably deprives one of all sorts of joys, it can't be put to any useful ends, it can't be eaten, it can't be given away, and it is damn difficult to get rid of in any other way. Only those who are totally ignorant about ignorance can believe that ignorance is bliss! But ignorance can also define and determine the value of scientific contributions. Its study should therefore be one aspect of the study of how scientific contributions can be assessed, and it should thereby become part of the philosophy of science. This fact, if it is a fact, holds a heartening hope for someone like me. It means that a cause of shame and embarrassment may yet turn out to be a source of professional expertise! My talk should be followed in the light of that hope. Dale Carnegie, that great existentialist, somewhere quotes Robert Maynard Hutchins, that great essentialist, in turn quoting Julius Rosenwald, that great former president of Sears and Roebuck, as saying: "When you have a lemon, make a lemonade." This is what I propose to do here, and I invite you to share the refreshment, sour though it may turn out to be.

2

The point of the sort of study that I have in mind will be more easily seen by recalling some developments in the contemporary history of the philosophy of science. Until recently, most prominent philosophers of science centered their professional attention on a conception of scientific theories aptly and succinctly described in a paper by Carl Hempel (1967):

The ... conception of a theory as consisting of, or being decomposable into two principal components: (1) An uninterpreted deductive system, usually thought of as an axiomatized calculus C, whose postulates correspond to the basic principles of the theory and provide implicit definitions for its constitutive terms; (2) A set R of statements that assign empirical meaning to the terms and the sentences of C by linking them to potential observational or experimental findings and thus interpreting them, ultimately in terms of some observational vocabulary.

Though the facts no longer warrant this, I shall refer to this conception as the *accepted view*.

It is important to remember that the proponents of the accepted view did not (or in any case need not and should not) claim that this conception correctly described what the word 'theory' means or that it described the form in which theories occur in the literature. Either claim would have been blatantly false. The claim was of a different nature altogether and might be put as follows: A theory is something that can be presented in many forms depending on one's objectives, one's audience, one's stylistic and pedagogic preferences, and other pragmatic considerations. However, every theory *can* be presented in the form of an abstract calculus paired with a set of interpretation rules satisfying the accepted view. Furthermore, the possibility of representing any theory in that form is of great philosophic significance. Why was it thought to be of great philosophic significance? The philosophers who developed the accepted view were committed to the task of making explicit the types of considerations that govern—or that ought to govern—the acceptance and the assessment of any alleged contribution to scientific knowledge, and, in particular, to the corpus of scientific theories. They also believed that a set of general criteria could be brought forth which (a) could be stated in ways that raised no philosophic difficulties, (b) would be unambiguously applicable to specific theories only in their guise of uninterpreted calculi paired with interpretation rules, (c) would rely in an essential way on the properties of calculi and interpretation rules, (d) would conform to the tenets of empiricism and the interests of enlightened scientists, (e) would mark as acceptable all and only those theories that scientists and empiricists would admit as acceptable on the basis of preanalytic intuitions and philosophic conscience. Thus the adherents of the view saw it as indicating how their task should be approached and completed. If a theory can always be represented as an uninterpreted calculus cum interpretation rules, and if criteria exist that satisfy (a), (b), (c), (d), and (e) above, then, in a sense that is difficult to analyze but easy to grasp, the task becomes "simply" that of formulating these criteria.

Those were not the only considerations that encouraged investment of time and thought and reputation in the accepted view. There are a number of concepts used in talking *about* theories—and particularly when evaluating them—that have long puzzled analytic philosophers. They include the notions of explanation, of theoretical terms, of predictive power, of empirical content, and others. Assuming the accepted view to be right, it seemed reasonable to seek out explications of these notions (in terms of the unproblematic notions that characterize interpreted calculi) that would constitute a solution of the analytic puzzles.

The accepted view is less and less accepted. Why? Some reasons for the decline are purely sociological, but there are less earthly reasons as well. The accepted view entailed at least four claims: (1) that every scientific theory can be axiomatized, that is, cast in the form of an interpreted calculus fitting Hempel's description above; (2) that a set of criteria can be stated that meets conditions (a) to (e) above; (3) that every accepted theory, once axiomatized, will satisfy these criteria; (4) that the notions of explanation, theoretical term, and the others mentioned above, can be reduced to the notions needed to formulate the accepted view. Three of these claims, (1), (2), and (4), entail the possibility of carrying out certain programs. These programs have not been carried out so far, and obstacles that appear insurmountable have arisen in their path. Thus the failure of the programs so far constitutes grounds for skepticism, that is, grounds for believing that there is something essentially mistaken about the accepted view.

I believe that the skeptics are right and that the accepted view is no longer tenable. But to say this is *not* to say that the problem that motivated it should also be dismissed. Remember the problem: to find and to state in philosophically unobjectionable ways the principles that govern or that ought to govern the acceptability of any alleged contribution to science, and especially to the corpus of theories. Let us call this the Appreciation Problem. Many people now deem also that the Appreciation Problem itself rests on a mistaken presupposition, namely, the presupposition that there are invariant, universal principles of acceptability which survive the continuous overthrow of scientific doctrines and which regulate their replacement. I do not wish to show here that the objections against that presupposition miss their mark. Nor am I prepared to defend the presupposition. I view it as an article of philosophic faith, supported by some clear intuitions, but possibly false. The only way to find out is by trying to solve the Appreciation Problem.

3

If I am right, we need a new approach to the Appreciation Problem. How shall we proceed? Let me first draw on my expertise as a master ignoramus to make a few initial suggestions that I shall refine somewhat later.

How do I know that I am such a good ignoramus? Well, I can cite a number of questions whose answers I don't know: 'What is the distance between London and Paris?', 'How many arithmetic steps are absolutely required in a program for solving a set of linear equations?', 'What is the Papago word for 'horse'?', 'What is the atomic weight of calcium?' Furthermore, some questions have me so utterly baffled that I can't even produce a plausible answer, for example, 'Why do tea kettles emit a humming noise just before the water in them begins to boil?', 'What are the heuristics by which a child discovers the grammar of his language?' Finally, there are problems that have me stumped. Give me the length of a ship, the weight of its cargo, the height of its mast, and I still can't figure out the age of the captain. Some people can. Or perhaps they can't do that, but give them the percentage of a solution of ethylene glycol in water and its density and they will figure out for you the vapor pressure of that solution at 20° C. In short, I know questions whose correct answers I can't tell from incorrect ones; I know questions to which I know only incorrect answers; I know problems that I can't solve.

But this now suggests that my ignorance is not one big undifferentiated glop, one huge unstructured nothingness. It is apparently made up of identifiable items. These items furthermore lend themselves to classification and comparison. It even looks as if they may stand in interesting relationships to one another and to other things. Let us tentatively refer to such items as *items of nescience*.

So far I have talked as if these items of nescience were my personal property. This is obviously presumptuous. Many are the common possession of a number of us and some are shared by all of us. It is therefore possible to think of them in abstraction of any specific owners. Thus a question that is an item of nescience of anyone who does not know the answer can be thought of as simply an item of nescience, without regard to its actual status in this or that person's ignorabilia.

Two more pieces of loose—but I hope suggestive—jargon will help to expedite matters. Let p be a correct answer to some question q. No one can count q among his items of nescience who knows that p. I shall say in that case that p *cancels* q. For instance, 'Dante was born in 1265 in Florence' cancels 'Where and when was Dante born?' Questions, as we shall see, are not the only type of items of nescience. Shortly, I shall describe other types and extend the concept of cancellation to cover them. Let x now be an item that cancels some item of nescience. I will then refer to x as an *item of yescience*.

With this last ugly new expression I can now state a philosophical hypothesis: Science is a set of actual or presumed items of yescience. It is no doubt a strange hypothesis. On the one hand, it looks like a truism; on the other, it hardly makes sense. The fact that it looks like a truism need not deter us. On the contrary! After all, philosophy consists in taking truisms seriously and squeezing depth out of them. The fact that it barely makes sense need not deter us either. It simply shows that we have some analytic work cut out for us. The important point to notice about the hypothesis is that it offers a new construal of the Appreciation Problem, for that problem can now be stated as follows: What principles determine whether a presumptive contribution to science is an item, or a set of items, of yescience? What determines whether it cancels what item of nescience, if any?

Is the hypothesis true? Well, it is too vague at this stage to enable us to decide. However, one thing must be clear: The hypothesis does not assert that every actual contribution or alleged contribution to science was initially sought in response to an awareness that something specifiable as an item of nescience needed to be canceled. There are innumerable contributions of which this is true. But there are many of which it is not. The truth of the hypothesis then should not hinge on the presence or absence of certain episodes in the intellectual biography of scientists. Furthermore, the test of the hypothesis lies in its entailments, and, particularly, in its programmatic entailment. In this respect it resembles the accepted view. I shall turn to that program in a moment. It constitutes an approach to the Appreciation Problem. If it can be carried out, this will constitute grounds for retaining the hypothesis, and for deeming that the Appreciation Problem can be solved. If it can't, then the hypothesis will have to be rejected and the Problem will have to be recast once more.

4

Before going any further, let us glance a little more closely at some of the flora and fauna of the land of nescience and yescience. I have mentioned questions and answers. 'Nixon is the President of the United States' cancels, unfortunately, 'Who is the president of the United States?' But now consider 'How is speech produced?', or 'What heuristics do good chess players use to spot possibilities?', or 'What would the universe be like if nothing existed?' We are, with regard to these questions, in what I have called elsewhere[1] a *p-predicament* (p here stands for 'puzzled' but as a mnemonic aid only), a predicament that I have described as follows: Someone is in a p-predicament with regard to a question q if and only if, given that person's assumption and knowledge, q must be sound, must have only true presuppositions (and hence have at least one correct answer), yet that person can think of no answer, can imagine no answer, can conjure up no answer, can invent no answer, can remember no answer to which, on that person's view, there are no decisive objections. A p-predicament is canceled by a correct answer. But less will do. Any answer not known to be false will do, even if not known to be true. It often requires the greatest geniuses to discover some answers of that sort. Consider also 'Why does the moon look larger when near the horizon?' If my information about that question is right, we do not know the answer, but a number of still viable possible answers are available. We are not in a p-predicament with regard to the question. Nevertheless, we also know that there probably are many other

---

[1] On the notion of p-predicament, see "An Approach to Explanation" and "Why-Questions," this volume.

possible answers that have not occurred to anyone yet. The discovery of such further possibilities would enhance our science and would thus also cancel some nescience. Answers that cancel p-predicaments of the sort illustrated by the last four questions are what I call *theories*. I have given an explicit definition of that term elsewhere.[2] Peter Achinstein, one of the very few people to have looked at that definition, has been kind enough to take a few whacks at it.[3] I believe that I can easily quibble my way out of his criticisms, but they do bring out certain very unfortunate unclarities that discourage me from repeating the definition here. I will reintroduce the term later.

If you wish to know the distance between Baltimore and Boston, you might get yourself a yardstick and measure the distance. It is a very tedious way of getting an answer to 'What is the distance between Baltimore and Boston?' and it may even be an impossible one. You can, however, get the answer by measuring the distance between the points corresponding to these cities on a good map and then computing the real distance from that one with the aid of the scale. Or again, if you wish to know the distance traveled by a free-falling body in half an hour, you can get yourself a big vacuum and drop objects from various heights until you find one that requires thirty minutes. This, too, would be tedious and probably impractical. But you can get the answer to 'What is the distance traveled by a free-falling body in half an hour?' simply by substituting '30' in the version of '$1/2\ gt^2$' that has the parameters in c.g.s. units. In each of these cases, there are thus at least two ways of arriving at an answer: a direct method, and one that derives the answer through computations on answers to other questions. Let us call the latter *procedures for carrying out vicarious investigations*, and the conglomerate they make up, we shall call *theory* (not *theories*; the word here is used as a mass-noun as in *electromagnetic theory* and no longer as a count-noun as in the *theory of relativity*). I mentioned earlier that if you gave me the length of the ship, the weight of the cargo, the height of the mast, I still would not be able to figure out the age of the captain. I could, of course, ask him. But there is, as far as I know, no available method for carrying out a vicarious

---

[2] See "A Theory about the Theory of Theory and about the Theory of Theories," this volume.

[3] See Achinstein 1968.

investigation that will yield an answer to the question about the age of the captain and that will rely solely on the information given in the problem. Our item of nescience here is the want of a formula for computing the answer from that information, and if it can be canceled, it will be canceled by such a formula, or by a method for deriving such a formula from general principles.

As we can see, items of nescience and items of yescience belong to very different species. We could, of course, say that there are only questions and answers, and that in the allegedly other sorts of cases we simply have slightly complex questions, such as, 'What is an answer neither known to be true nor known to be false to 'How is speech produced?'?' or 'What would be a method for carrying out a vicarious investigation using the answers to 'what is the length of the ship?', 'what is the weight of the cargo?', 'what is the height of the mast?' to obtain the answer to 'what is the age of the captain?'?'. We could say this, but we would then blur distinctions that are important in our approach to the Appreciation Problem. Since I do not wish to blur any more distinctions than I shall be compelled to blur anyhow, I shall pretend throughout that we do not ask questions about questions, except when we do philosophy.

5

Back now to the Appreciation Problem. You will recall its new construal: What principles determine whether a presumptive contribution to science is an item or a set of items of yescience, that is, what determines whether it cancels what items of nescience?

To solve that problem we need a general theory of nescience and yescience that will exhibit such principles in a form applicable to actual cases (though these may themselves have to be put first in some canonical form—as in the case of the accepted view) and satisfy ourselves, perhaps by looking at actual cases, that these principles yield the very evaluations we make when flying by the seat of our rational pants.

This is an enormous order which I cannot hope to fill in this talk or even in my lifetime. I can and will indicate the broad outlines of that theory and thus describe the program that will test the hypothesis I am entertaining. I shall do this by outlining the chapters of an imaginary treatise through which the theory of nescience and yescience might be taught. This treatise will contain at least three chapters: I. Erotetic Logic, II. Theory of Theories, III. Theory of Theory. Each chapter will in turn be divided in two sections, a deductive section and an inductive section. What will these chapters and sections contain?

I.   Erotetic Logic

Erotetic logic is the logic of questions and answers. This chapter starts from the assumption that every question stands in three different relations to specifiable propositions. Some propositions *give rise* to it; some propositions are *presupposed* by it; some propositions are *direct answers* to it. For instance, 'The Empire State Building is heavy' gives rise to 'How heavy is the Empire State Building?'; 'There is a King of France' is presupposed by 'What is the age of the present King of France?'; and 'The present King of France weighs five hundred pounds' is a direct answer to 'What is the weight of the present King of France?' (So is 'The present King of France weighs two hundred pounds'.) Roughly put, a proposition *gives rise* to a question if it entails that the question has a correct answer. A proposition is a *presupposition* of a question if its falsehood entails that the question has no correct answer. A proposition is a *direct* answer to a question if, if true, it is a correct answer.

Notice that if a proposition gives rise to a question, then it entails the presuppositions of that question. The converse does not hold. Notice also that every direct answer (whether correct or not) entails the presuppositions of the question, but does not necessarily entail that which gives rise to that question.

The deductive section of erotetic logic concerns itself with all those relations. If the approach is formal, then this section will first develop ways of representing propositions and questions and it will then explicate the relations of *giving rise*, *presupposing*, and *being a direct answer* in terms of these methods of representation. In other words, it will develop methods of representation, and concepts about these methods of representation, and explications that together will satisfy the following conditions: if p gives rise to q, then the fact that p gives rise to q can be inferred from the form in which p and q are represented. If p is presupposed by q, then this too can be inferred from the forms of p and q as represented by our method. If p is a direct answer to q, then this again can be inferred from the forms. In all these respects a formal erotetic logic simply apes formal deductive logic. In fact, a wise approach will try to develop this chapter so that it can be amalgamated with some system of formal "assertoric" logic (we owe the term to Nuel Belnap). If the approach is not formal, then a theory of nonformal features of some sort will have to be developed which satisfies the condition that if p gives rise to q then it will turn out that p and q share some features common to all and only pairs which stand in that relation. Analogous nonformal features will have to be found for the other two relations.

So much for the deductive section of erotetic logic. The inductive section concerns itself with the relation between a question and direct answers deemed correct or probable, or at least warranted by evidence. If this part is formal too, then the methods of representation will have to be such that if q is a question and R is a set of propositions which entail that p is a correct (or probable or warranted) direct answer, then this fact will have to be inferrable from the form of their representation. Parts of the inductive section will have to wait for developments in the theory of theory, as will become evident shortly. Furthermore, this section will also have to include most of the traditional domain of inductive logic since it concerns itself with the grounds for assigning truth, or probability, or warrantedness to propositions that give rise to or are presuppositions of questions, as well as to those that express answers.

So far I have not used the words 'item of nescience' or 'item of yescience' or mentioned the Appreciation Problem. Questions are genuine items of nescience if and only if their presuppositions are true. A question is a spurious item of nescience if at least one of its presuppositions is false. Any proposition that gives rise to a question generates, if true, an item of nescience. Nothing can cancel a question unless (a) it is a direct answer to that question and (b) the question is not a spurious item of nescience. A question is canceled when one of its direct answers is confirmed. It is tentatively canceled when one of its direct answers is shown to be probable or warranted. The Appreciation Problem requires that we work out the conditions under which any of these contingencies hold, and the chapter we have not written just now informs us about these conditions.

II. The Theory of Theories

The theory of theories concerns itself with p-predicaments and their cancellation. A person was said to be in a p-predicament with regard to a question q, you will recall, if, given that person's knowledge and assumptions, q must be sound, that is, have no false presuppositions, yet the person can think of no answer, can conjure up no answer to which, given that knowledge and those assumptions (and nothing else, I should add), there are no decisive objections. A p-predicament with regard to a question is canceled by any direct answer compatible with that knowledge and those assumptions. But the theory concerns itself also with the cancellation achieved by the discovery of new compatible answers, when some compatible ones are already known. In view of this, the discussion can be simplified if we modify the characterization of p-predicaments slightly to cover all the relevant cases. Let us then say that a person is in a p-predicament with regard to a question q if there is *some* answer compatible with his knowledge and assumptions that that person cannot think of, cannot excogitate. Under this new description one need not be as much in the dark to be in a p-predicament: one may have conjured up some direct answers that are compatible with one's set of beliefs; one may even know some correct answers. I, for instance, am now in a p-predicament with regard to 'Why did that cup I dropped this morning break?' even though I can think of 'That cup broke because it was brittle and hit a hard floor', for there are many other answers, some of which will undoubtedly occur to physicists, that do not occur to me.

The deductive part of the theory of theories must explicate the notion of p-predicament. To accomplish this it will have to incorporate and build on many parts of erotetic logic. The systems of erotetic logic presently available, such as, those of Kubinski, Harrah, Belnap, and Aqvist, all use relations of direct answerhood that are *constructive*. In other words, in each of these systems the whole set of direct answers to a question can be generated by an algorithm. Offhand it may seem that in order to represent adequately the notion of p-predicament the theory of theories should rely on a system of which this is not true. However, Harrah (1969) has shown that systems that incorporate such algorithms are *incomplete* in the non-pejorative sense that they entail the existence of sets of propositions that are not the set of direct answers of *any* question. The proof is very simple and need not detain us. The theorem itself accords with intuition, that is, it seems to be true not only of artificial systems, but also of the ones embodied in us. For this reason, as well as because of some other premonitions—not to be mentioned here—

about the eventual character of an adequate erotetic logic (the systems presently available are simply not rich enough), I assume that in the system of our theory the relation of direct answerhood will have to be constructive. The algorithms however will in many cases turn out to be either not obvious or not simple or not manageable within human limitations. But I complement this assumption with the further assumption that we will be able to define *search algorithms*, that is, algorithms that enumerate proper subsets of the set of direct answers of some questions and that express heuristics for the excogitation of possible answers.

A p-predicament can then be thought of as involving five elements: (1) a person; (2) a set of propositions expressing the knowledge or assumptions of that person; (3) a question whose set of direct answers can, in principle, be generated by an algorithm; (4) a finite (possibly empty) set of direct answers to the question available to the person and compatible with the propositions in the above set; (5) a search algorithm that generates only direct answers incompatible with the set of propositions in (2)—unless already members of the finite set of direct answers in (4)—and that models the heuristic the person would use (consciously or unconsciously) in seeking possible direct answers. Since we are dealing with a philosophic theory, our purposes will be best served by forgetting persons. Let us then define a p-predicament as an ordered quadruple consisting of a set of propositions, a question, a finite (possibly empty) set of direct answers to that question, and a search algorithm. I shall refer to the set of propositions as *the constraint* and require that the constraint never include propositions that give rise to the question. This will simplify the discussion. The search algorithm generates only direct answers to the questions that are either members of the finite set of direct answers or are incompatible with members of the constraint.

Each p-predicament, that is, each such ordered quadruple, is an item of nescience. What of the question in it? It, too, is an item of nescience. Each p-predicament represents then two items of nescience: itself, and the question in its bosom. The difference between them is in their structure and in the manner in which they are canceled. The p-predicament (unlike the question) is canceled by any direct answer (to the question) that is not produced by its search algorithm and that is not in its finite set of direct answers, but that is compatible with the members of the constraint.

The deductive part of the theory of theories explicates all these notions along lines similar to those in the corresponding section of erotetic logic. If the theory is formal, then it will incorporate representations with the power to reveal whether a given quadruple is (or fails to be) a p-predicament from the way the elements are represented. These methods of representation will have the same power for the relation of cancellation. If the theory is not formal, then it will reveal nonformal features shared by all and only p-predicaments, and nonformal features shared by all and only pairs consisting of a p-predicament and an item of yescience that cancels it.

The inductive section of the theory of theories repeats most of the inductive section of the previous chapter, but it adds some elements of its own. We shall only glimpse these here. First, two definitions.

A proposition s is an *explanation relative to a p-predicament* x if (a) s is true and (b) at least one of the following conditions holds: (i) the members of x's constraint are true, the presuppositions of the question in x are true, and s cancels x; or (ii) the members of x's constraint are true, some of the presuppositions of the question in x are false, and s is a denial of these false presuppositions; or (iii) some of the members of x's constraint are false, the presuppositions of the question in x are true, and s is a conjunction of an answer to the question in x and of denial of the false constraints incompatible with that answer.

A proposition t is a *theory relative to a p-predicament* x if (a) t is neither known to be true nor known to be false and (b) at least one of the following conditions holds: (i) t cancels x; or (ii) t is the denial of some presuppositions of the question in x; or (iii) t is a conjunction of a direct answer to the question in x and the denial of members of x's constraint incompatible with that answer. Roughly then, a theory is a possible explanation in that it is an explanation if true.

I will not defend these definitions here. Their rationale, if there is any, can readily be extracted from my other papers on this subject.[4] The inductive section deals with both explanations and theories, but especially the latter. It concerns itself with the conditions on data, p-predicaments, and propositions (remember that direct answers are

---

[4]See "An Approach to Explanation," "Why-Questions," and "A Theory about the Theory ...," this volume.

also propositions) that determine when the latter are theories and, if they are, relative to what p-predicament and to what body of data. The approach here again may turn out to be either formal or nonformal. The inductive section also concerns itself with the conditions under which a theory becomes a warranted proposition by virtue of being the only theory available relative to a specific p-predicament.

The details of this section are bound to be gruesome. When available, they will constitute another part of the solution of the Appreciation Problem.

III. The Theory of Theory

The theory of theory concerns itself with procedures for the conduct of vicarious investigations. The topic is vast and has been outlined in some detail elsewhere.[5] Brief suggestions will have to serve here. Remember our examples: the determination of a distance between two cities, and the computation of the distance traveled during a given time interval by a free-falling body. In each case there was a question whose answer we wanted, there were questions whose answers we knew or assumed, and there was a computation that led from the latter answers to the former ones. A problem as envisaged here is thus representable as a set of questions, some of which are marked as answered and one of which is marked as unanswered. As an item of nescience it is canceled by a partial recursive function which maps some direct answers of the questions marked as answered on some direct answers of the question marked as unanswered. The partial recursive function must, however, map correct answers only on correct answers. But problems fall into certain natural types. Thus the formula used to compute the distance traveled by our free-falling body could have been used to solve *any* problem whose unanswered question was about a distance traveled by a free-falling body and whose answered one was about the duration of the fall. Even without the formula we could have predicted from the similarities of these problems that there should be one formula for all of them. Problem types then also constitute items of nescience. They are canceled when a partial recursive function is found that map as above for any member of the type.

---

[5] Ibid.

The deductive section of the theory of theory explicates the notions of problems, problem types, and of their cancellation. For instance, it offers ways of representing (or features of) functions and problems that determine whether a given function maps direct answers marked as known on answers marked as unknown in a given problem. It also presents ways of determining whether a set of problems constitutes a type.

The inductive section of the theory of theory investigates the conditions under which formulae (i.e., the sort of partial recursive functions discussed above) can be trusted to map true, or probable, or warranted answers on true, or probable, or warranted ones in a problem. It also investigates when an answer can be deemed warranted *by virtue* of *the fact* that it is the value of a formula for certain known answers of a given problem. It is thereby also relevant to the intuitive section of erotetic logic.

6

Composing the treatise that I have just outlined will be only one half of the program required to solve the Appreciation Problem and to show that science is a set of actual or presumed items of yescience. The other half requires that we see whether the actual corpus of admittedly scientific doctrines conforms to the theory. We will therefore have to cast elements of that corpus in the form of confirming or disconfirming instances.

Is there any reason to believe that either half of the program can be accomplished? The question is vacuous until we impose constraints on what devices, what concepts, what symbols may enter into the theory of nescience and yescience. But what would be reasonable and plausible constraints? I would like to suggest the following, at least for the deductive sections: that the devices be essentially those also required in an elaboration of the syntax and semantics of *natural* languages, but an elaboration that presents explicitly aspects of grammars and of semantics internalized by human beings. A constraint on a philosophic theory is reasonable and plausible when it reflects a reasonable and plausible point of view. The constraint that I have suggested would reflect the view that expressibility in a human language is of the essence in scientific knowledge, that is, that nothing can constitute an addition to our scientific knowledge unless it can be stated in some language or other, some *human* language or other, and thus be taught and shared, and that nothing counts as an instance of ignorance amenable to scientific research unless it too can be conveyed in a human language and jointly recognized.

This may seem to mean that we must postpone our program until further progress is made by linguists. But not really. Enough is known or can be guessed to enable us to draw tentative sketches and to peruse the works of scientists for plausible items of yescience. Anyone can take a text and ask himself: what questions are answered here, what theories are proposed, what methods for carrying out vicarious investigations are offered? After a while, patterns begin to emerge and generalizations suggest themselves that can be put in terms that we also know how to apply to our language. This already gives some prima facie support to our hypothesis. It can also be quite exhilarating. It brings the works of scientists alive in a way that is not matched by any other philosophic perception. Karl Popper invites us to look upon scientific progress as a series of combats in which each contribution is either a chip on someone's shoulder or an attempt to knock off a chip. Thomas Kuhn invites us to think of scientific progress as exercises in imitation interrupted by changes in fashion. The view proposed here sees scientific progress as something more worthy of emulation by other human endeavors, as work designed to overcome identifiable shortcomings shared by many, as production for consumption, or, more simply, as one aspect of the eradication of ignorance.

6

Rational Ignorance

1 Introduction

Different people know different things and are ignorant about different things. For instance, much that inhabitants of Massachusetts know and don't know is different from what inhabitants of Provence know and don't know, and much of what physicists know and don't know is different from what linguists know and don't know. These differences are to a large extent traceable to differences in circumstances and opportunities. But some are traceable to deliberate choices: People can and do choose to find out certain things and to remain ignorant about others. And they don't all make the same choices, even when the same choices are available to them.

In this paper, I want to explore some aspects of these choices, and of the constraints that limit them. My ultimate reasons for being interested in these choices have to do with concrete issues in epistemology and the study of cognitive development. I will say a few words about those before concluding. But they will not be my major focus. For the time being, I want to concentrate on preliminary conceptual matters that need to be appreciated before we can make real progress with the more concrete problems.

Let me set the stage with a few stipulative definitions.

1. *Ignorance* is the relationship between a person P and a set of questions Q, when P does not know the correct answer to any of the members of Q and has no strong views as to what the correct answer to any of them is.[1]

---

[1] In what follows, I will indulge in a number of idealizations and simplifications that a lengthier discussion would avoid. For instance, I will pretend that all

2. A *person's (P's) ignorance at time t* is the set of questions that is the maximal Q_t to which P stands in the ignorance relation at time t. (I use 'Q_t' as a variable ranging over sets of questions that constitute someone's ignorance at time t.)

3. A person is *less ignorant at time t_2 than at time t_1* if and only if $Q_2 < Q_1$, that is, if and only if there is at least one question that is a member of Q_1 but not of Q_2 but not vice versa.

   A decrease in P's ignorance between t_1 and t_2 can come about by chance, or it can come about as a result of deliberate action. Deliberate action requires two stages: first, the selection of a question from Q_t, and then, second, the carrying out of whatever activities are required to get the answer to that question.

4. The first stage of a decrease of ignorance is *rational* if and only if it consists in selecting a question in a rational way, that is, with a view to maximize values and to minimize costs.

5. A person P is a *rational ignoramus at time t* if and only if at time t, P has and uses a rational policy for selecting the next question to be eliminated from P's ignorance.

In what follows, I will explore implications of these definitions. How much and what sorts of things must one know to be rationally ignorant? How do what values come into play in the choices of a rational ignoramus? What problems must a rational ignoramus solve?

2 Knowing What One Does Not Know

Since a rational ignoramus must deliberately select from his ignorance at time t one question for elimination, he must be able to survey the membership of his ignorance. How else can he establish his preferences? But to be able to do this, our ignoramus must be quite knowledgeable!

2.1 Representation and Understanding of Questions

A rational ignoramus must be able to represent questions, that is, be able to formulate and to understand interrogative sentences in some

---

questions have at most one correct answer. That is blatantly false, but should not affect the main thrust of the discussion. I will also disregard the fact that one may be said not to know the answer to a question when one mistakenly takes a false answer to be a correct answer. In fact, I will use the word 'know' rather loosely.

language.[2] Offhand, that may not seem to be a very constraining requirement. Most people we know will easily meet it. Even so, we should be mindful that it is a very complex requirement. In fact, at present, no semanticist can fully describe it.

To get an idea of the difficulty—and without even considering what is required to be able to formulate questions—compare what is involved in understanding a declarative sentence with what is involved in understanding an interrogative sentence. To understand a declarative sentence one has to be able to determine what semanticists call its *truth-conditions,* that is, what has to be the case if the sentence is to be true. What that involves is not understood completely either, but at least there are a number of theories that give us a very good inkling. But what constitutes understanding an interrogative sentence? What constitutes understanding

(1)   What is the distance between London and Paris?

or Heidegger's beloved question

(2)   Why is there something rather than nothing?

It can't be knowing truth-conditions, since questions do not have truth-conditions.

Could it be knowing (or being at least in a position to determine) the truth-conditions of every possible answer to the question?[3] For instance—in the case of the first example above—could it be knowing the truth-conditions of

(3)   The distance between London and Paris is one inch.

(4)   The distance between London and Paris is two inches.

(5)   ...

and so on ad infinitum?

That hardly seems plausible: we do understand many questions whose possible answers we are in no position to state. Think of the second example above. Or for that matter think of

---

[2]I use 'interrogative sentence' to refer to linguistic entities and 'question' to refer to what these linguistic entities express. Some complex issues related to the existence of propositions, senses, Fregean thoughts, etc., are masked by this terminology. However nothing in what follows hinges on the stand one takes on any of these issues.

[3]'Possible answer' is a semantic notion that covers correct, incorrect, plausible, implausible, etc., answers and excludes only things that are not answers at all.

(6)   What does one need to know in order to know that one does not know something?

How many of us could state all the possible answers to that one, even if we had all the time needed to utter them? And in any case, knowing these truth-conditions would not be enough. We would also have to know that each possible answer *is* a possible answer, in other words, that it stands in the proper answerhood relation to the question. And that is very different from knowing truth-conditions. Thus understanding an interrogative sentence cannot come down to knowing the truth-conditions of each of its possible answers.

2.2   Knowing of Each Item of Ignorance That It Is a Bona Fide Item of Ignorance

Our ignoramus must not only be able to formulate and understand questions, he must know that some of them represent genuine items of ignorance, that is, he must know or have good reasons to believe that he does not know their answer. To know that one does not know that, one has to know quite a bit!

First one has to know, or at least believe, that the *presupposition* of the question is true. Let me explain with an example:

(7)   What is the age of the King of France?

That question does not represent a genuine item of ignorance. No one does not know what the age of the King of France is. Not because everyone knows: no one knows what the age of the King of France is either, and not because it is a universal mystery. But because there is no King of France. The question presupposes that there is a King of France, and because there isn't, the question has no answer.[4]

Contrast that with

(8)   What binds neutrons and protons in an atomic nucleus?

It presupposes that there are atoms, protons, and atomic nuclei.

---

[4]Of course, someone who thinks that there is a King of France might think that he does not know. But he would be mistaken. Admittedly, such a person will gain new information by learning that there is no King of France. But to learn that is not to learn the age of the King of France. Similarly, there was a time when people thought that they did not know the specific gravity of phlogiston, the ratio of fire to earth in wood smoke, the distance from the earth to the sky. Later discoveries did not cure that ignorance; they dissolved it.

Since that is true, the question can—in my case does—represent a genuine item of ignorance.

Put somewhat roughly, the presupposition of a question is a proposition to the effect that some thing or things of a certain character exist that the question is about.[5] To know a question represents a bona fide item of ignorance, one must thus not only know that one cannot answer it, one must know that its presupposition is true.

Second, one must know that *the question arises*. What I have in mind here is—like so many of the other topics in this discussion—complicated to analyze, but easy to illustrate. Consider

(9)   How long is the number 5?

(10)   What is the main verb of an electron?

(11)   What is the square root of the Empire State Building?

None of us, I presume, can give the answer to any of these questions, not because we do not know the answer, but because there are no right or correct answers. On the other hand there is presumably an answer to the question

(12)   With how much force does the earth attract the moon?

though once upon a time that question would have seemed crazy to people.

Knowing that a question arises—as I use the term—requires knowing general principles of a peculiarly abstract kind, for example, that all objects attract each other with a force that has magnitude and direction (hence the question 'What is the force with which the earth attracts the moon?' arises); that atoms have mass (hence the question 'What is the mass of a lithium atom?' arises); that every event has a cause (hence the question 'What was the cause of the fire?' arises for every fire); that objects have inertia (hence 'What force is responsible for change of direction or velocity?' arises in connection with every deviation from straight uniform travel). Let me call such principles *question-raising principles*.

Knowing that a question arises is very similar to knowing that the presupposition of the question is true.[6] The difference lies in the fact that knowing that a question arises requires knowing general

---

[5]That "some thing of a certain character" need not be a physical object but can be a state of affairs or fact or event. Thus 'Why does copper turn green when exposed to air?' presupposes that copper turns green when exposed to air.

[6]In "What We Don't Know When We Don't Know Why" (this volume) I

principles of a relatively high level of abstraction. Knowing that the presuppositions hold requires knowing that a certain thing or certain things exist (or that certain events have occurred, or that certain facts hold).

Third, one has to know that one does not know the answer. That covers the following different kinds of situations.

There is, to begin with, the kind of situation in which one is able to cite many possible and plausible answers, but has absolutely no reason to prefer any of them (has no evidence that favors one above the others). That is probably how most of us stand with regard to

(13)   What is the distance between London and Paris?

(14)   What will be the name of the last person admitted to next year's freshman class of M.I.T.?

To recognize instances of it one must—among other things—be able to evaluate and to compare evidence.

Next, there is the kind of situation in which one does have evidence that makes some answer more likely than others, but the evidence is not conclusive.

(15)   What will the weather be like tomorrow?

To recognize that sort of situation one must be able to determine when evidence is conclusive, or at least strong enough to warrant the belief that one knows the answer.

Next still, there is the kind of situation in which one can come up only with answers one knows to be false and yet has reason to believe that the question is sound, that is, arises and has true presuppositions. Until recently no one knew why the moon looked larger when near the horizon than when right overhead. A number of theories existed, but each was refuted by good evidence. To recognize that type of situation one must have all the knowledge mentioned above and furthermore be able to determine that a certain set of possible answers is not complete even though one cannot extend it.

2.3   Knowing Enough about What One Does Not Know

We are examining what an ignoramus must know in order to be able to function as a rational ignoramus. We have said that he must be

---

explicitly identify this "knowledge" as knowledge of a certain kind of presupposition, which I call there "attributive presupposition."

able to represent items in his ignorance. We have said that he must know that these are items of ignorance. But of *how many* items of his ignorance should he know this? How large a list should he have? Which questions from his ignorance should it contain?

Unless rationality can require the impossible, it cannot be a complete list. It cannot contain every member of his ignorance. That follows from fairly straightforward considerations. There are an infinite number of objects, events, and states of affairs whose existence any individual is doomed not to know about. Each of these gives rise to an indefinitely large number of questions. And he is thus doomed to remain ignorant about the fact that he does not know the answer to those questions.

It also follows straightforwardly from the fact that the cardinality of any expressible list cannot be as large as the total number of objects about which questions arise. There are nondenumerably many real numbers. About each such questions as, for example,

(16)   What is the largest prime natural number smaller than it?

arise. But of course these cannot all be formulated in one language, since at most denumerably many questions can be formulated in a single language.

Finally it follows from the fact that many questions implicate concepts of a very special kind, namely, determinables,[7] of which the following are examples: 'distance in inches', as in

(17)   What is the distance in inches between John's two nostrils?

or 'mass', as in

(18)   What is the mass of the moon?

or 'D-structure', as in

(19)   What is the D-structure of 'Jean est facil à convaincre'?

'Voltage', 'chemical composition', and 'anatomical structure' are further examples. Determinables can express functions that map objects on questions. But to grasp a determinable one has to have a fair amount of theory. Thus, before Newton's gravitational theory became available, no one was in a position to entertain the questions that we are able to express in English by using the expression 'grav-

---

[7]No "theory" of determinables, i.e., explicating their semantics, is currently available, and hence the class is difficult to demarcate, though its most typical members are easily recognized.

itational mass'. Aristotle—rational though he was—not having the concept of mass, would not have been in a position to know that he did not know the answer to

(20)   What is the mass of the Parthenon?

or to include it in a specification of his ignorance. It seems therefore unlikely that anyone will ever grasp all the determinables that generate sound questions about actual objects, events, or states of affairs.

To what subset of his ignorance must an ignoramus then apply his policy to be deemed rational? The enumerable subset consisting of all and only the questions that he is in a position to formulate and to entertain (that is, whose presupposition he knows to be true, and whose determinables he has grasped, etc.)? But the construction of such a list would require an infinite amount of time, since the list would include, for example, questions about each natural number, that is, the list would be infinitely long: rationality would defeat itself by preventing itself from getting off the ground!

There may be a way out of this paradox.[8] But I do not know what it is. So let us set it aside for the time being by dropping the notion of rational ignoramus at time t as too strong for present purposes, and let us replace it with a weaker notion: that of a rational ignoramus relative to a set of questions Q at time t:

(21)   A person P is *a rational ignoramus at time t with respect to a finite set of questions Q* if and only if, at time t, Q is an accessible[9] proper subset of P's ignorance, and P has a rational policy for selecting the next question in Q to be eliminated from P's ignorance.

Let us now think about that rational policy. It is presumably designed to maximize certain values and to minimize certain costs. What value should it seek to maximize?

---

[8]There may be a rational policy whose application does not require that questions be selected or eliminated or ranked one by one, but that treats some of them en bloc. In all the cases that I have examined difficulties similar to the above reemerge.

[9]That is, P can express each member of Q, P knows—or has at least good reasons to believe and no good reason not to believe—that its presupposition is true; P knows that it arises; P is in a position to know that he does not know its answer.

3   The Value of Questions and Their Types

3.1   Intrinsic Value and Added Value

The correct answer to a question can be of value to us for many
different reasons. For present purposes I will sort these under three
headings. It may provide us with an *intellectual* benefit, namely,
satisfy our curiosity. There are different degrees of curiosity. And
hence, from that point of view, answers to different questions may
turn out to have different values. Let us call that the *gosh value* of an
answer, a measure of the intellectual pleasure derived from coming
to know the answer or of the relief of no longer not knowing it.

We may also prize the answer to a question because it enables us
to construct something, to repair something, to find something, to
obtain some *material* benefit. Let us call that the *cash value* of the
answer.

I have defined the gosh and cash value of an answer in terms
of certain properties of that answer. Of course one may not know
the value of the answer before coming in possession of it or while
still contemplating the question. Yet estimates of such values should
obviously play a role in any policy designed to select questions to be
answered. To refer to such estimates, when we talk of *the gosh and
cash values of a question* (rather than of an answer), let us mean
the estimated value of the gosh and cash value of the answer to that
question.

Let us call the sum of the gosh value and cash value of a question
the intrinsic value of the question. Intrinsic value is obviously a
notion that has to be relativized to individual preferences, to time,
to background knowledge, and perhaps to other circumstances. So
when we talk about the intrinsic value of a question, let that be
shorthand for the intrinsic value of that question as estimated by
our hypothetical rational ignoramus in the light of his circumstances
at a time when he is using his selection policy.

3.2   Added Value

Besides having gosh and cash value, an answer may be of further
value because it puts one in a position to obtain answers to other
questions with values of their own. Thus if one knows the width
and the length of a floor, and one knows the formula for computing
the area of a rectangle one is thereby put in a position to find the

answer to 'What is the area of the floor?' If the latter is of value, then surely some of that value should accrue to the answers to 'What is the length of the floor?' and to 'What is the width of the floor?' Let us call that the *added value of the answer.* And let us use *added value of the question* as shorthand for the estimated value of the answer relativized for preference, time, background knowledge, and other relevant circumstances.[10]

3.3   Value Adders

Questions get added value through devices and algorithms, that is, *value adders,* that transform their answers into answers to other questions. Let us look at these value adders for a bit. They come in various shapes and forms. Consider

(22)   All men are mortal

(23)   Is Fido a man?

If the answer to (23) is 'yes' then (22) puts one in the position to compute the answer to

(24)   Is Fido mortal?

If the answer is 'no' then it does not. That sort of a value adder is a *gappy* value adder, or at least gappy for a certain question. It generates added value to that question only for some answers and not for others. What the correct answer is matters to it. If it does not like the answer, it does not add value.

Contrast that with the pair

(25)   The distance between A and B is twice the distance between B and C.

(26)   What is the distance between B and C?

Here (25) puts one in the position to compute the answer to

(27)   What is the distance between A and B?

no matter what the answer to (26). It adds value to the question (26), no matter what the answer turns out to be. Let us call that sort of value adder an *erotetic* value adder relative to a certain question.

But now consider the formula for the pendulum

---

[10]These "other circumstances" include many sorts of contingencies that cannot be discussed here. For instance, added value depends not only on the availability of value adders—see below—but also often on the availability of answers to other questions required by the value adder.

(28) $T = 2\pi\sqrt{l/g}$.

It will add value to the question

(29)   What is the length of the pendulum?

for any pendulum under consideration that is influenced only by local gravitational force. But it is much more powerful than that. It will add to the value of any question (and no matter what the answer) constructed on the determinable

(30)   What is the length of ... (name a pendulum) ... ?

the value of the corresponding question of the form

(31)   What is the period of ... (name same pendulum) ... ?

Let us call that sort of value adder *super-erotetic* value adders.[11] We have here a hierarchy that can clearly be extended further. Thus differential equations of a certain kind will generate super-erotetic value adders, and theories—or at least certain kinds of theories—will in turn generate super-super-erotetic value adders.

3.4   Science and Value Adders

Many contributions to science are designed—either explicitly or implicitly—to provide us with value adders. The value adders they provide can vary in attractiveness along a number of dimensions: they can vary in reliability; they can vary in precision; they can vary in subject matter; and of course, they can vary in power along the hierarchy that I have just sketched. They can vary in the amount of gosh and cash value of questions under their jurisdiction. The practical sciences are built around a concern about questions with high gosh and cash value. Theoretical sciences seek powerful value adders. Primitive sciences tend to wallow at the level of gappy value adders of low precision, questionable reliability, remote subject matter, and little cash value, but very high gosh value. Theology, much psychology, a fair amount of what comes under the heading of semantics and pregenerative linguistics belong here. Of course, this does not mean that they should not be pursued: low-level sciences have a way of blooming into high level ones. And high-level sciences like physics, biology, chemistry, and more and more of linguistics of the right sort,

---

[11]Super-erotetic value adders turn into erotetic value adders when provided with specific objects as arguments (in the case at hand when '... a pendulum ...' is replaced by an expression referring to a specific pendulum).

spew forth value adders that shine in all directions: precision, reliability, power, and intrinsic value of many of the questions in their domain.

But value adders vary not only along the valuational dimensions just described. They also vary drastically in ontological character and in the competences that they demand of their users. To see this, let us look briefly at some banal examples.

3.4.1 Models

What is a model? Think of small models of a big airplane, or of plastic models of DNA molecules, or of maps. What makes one of these objects a model of another? The fact that by finding out certain things about the model one can then find out certain things about the thing modeled. By counting the stacks on the plastic model of the Queen Mary one can find out the number of smokestacks on the real Queen Mary. By counting the number of black spheres on a wire and wood model of methane, one can find out the number of carbon atoms in a real methane molecule. Artificial models are designed with just that sort of relationship in mind. To fix ideas, think of maps and of the territories they represent. By measuring distances on a map one can find the answer to the following sorts of questions: 'What is the distance between such and such a point on the map, and such and such another point on the map?' Anyone versed in map reading can translate the answer to such questions about the map into questions about the territory mapped, such as, 'What is the distance between such and such a place in the territory and such and such another place in the territory?'[12]

Thus, as a first approximation, we might define a model as follows:

(32) M is a model of O relative to a set of triples $\langle Q_m \, Q_o \, A \rangle$ if and only if in each triple Q_m is a set of questions about M; Q_o is a set of questions about O; and A is an algorithm that translates any answer to a member of Q_m into an answer to a member of Q_o, and *correct* answers to the former into *correct* answers to the latter.

---

[12]Of course, many questions that can be answered by looking at the map do not translate into questions about the territory, e.g., 'What is the name of the publisher printed on the map?' And the converse is also true, i.e., many questions about the territory can usually not be answered through questions about the map.

In the case of maps as in the case of other models, the set Q_m and the set Q_o are sets whose members are built around common determinables (e.g., 'distance'). But that is not an essential feature. Population graphs, for instance, do not have it.

Maps are clear instances of super-erotetic value adders, and so are other models that conform to our definition of a model. This definition is almost identical to that of a super-erotetic value adder.

Maps and other models are physical super-erotetic value adders[13] but there are other kinds of physical super-erotetic value adders, such as gauges. A pressure gauge, for instance, is a device that enables one to obtain the correct answer to instances of 'What is the pressure of ... (name a sample of gas to which the gauge is connected) ... at ... (name a time) ... ?' from instances of 'What is the position of the needle at ... (name the same time) ... ?'.

But there are also ways of conceptualizing things that yield supererotetic value adders. I'll briefly mention two.

3.4.2 Natural Kinds

A class of objects constitutes a natural kind only when each member can serve as a model for every other member. In other words, associated to every natural kind, there is (or is presumed to be) a set of *projectible questions*, a set such that when the answer to one element is obtained for one member of the kind, the answer to the same element for every member of the kind is also obtained, because the answer is necessarily the same.[14] For instance, by finding the answer to

(33)   What is its boiling point under standard conditions?

for one sample of water, one ipso facto gets the answer for every sample of water. And the same goes for

(34)   What is its density?

(35)   What is its freezing point?

3.4.3 Categories

Natural kinds arrange themselves into categories. For example, tigers are animals, a *category* that includes cats, dogs, and earthworms, as well as tigers. Samples of water are samples of substances,

---

[13]At least in part: the algorithms are obviously not physical.

[14]This feature, though essential, is not sufficient to characterize natural kinds. The notions of projectible questions and of categories are discussed in more detail in "Types and Tokens in Linguistics," this volume.

and substances include gold, alcohol, iron, and so on. Tokens of the word 'Apotheosis' are tokens of an English word. English words include 'dog', 'cat', 'apocalypse', 'Ticonderoga'. Members of categories share projectible questions. Thus every animal kind shares with every other animal kind the projectible question 'What is its anatomical structure?' though, of course, different kinds get different answers. Every substance kind shares with every other kind the projectible question 'What is the boiling point under standard conditions?' (but gets a different answer).

It is at the level of categories that formulas come into play. Consider the formula governing simple pendula. Simple pendula that have the same length and period can be viewed as forming a natural kind, and all simple pendula together, collected regardless of their length, can be viewed as forming a category; the formula is thus a device that enables us to compute the answer to one projectible question for any pendulum whatever its kind, from the answer to other projectible questions about the same pendulum. The formula covers the entire category. Of course, we do not usually think of simple pendula as forming natural kinds: nature has created very few simple pendula. But formulas that enable us to compute the boiling point for any substance from the structure of its molecular bond, or to compute across species some traits of plants from other traits, function essentially in the same way as the formula of the pendulum.

4   Types of Costs

Let us return to our ignoramus. One might think that a rational policy should always select questions according to their total (gosh plus cash plus added) value, that is, should always go for the ones with greatest total value first. But that would overlook at least two facts: (a) answers to questions with highest total value can be beyond reach; (b) even if they are within reach, the cost attached to finding them can be too high.

The first of these possibilities will obtain when answers to highly valued questions cannot be had "directly" by observation, or through intuition, or by asking someone, and when no value adders are available that will generate them from answers that can be had directly, or that are otherwise forthcoming. A rational policy should obviously pass over such questions, regardless of their value.

This fact, by the way, puts our rational ignoramus in a difficult predicament; it requires him to find out whether the answer to the most highly valued question is actually obtainable, and when he finds that it is not, to go on searching until he comes to a question whose answer is obtainable. How is he to determine the likelihood of getting an answer? And how is he to estimate the value of these *subsidiary* questions about questions (and their cost) raised by his very decision to use his policy? And how are *we* to analyze the place of such higher-order questions in a rational scheme?

The second of these possibilities is created by the reality of costs. That is a very messy topic. There are many kinds of costs: cost in time required for retrieval of information, for computation, for mastering value adders; financial costs of instrumentation, assistance; and emotional costs of boredom, anxiety, or frustration. How these costs are to be measured and compared is far from obvious. Their bearing on the formulation of a rational policy, on the other hand, is all too obvious.

5   M.I.T.

A rational ignoramus, as described so far, is someone engaged in making decisions based on assessments of risks, assessments of gains, and assessments of costs, in short, someone engaged in a game-theoretical situation. Simulating his situation as an actual game may therefore help us see a little more clearly the strategic demands on a rational policy. The name of the game is clear: it must be either *Minimizing Investigative Travails* or *Maximizing Investigative Tradeoffs* but in any case, be a name that abbreviates as *M.I.T.* Other aspects of the simulation are less obvious. Here is one way of picturing them.

Think of the game as played by two agents, A and B. A is pitched against A and against luck. B plays a subsidiary role.

M.I.T. is won or lost in sets.

- A set consists of n games.
- At the beginning of each game, A announces a question.
- During the game A can do a number of things: (1) He can put questions to B—these may not include the one he announced at the outset of the game, or of any previous game, or of any future game, and must pertain to specific individuals, or events,

or state of affairs. (If B answers at all, B answers truly. And B answers whenever he can.) Each question costs A 10 points, whether B answers it or not. (2) He can buy value adders. Gappy value adders cost 100 points each; erotetic value adders cost 1,000 points each; super-erotetic value adders cost 10,000 points; theories cost 100,000 points. (3) He can compute; cost of computation is 1 point per minute.

- A game ends as soon as A has figured out the answer to the question he announced, or after one year, whichever comes first.

- The score for the game is computed as follows: if A gets the answer to his question, he scores the intrinsic value (gosh plus cash value) of the question minus the costs he has incurred. If he does not get the answer to his question, he scores a negative value amounting to the costs he has incurred during the game.

- The games are not completely independent. When A starts a new game, he can come equipped with all the answers and all the value adders he has accumulated in previous games.

- If at the end of a set, A has scored 100,000 points, (the equivalent of a theory) he is declared a winner and gets a prize called *tenure*, and playing comes to an end or goes on, but for higher stakes (an endowed chair, a Nobel prize). If he gets less than 100,000 points he must play another game, only this time he has to be the research assistant, and B gets to ask the questions.

M.I.T. is too simple and unrealistic to represent adequately the strategic decisions faced by a real rational ignoramus even at the real M.I.T. But it does indicate the network of problems that his policy must handle, the different roles that knowledge will play in its execution, and brings out that the best strategy in most situations will be far from obvious.

6   Why Bother with All This?

The time has come to stop wondering about rational ignoramuses and to start acting like one. And so let us ask: of what value are the questions that we have been asking? What could their gosh or cash value possibly be?

As far as I can see, it is not very great. Nor do I think that these questions are likely to accrue added value from elsewhere. Their value is of a different nature. The value of their answers lies in their potential as question *generators*! They will generate at least two sets of questions with high gosh value.

First, they generate a set of questions in philosophic epistemology. Does our rational ignoramus embody plausible normative aspirations, that is, does he represent cognitive traits and intellectual attitudes that we aspire to embody, and does his policy exhibit standards by which we measure aspects of our worth and that of other human beings? Or does he represent an unattainable, illusory, and uninteresting ideal of no relevance to a responsible epistemic conscience?

Second, they generate a set of cognitive-psychological questions. Are human beings rational ignoramuses at any points of their development? More specifically, are infants rational ignoramuses? To conjecture that they are is to conjecture that at various stages of their development they are endowed with representations of part of what they do not know, with weights attached to some of these representations, with concepts of determinables, with question-raising principles, and with value adders; it is to conjecture that they may come innately equipped with such things, and that they may guide their attention by such things. It is to invite ourselves to find out concrete features of that endowment and of its evolution. Thus the answer to our questions about rational ignoramuses raises new issues about the nature of innate and acquired cognitive capacities.

But note that this is a dimension of value that has been given no weight so far in the policy of our rational ignoramus: it is not gosh or cash or added value, but the value that a question derives from the fact that its answer may open up new fields of ignorance, a value even less predictable than the others. Let us call it *golly* value, and stop.

7

What We Don't Know When We Don't Know Why

Some twenty years ago, I gave a paper on why-questions to the University of Pittsburgh Center for Philosophy of Science. The occasion was—at least for me—a happy one. Later when I was invited to join in the twenty-fifth anniversary celebration of the Center, it struck me that a talk on the same topic would make a fitting birthday present. So this talk too will be on why-questions. But unlike the previous one, it won't be on *answers* to why-questions. It will be on a certain predicament to which why-*questions* themselves can give rise. That predicament interests me mainly because of its consequences for something I call "rational ignorance." Therefore, I will begin with a brief discussion of rational ignorance. It is also crucially related to the fact that why-questions do not have what linguists call "traces." I will therefore go on by explaining the notion of a trace and give reasons for believing that why-questions don't have any. I will turn to the predicament itself only in the last part of the paper.

1 Rational Ignorance

According to received history, Eratosthenes was the first person to come close to figuring out the circumference of the earth. You re-

*I thank Ken Hale, Morris Halle, Jim Higginbotham, Richard Larson, Guiseppe Longobardi, and David Nash for much of the information in and behind this paper, and for other forms of help; Tom Kuhn for comments on a previous draft and for many useful discussions around these topics; and Nancy Bromberger for editorial and orthographic advice. I owe much to Jaakko Hintikka's work on topics related to what I call "rational ignorance" and to our conversations about the subject.

member how he went about it. He knew that at noon on the summer
solstice, the sun would be straight overhead in Syene and that no
shadow would be cast there by any gnomon. He assumed (almost
rightly) that Alexandria was straight north of Syene. He also knew
the distance (d) between Syene and Alexandria. He erected a vertical gnomon in Syene and another in Alexandria and, at noon on the
summer solstice, he measured the angle (θ) formed by the gnomon
in Alexandria and the sun ray skimming its top. He had correctly
reasoned that θ would be equal to the angle at the center of the earth
subtending the arc between the gnomon in Alexandria and that in
Syene. Then using some version of the formula

(1) $C = (2\pi \div \theta) \times d$

he calculated that the circumference of the earth was 250,000 stades,
a good approximation that we can adopt for present purposes.

Eratosthenes's discovery was not an accident. He did not stum-
ble on the answer to 'What is the circumference of the earth?' the
way, for example, Roentgen stumbled on radiation phenomena or
Oersted on electromagnetic ones. Eratosthenes knew that he did
not know the answer and set himself to find it. In doing so, he
engaged in a pivotal human activity: the pursuit of answers to pre-
chosen questions. I say "pivotal" for good reasons: human cognitive
growth turns on it. Children must engage in it if they are to learn
the phonemes, words, phrases, and parameters of the ambient language; we must unconsciously engage in it if our vision is to find
the properties of distal stimuli on the basis of proximate ones; and,
of course scientific research and pooling of knowledge wouldn't be
possible without it.

An activity that central to our mental, intellectual, and communal life calls for investigation. Philosophers in particular should
try to clarify how knowledge and rationality can influence it. What
we need to clarify can be put a little more explicitly. Imagine an
ideal but intellectually ambitious rational agent—call him Rational
Ignoramus—and let Q_1 be the set of all the sound questions[1] to
which Rational Ignoramus does not know the answer at t_1. Being
intellectually ambitious, Rational Ignoramus wants to remove questions from Q_1, that is, wants to bring it about that at some later

---

[1]By a sound question, I simply mean a question that has a correct, true
answer.

moment t_1 he will have the answer to some member of Q_1. Under what conditions can he rationally undertake to do this?[2]

Four conditions come immediately to mind.[3]

First Condition: Representations. Rational Ignoramus must be able to formulate and to understand interrogative sentences that express members of Q_1. He must therefore have access to some system in which some members of Q_1 can be represented. How else can he target any of them?

Many things about that requirement will remain obscure until we see clearly what is distinct about the systems of representations that humans can use. One thing is clear, however: some questions are beyond the reach of some systems of representation.

Consider for instance a system that admits only single-clause surface interrogative sentences of English.[4] Such a system could not represent the question now represented by

(2)   There is something whose destruction calls for explanation. What is it?

since (2) is not a single-clause surface interrogative sentence. The single clause

(3)   what does the destruction of call for explanation?

does express what (2) does, but is ungrammatical.

Such a system, by the way, would in all likelihood not be able to avoid ambiguities. For instance,

(4)   Who did John tell what to do when?

though a single interrogative sentence, is ambiguous in that it can be construed with 'when' questioning either 'tell' or 'do'.[5]

---

[2] By defining Q_1 as made up of only sound questions we leave out of consideration, for the present, problems caused by the fact that Rational Ignoramus must also cope with questions he mistakenly believes to be sound.

[3] These are not the only ones, but they are the only ones that matter for present purposes.

[4] English is *not* such a system.

[5] Ambiguity of interrogative sentences raises a vexing problem. To say that an interrogative sentence is ambiguous is to say that it can be used to express more than one question. If there are ambiguous interrogative sentences—as there obviously are—this means in effect that we cannot identify a question by just any sentence that expresses it. How then shall we identify questions? In the case of declarative sentences helpful notions of ambiguity are available: for example, that a declarative sentence is ambiguous if and only if it can be evaluated through

Another thing is clear: Rational Ignoramus may be able to formulate and to understand a question and yet not be able to formulate and understand all its possible answers. Most of us understand 'Who will be the President of the United States in 2054?' yet cannot begin to express all the possibilities.

Second Condition: Soundness. Rational Ignoramus must know[6] of some questions in Q_1 that they are sound, that is, that they have a correct answer. This does not mean that he must know the answer! In most cases he only needs to know that two sorts of presuppositions are satisfied.

First Rational Ignoramus must know of some questions in Q_1 that their *existential* presuppositions are satisfied, that is, that their referential constituents have actual references.[7] The idea is a familiar one. The question expressed by[8]

(5)   What was the age of the King of France in 1945?

presupposes that there was a King of France in 1945. There was none, and the question is not sound, has no true answer. On the other hand

(6)   How are neutrons and protons bound in an atomic nucleus?

presupposes that there are neutrons, and protons, and atomic nuclei. This is true, and the question is sound, must have an answer.

---

more than one set of truth-conditions. This suggests that what a declarative sentence expresses may turn out to be identifiable by a set of truth-conditions. Working out this notion is fraught with difficulties. But it gives us some sort of grasp. Nothing of the sort is available for interrogative sentences: interrogative sentences do not have truth-conditions. Identifying them through the truth conditions of the declarative sentences that express their possible answers or their presuppositions doesn't work either. In a later section I will presume that these sentences have unambiguous logical forms.

[6] "Know" here and elsewhere may seem too strong. "Believe" or "believe on good grounds" may seem better. These subtleties are beyond the accuracy of this discussion.

[7] This way of putting the point implies that questions can have referring constituents, that is, are sentence-like objects. I happen to think that this is true, but the condition can, in any case, be restated so as to mention only constituents of the sentences used by Rational Ignoramus to express questions. The restatement is joylessly convoluted and forces issues about ontological and conceptual relativity to the surface. I will bypass it.

[8] From here on, I will drop this awkward "the question expressed by" and let context indicate whether the example is to be taken as a question expressed by the sentence or the sentence itself.

However, that answer cannot be deliberately sought by anyone who does not know that there are neutrons, protons, or atomic nuclei.

Second, Rational Ignoramus must know of some questions in Q_1 that their *attributive* presuppositions are satisfied. So, for instance

(7)   What is the height of the Empire State Building?

presupposes not only that the Empire State Building exists, but also that it has a height. This is true, and hence (7) is sound, must have a true answer. On the other hand,

(8)   What is the square root of the Empire State Building?

presupposes that the Empire State Building has a square root. It does not, and hence (8) cannot have a true answer.

There are a number of ways of looking at what I have called attributive presuppositions. I will come back to the topic later, but here is a rough sketch of what is involved. (7) expresses a question built around the predicate function

(9)   ... is the height of ...

which pairs distances and objects. The attributive presupposition of the question is satisfied if and only if the related predicate represented by the open sentence

(10) $(\exists x : x$ a distance$)(x$ is the height of ...$)$

is satisfied at the Empire State Building,[9] that is, if the Empire State Building has height, which it does.

On the other hand, (8) is built around

(11)   ... is the square root of ...

and would be sound only if the predicate represented by the open sentence

(12) $(\exists x : x$ a number$)(x$ is the square root of ...$)$

were satisfied at the Empire State Building, that is, if the Empire State Building were a square, which it isn't.

Questions are built around such predicates. Many are intimately related to what used to be called determinables, that is, height

---

[9]The use of a (restricted) existential quantifier in (10) may suggest that we are simply dealing with another existential presupposition. Note however that (7) can be expressed with 'how' rather than 'what' ('How high is the Empire State Building') to mark the difference between existential and attributive presuppositions. Which is which in specific cases cannot be settled without settling general and specific issues of ontology and ideology.

('What is the height of ... ?'), color ('What is the color of ... ?'), mass ('What is the mass of ... ?'), voltage ('What is the voltage between ... ?') and so on, a class of notions that has for too long been ignored by erotetic logicians.

Rational Ignoramus cannot know whether a given attributive presupposition is satisfied unless he has the concept of its corresponding predicate function in his intellectual kit. That fact can severely narrow his choices. To see this, imagine what things were like before the concepts of mass, electric resistance, atomic number, standard deviation, marginal utility, constituent structure, and other technical determinables were available.

He must also have some knowledge of that function's range and domain. For example, he must know that square root is defined at numbers but not at buildings or even plants, that height is defined at buildings, but not at oceans or snakes, and so on.

The grounds for that sort of knowledge, and how it can be acquired, are far from clear. Whence do we know that all physical forces have direction and magnitude, that material objects have mass, that events may have causes, that pairs of numbers have products, that sets have cardinality?

The knowledge in many cases, perhaps in all, must be grounded on the conceptual structures in terms of which we categorize, classify, taxonomize, and otherwise group things for the projection of properties and principles. Thus it is a feature of the concept of a building that a building is the sort of thing for which there must an answer to the questions 'What is its height?', 'Where is it located?', 'Who built it?', and so on. It is a feature of our concept of a sphere that a sphere is the sort of thing for which there must be an answer to the questions 'What is its volume?', 'What is its radius?', 'What is the area of its surface?', and so on.[10] If anything is a priori knowledge, that sort of thing surely is.

Third Condition: Awareness. Rational Ignoramus must know of some questions in Q_1 that he does not know their answer. In other words, he must be occurrently, not merely dispositionally, attending to some questions in Q_1 through some of their representations, be

---

[10]But there can be conceptual changes. It is no longer a feature of the concept of physical object that a physical object is the sort of thing for which there must be an answer to the questions 'What is its mass?', 'Where was it located when?', 'What was its velocity relative to what frame of reference when?', and so on.

aware of them as sound, and know that he lacks sufficient reasons for accepting any particular answers to them.

The third condition obviously entails the first two. But it also goes beyond them. It demands that the questions have "arisen" for Rational Ignoramus, a matter over which he himself has very little control, and which his rationality can no more influence than it can influence the flow of inner and outer events of which he is aware. And it furthermore demands that he should not mistakenly believe that he knows the answers when he does not. That too is a matter over which he may have very little control and on which his rationality has less influence than some philosophers have acknowledged: insufficient reasons can be unrecognizably disguised as sufficient ones when possible answers—including perhaps the right one—fail to come to mind, or are unrepresentable, in spite of the most assiduous and appropriate intellectual efforts.

Let us call members of Q_1 that meet the first three conditions at t_1 the questions *accessible* to Rational Ignoramus at t_1.

Even under the best of circumstances, there will be members of Q_1 that are not accessible to Rational Ignoramus. This follows first from technical considerations.[11] It also follows from predicaments that Rational Ignoramus cannot avoid. Rational Ignoramus cannot possibly know of each thing, present, past, future, nearby, and far away, that it exists. Nor can he be aware of all the attributes manifested somewhere. How likely is it, for instance, that Eratosthenes could have conjured up the notion of space curvature or of valence? And it follows from the fact that the circumstances in Rational Ignoramus's life cannot raise every member of Q_1 for him, not even every member otherwise accessible to him.

---

[11]For instance, there are as at least as many questions as there are real numbers—that is, nondenumerably many—since there are questions of the form

  (a) What is its square?
  (b) What is the prime number closest to it?
  (c) What is the difference between it and the average population of New York in 1924?

for each real number. But the total number of questions expressible in Rational Ignoramus's language can be at most denumerably infinite, since each must be expressed in a finite structure constructed out of a finite—or at best denumerably infinite—vocabulary. Thus, after taking into account all the expressible questions to which Rational Ignoramus knows the answer (a denumerable set), we will still be left with nondenumerably many sound questions.

Fourth Condition: Value. Since the subset of accessible questions in Q_1 is apt to be enormous, Rational Ignoramus can't try to answer them all and must make choices. If the choices are to be rational, he must seek to maximize values and to minimize costs.[12] What values? The main relevant values come under four headings. I have named each after a philosopher biased in its favor.

1. Peircean value: The value that a question gets from the expected intellectual value of its answer, that is, the pleasure, or relief, or cognitive stability expected from its answer.[13]

2. Jamesian value: The value that a question gets from the material benefits expected from its answer.[14]

3. Collingwood value: The value that a question gets from the prospect that its answer will raise new questions with expected values of their own.[15]

4. Machian value: The value that a question gets from the prospect that its answer will yield answers to other questions with values of their own.[16]

All these values obviously are relativized to Rational Ignoramus's preferences and background knowledge at the time the choices have to be made.

Machian value depends on devices that turn answers to some questions into answers to other questions, that is, things like (1) and the algorithmic procedures associated with it.[17] Let us call such devices "value adders."[18]

---

[12] I omit discussion of costs and of certain other relevant considerations such as likelihood of success in the pursuit of an answer.

[13] Elsewhere I have called this "gosh" value.

[14] Elsewhere I have called this "cash" value.

[15] Elsewhere I have called this "golly" value.

[16] Elsewhere I have called this "added" value. Naming it after Mach is a little misleading. I do so because he valued laws and theories for the "intellectual economy" they made possible. That comes close to valuing them as means for yielding what I call Machian value to questions.

[17] (1) gave added value to both 'What is the value of θ?' and to 'What is the value of d?' The added value given to each of these depended, of course, on the prospects of getting the answer to the other.

[18] Intellectual value adders differ along such dimensions as precision, reliability, accuracy. But they also differ in power. Consider for instance

(a) All elephants have warm blood.
(b) Is Jumbo an elephant?

Let me summarize where we are by returning to Eratosthenes, our near-incarnation of Rational Ignoramus.

Before his discovery of the circumference of the earth, Eratosthenes knew that the earth existed; knew that it was spherical; knew that spheres have circumferences; knew that there was a gnomon in Alexandria; knew that there was one in Syene; knew that at noon on the summer solstice, sun rays near the gnomon in Syene would cast no shadows, and therefore be on a line through the center of the earth; knew that at that very time, a sun ray skimming the top of the gnomon in Alexandria would form an angle with that gnomon, equal to the angle at the center of the earth, subtending the arc between Alexandria and Syene. The questions

(13)   a. What is the sun ray-gnomon angle in Alexandria?
       b. What is the circumference of the earth?

were accessible to him. The first had little intrinsic value, but the second had enormous Peircean and possible Jamesian value. Eratosthenes knew how to use the value adder (1). That added the value of (13b) to that of (13a). Long before, others had considered

(14)   What is the shape of the earth?

   (c) Is Jumbo warm-blooded?

The value adder (a) adds the value of (c) to the value of (b) only if the answer to the latter is 'yes'. Otherwise it adds no value to (b). It is a conditional value adder. Contrast that with

   (d) The distance between Memorial Hall and Kresge is twice the distance between Central Square and the middle of Harvard Bridge.
   (e) What is the distance between Memorial Hall and Kresge?
   (f) What is the distance between Central Square and the middle of Harvard Bridge?

(d) adds the value of (f) to the value of (e) no matter what the answer to the latter. It adds value unconditionally. And now consider

   (g) $T = 2\pi \sqrt{l/g}$
   (h) What is the length of the pendulum built by Foucault?
   (i) What is the period of the pendulum built by Foucault?

(g) adds unconditionally the value of (i) to the value of (h). But, more important, it adds to any question of the form

   (j) What is the length of ... ?

about some pendulum, the value of the corresponding question of the form

   (k) What is the period of ... ?

about the same pendulum. We have here the beginnings of a hierarchy that extends to the farthest levels of theory.

which had the Collingwood value of generating (13b).

So far so good. But now consider the question

(15)   *Why* is the circumference of the earth 250,000 stades?

Eratosthenes clearly did not answer that question. Nor did his discovery of the answer to (13b)—even with all the rest of his knowledge—put him in a position to answer that why-question. But did it at least make that why-question accessible to him? Did it put him in a position to see that it was sound (assuming that it is sound), that it had an answer (assuming that it has an answer)? It obviously didn't.

What else did he need to know? Was he at least in a position to figure *that* out? We know that he wasn't! But why-questions must then be different, must stand in a different relation to their presuppositions. What is the difference?

Linguistic facts provide an important clue, namely that why-questions bind no traces. Let us then look at that clue.

2   Traces and Why-Questions

2.1   Traces

To begin with, what is a trace?

Think of a trace on the analogy of a variable bound to a quantifier.

(16)   John hit someone.

for many purposes is analyzed as having the form

(17) $(\exists x)(\text{John hit } x)$

Think then of

(18)   Who did John hit?

as having the form

(19)   (Who t)(did John hit t)

where the t in mid-sentence is the trace of 'who' and is bound to it as x is bound to '$\exists x$' in (17). Note that the x and the t—that is, the bound variable and the bound trace—both occur in a position dictated by meaning considerations: the position in which the target of 'hit' is indicated. That is the interpretive job of that position. The interpretive job of the operator's positions—that is, of the position occupied by '$(\exists x)$' and '(Who t)'—is to indicate scope.

Traces are associated syntactically with a "movement" of the interrogative operator. In the example above, (18) and (19) derive from the deep structure[19]

(20)   John hit who

—in which 'who' is in a position indicating the target of 'hit' — through a transformation that "raises" 'who' to a sentence-initial position but that leaves a trace bound to it. The trace preserves the information that the target of 'hit' is the questioned.[20] It therefore plays a semantic role.

Traces have as much reality as real words. They not only affect what an interrogative sentence means, but, like real words, they can affect pronunciation. Chomsky (1977) brings out evidence of the following sort:

The interrogative sentence

(21)   Who do you want to eat?

is ambiguous. It can express either a question that can take (22a) as answer, or one that can take (22b) as answer:

(22)   a. I want to eat the missionary.
        b. I want the missionary to eat.

The ambiguity is easily explained: 'Who' can "start out" in situ—that is, in a location indicating what is being questioned— as either the theme or the agent of 'eat'. And (21) may thus be the perceptual shape of either (23a) or (23b):

(23)   a. (Who t)(do you want to eat t)
        b. (Who t)(do you want t to eat)

What is more, the ambiguity of (21) vanishes when 'want' and 'to' are contracted into 'wanna'.

(24)   Who do you wanna eat?

---

[19]The expressions 'deep structure', 'surface structure', and 'logical form' are shunned nowadays because they call up misleading associations. Linguists prefer to use 'D-structure', 'S-structure', 'L-form'. I will use the old terminology in the belief that some mnemonic association is better than none.

[20]Linguists use the term 'raise' because the transformation moves 'who' from the end of a lower branch to that of a higher one in a tree-like representation of the sentence's structure. Other transformations—of no interest here—are also required to get (18) and (19): one that inserts 'did', for example. All this talk of transformation is not to be taken literally: it is a picturesque way of talking about relationships among various levels of analysis.

can only mean (23a), it cannot mean (23b). This is accounted for if the trace in (23b) stands like a real word between 'want' and 'to' and blocks their contraction.[21,22]

English interrogative sentences then contain mid-sentence traces in their surface structure. But they also contain traces in their *logical form*. To see this, let's look again at quantified sentences.

(25)   Someone is loved by everyone.

is ambiguous: it can be interpreted either with 'someone' in the scope of 'everyone' or with 'everyone' in the scope of 'someone'. We account for this by distinguishing between surface structure and logical form, and by imputing to (25) two logical forms, namely, to a first approximation

(26)   a. $(\exists y)(\forall x)(y$ is loved by $x)$
       b. $(\forall x)(\exists y)(y$ is loved by $x)$

in which the ordering of the quantifiers indicates their relative scope. Scope ambiguities of surface structures thus indicate the existence of multiple logical forms.

But interrogative operators can also be the source of scope ambiguities. For instance,

(27)   Where did everyone go?

can be construed as presupposing that everyone went to one place, or as not presupposing it. We account for this by imputing two logical forms to (27) also, namely, to a first approximation,

(28)   a. (Where $t)(\forall x)(x$ went to $t)$
       b. $(\forall x)$(Where $t)(x$ went to $t)$

in which the ordering of the quantifier and the interrogative operator indicates their relative scope. The account obviously requires that

---

[21]This argument must be handled with extreme caution: traces are "visible" and block contractions only under specific conditions. Many traces do not block contraction. But for present purposes, it is sufficient that some do.

[22]The data are from a dialect of English that does not have 'whom'. Speakers of dialects that have 'whom' may find 'What do you want to smell?', 'I want the flowers to smell', 'I want to smell the flowers', 'What do you wanna smell?' more convincing. But since their dialect probably does not tolerate 'wanna' in any case, they should look at the data as taken from a dialect that happens not to be theirs. That does not make it less real.

traces occur in the logical form of interrogative sentences as well as in their surface form.[23]

English interrogative sentences then have traces in both their surface structure and their logical form. That is not true of interrogative sentences in every language. In Chinese, for instance, no traces of interrogative words occur in surface structures: the interrogative words corresponding to our 'who', 'where', 'what', 'when', and so on, remain in situ there; they never move to the sentence-initial position. In other words, they behave very much like quantifiers in English,[24] which occur in situ in the surface structure and "move" only in the logical form. But there is evidence that Chinese interrogative operators do move in logical form. For instance, they can be the source of scope ambiguities that English interrogative operators never produce.[25] In view of these ambiguities, Chinese sentences must have logical forms distinct from their surface structure. More to the point, these logical forms, when interrogative operators are present, must contain traces. How else could they mark both the relative scope of the operators and the position questioned?[26]

2.2   No Traces In Why-Questions

I said that why-questions don't have mid-sentence traces.[27] I can now be more specific: first, they do not have mid-sentence traces bound to 'why' in their surface structure, and, second, they don't

---

[23]There are many other grounds for holding that sentences have logical forms besides surface and deep structures.

[24]Or like all but one wh-operator in English multiple questions. For example, 'Who went where, when, how?' See (29a).

[25]The sequence 'John know his mother see who?' matches the sequence of words in a Chinese sentence that can be interpreted as either 'Who does John know that his mother saw' or 'John knows who his mother saw'.

[26]Everything has to be qualified! We have known ever since Schönfinkel that sometimes combinators properly arranged can perform the two corresponding jobs for quantifiers without binding anything. The same is probably true of traces. Offhand, I don't know how to handle that complication and save the rhetorical point of my question. But the thesis that why-questions have no mid-sentence traces should translate into an equivalent thesis in a scheme using combinators, if it turns out that the logical forms of sentences in a natural language are representable with combinators.

[27]I use "mid-sentence" out of technical caution. As far as I know, 'why' may bind traces in sentence-initial positions, that is, in what will be called COMP below.

even have mid-sentence traces bound to 'why' in their logical form. Furthermore, since translation across languages must share binding relations and relative scopes in the logical forms, it is a good bet that their expression in other languages doesn't have 'why'-bound (or whatever the word for 'why' in the other language) traces in the logical form either.[28]

But what reason is there to believe that 'why' does not bind mid-sentence traces?

Here is one well-known argument.

Both of the following are acceptable sentences:

(29)   a. Who did John hit where?
       b. Where did John hit who?

The explanation is straightforward: (29a) and (29b) both start with the deep structure

(30)   John hit who where

(29a) results when 'who' is raised to the sentence-initial position,[29] and (29b) results when 'where' is raised to the sentence-initial position.[30]   It happens that in English only one wh-operator can be raised to a sentence-initial position at surface structure. The other wh-operators, if any, must stay in situ. Therefore either 'who' or 'where' (though not both) can leave a trace and move to the sentence-initial position, and either (though not both) can end up in a mid-sentence position.

On the other hand, though at first sight related exactly like (29b) and (29a), the following are not both acceptable sentences:

(31)   a. Why did John hit who?
       b. Who did John hit why?[31]

(31a) is acceptable, but (31b) is not.

The explanation is straightforward if 'why' cannot occur in mid-

---

[28]Another qualification! 'How come' questions do have a trace bound to 'how' after 'come'. Doesn't that pose a problem if—as seems plausible—'(how t) (come t that p)' turns out to be a synonym of 'why p', or if some expression much like it turns out to be the translate of 'why' in some other language? Not really. The argument below hinges on the absence of a trace bound to 'why'—or to any of its translates—inside of p—or any of p's translates. The innards of p are what matters. I thank Ken Hale for helping me with this point.

[29]When the trace is made visible, (29a) is '(Who t)(did John hit t where?)'.

[30]When the trace is made visible (29b) is '(Where t)(did John hit who (at) t?)'.

[31]Not to be confused with 'Who did John hit and why?'

sentence position in deep structure; in other words if there is no deep structure (32)

(32)   John hit who why

but there is a deep structure (33).

(33)   Why John hit who

The unacceptability of (31b) then follows from the fact that since 'why' never occurs in mid-sentence, it cannot be "left" there while 'who' moves to the front of the sentence. The acceptability of (31a) follows from the fact that 'why' can occur in sentence-initial position in deep structure and can occupy that position in (31a) without having to "move" into it.

Since wh-words in surface structures bind traces only in positions from which they have moved, it also follows that 'why' does not bind a mid-sentence trace in (31a). And from general considerations it follows that it does not bind a mid-sentence trace in any surface structure.[32,33]

The argument shows that 'why' does not bind a mid-sentence trace in surface structure. I now want to offer an argument that shows that 'why' does not bind a trace in logical form. That is of greater import for Rational Ignoramus since it carries cross-linguistic consequences. The argument is also philosophically important. It is based on data that have deeply shaped recent philosophic conceptions of what why-questions are about. In fact, the argument occurred to me while I was mulling over examples used by van Fraassen in *The Scientific Image* (1980, chap. 5, sect. 2) and viewed by him

---

[32]The account also implies that 'why' cannot carry the sort of thematic role that arguments of verbs or prepositions carry.

[33]This argument, being an induction to a (best?) explanation, needs strengthening from further evidence. Such evidence exists. For instance, Giuseppe Longobardi, in conversation, has shown me a beautiful argument based on the observation that whereas both members of a pair like

(a) Why do you think John left?
(b) Why do you think that John left?

—construed as about the reasons for John's leaving, not for thinking that he left—are acceptable, only (c) of the pair below is acceptable:

(c) Who do you think went to London?
(d) Who do you think that went to London?

Yet at first sight, the difference between the members of both pairs is the same, namely the absence or presence of 'that'.

as proving that all why-questions have an essential indexical aspect. To underline this connection, I will use an example taken from the discussion of why-questions in that book. Consider

(34)   Why did Adam eat the apple?

This can be uttered with different intonation contours. It can be uttered with a normal intonation contour or with emphatic stress on one of the words as below:

(35)   a. Why did Adam eat the apple?
        b. Why did ADAM eat the apple?
        c. Why did Adam EAT the apple?
        d. Why did Adam eat the APPLE?

These differences affect the question expressed in two ways.

First, different placements of emphatic stress create different implicatures. So (35b) implicates that someone else than Adam might have eaten the apple but didn't. (35c), on the other hand, implicates that Adam might have done something else to the apple but didn't. (35d), in turn, implicates that there was something else that Adam might have eaten but didn't. (35a) has none of these implicatures.

Second, different placement of emphatic stress imposes different conditions on what counts as an answer.[34] For instance, (35a) can tolerate as an answer

---

[34] The fact that stress affects what counts as an answer has wrongly been taken to show that the construal of why-interrogative sentences like (34)—even if we abstract from the presence of explicit indexicals—is more crucially dependent on context of utterance than that of other sentences. It shows nothing of the sort. What it does show is that accentuation is one of the individuating features of sentences. It has also been taken to show that (35b), (35c) and (35d) express different ways of construing (35a). They don't. Their readings are not among the readings of (35a) even if—as some believe—the answers they tolerate are among the answers that (35a) tolerates. (The converse is not true, as lovers of poor jokes well know.) (35b) is no closer to expressing a way of construing (35a) than the cleft interrogative sentence 'Why was it Adam who ate the apple'—with which it shares logical form—is. (35a), (35b), (35c), (35d) are different sentences each with its own construal. (35b), (35c), (35d)—though not (35a)—happen to share logical form with clefted interrogative sentences, and each therefore expresses the same question as its corresponding clefted interrogative sentence. But interrogatives with different logical forms express different questions, regardless of the similarities in their surface structure. The point may be obvious but it is overlooked by theories that take why-questions with emphatic stress (or clefted) as paradigmatic cases of why-questions, and that do so on the mistaken presumption that every why-question can be expressed with emphatic stress on one of the

(36)   Because God intended that to happen.

(35b) can tolerate

(37)   Because he (Adam) was the one that Eve worked on.

(35c) can tolerate

(38)   Because he couldn't think of anything else to do with it.

(35d) can tolerate

(39)   Because it (the apple) was the only food around.

Compare this with non-why-questions.

Non-why-questions, of course, can also be uttered with normal intonation contour or with emphatic stress placed on one of the words. Take 'when',[35] for instance. We have

(40)   a. When did Adam eat the apple?
       b. When did ADAM eat the apple?
       c. When did Adam EAT the apple?
       d. When did Adam eat the APPLE?

But these different placements of emphatic stress don't have the consequences they have for why-questions.

First, though emphatic stress still creates implicatures that vary with the location of the stress, these are not the ones created for why-questions. Thus (40b) implicates that others also ate the apple,[36] not that they could have but didn't. (40c) implicates that Adam also did other things with the apple, not that he could have but didn't. (40d) implicates that Adam ate also other things, not that he could have but didn't.

Second, different placements of emphatic stress do not impose different conditions on what counts as an answer. Thus (40a), (40b), (40c), (40d) all tolerate the answer:

(41)   At 4 p.m. on July 7, 24,000,000 B.C.

or any other answer that one of them tolerates. And they must all share the same correct answer, if there is one.

How shall we account for all this?

First note that English declarative sentences too can be produced either with normal intonation contour or with stress placed on one

---

words, or by a cleft interrogative. Such theories start off on the wrong foot in any case, since their inductions rest on biased samples with idiosyncratic logical forms.

[35] 'How' or 'where', and so on, would do just as well.

[36] Admittedly *that* implicature is rather difficult to swallow.

of the words, and that stress placed on one of the words results in a sentence logically equivalent to a so-called cleft sentence.[37] So (42a) is logically equivalent to (42b), and (43a) is logically equivalent to (43b):

(42) a. ADAM ate the apple.
      b. It was Adam who ate the apple.

(43) a. Adam ate the APPLE.
      b. It is the apple that Adam ate.

To a first approximation,[38] (42a) and (42b) share the logical form

(44)   ( ){($\exists x : x = $ Adam){( )(x ate the apple)}}

whereas (43a) and (43b) share

(45)   ( ){($\exists x : x = $ the apple){( )(Adam ate the apple)}}

The blanks between parentheses indicate sentence-initial positions. Those are the positions into which interrogative words, if any, are "raised." Because they are also the positions in which complementizers (words like 'that' which initiate subordinate sentences) would occur, linguists label these positions COMP (for "complementizer").

With these analyses of declaratives in mind, we can look at our when-questions again.

Their logical forms must be similar to those of the declarative sentences, but with the interrogative operator 'when' and its trace added. The logical form of (46a), in which there is no emphatic stress, is, to a first approximation, simply (46b), that of (47a) is (47b), and that of (48a) is (48b):

(46) a. When did Adam eat the apple?
      b. (When t)(Adam ate the apple at t)

(47) a. When did ADAM eat the apple?
      b. ( ){($\exists x : x = $ Adam) {(when t)(x ate the apple at t)}}

(48) a. When did Adam eat the APPLE?
      b. ( ){($\exists x : x = $ the apple) {(when t)(Adam ate x at t)}}

---

[37] This is not the only instance in which departure from normal intonation contour changes logical form. Declarative sentences produced with an interrogative intonation contour have the logical form of an interrogative sentence.

[38] I say "to a first approximation" because many details are left out and because the '($\exists x : x = N$)' representation of the focusing operator is crude.

These analyses account for the differences among the implicatures. (46b) does not have a focusing operator; (47b) and (48a) have different ones.

They also account for the common answers: all the constituents under the scope of 'when' have the same interpretation since their referential expressions and variables have the same assignments.

Note that in each case, 'when' binds a mid-sentence trace, for that turns out to be crucial.

There are two sentence-initial positions—two COMPs—in the logical forms of the stressed when-questions, one with the focusing operator under its scope of that operator; or, to put things a little differently, one that prefixes the whole logical form, and one that prefixes the inner clause only. 'When' cannot occur in the former because it binds a trace. Traces of wh-operators are anaphors, that is, they behave like reflexive pronouns and must be in the same innermost clause as their antecedents.[39] If 'when' were in the outermost initial position, it would be too far from its trace, it would be outside the innermost clause containing its trace, outside the domain it must cohabit with its trace.

Now let us return to why-questions.

The logical form of (49a), in which there is no emphatic stress, is to a first approximation, simply (49b), that of (50a) is (50b), that of (51a) is (51b):

(49) a. Why did Adam eat the apple?
      b. (Why)(Adam ate the apple)

(50) a. Why did ADAM eat the apple?
      b. $(Why)\{(\exists x : x = Adam) \{(\ \ )(x \text{ ate the apple})\}\}$

(51) a. Why did Adam eat the APPLE?
      b. $(Why)\{(\exists x : x = \text{the apple}) \{(\ \ )(Adam \text{ ate } x)\}\}$

Note that 'Why' occurs in each case in the initial position (COMP) of the whole sentence. Nothing prevents it from occurring there;

---

[39]That this is the case for reflexives is illustrated by the contrast between (a) and (b):

(a) John helped himself.
(b) John asked Mary to help himself.

In (b), unlike in (a), 'himself' is not in the same innermost clause as 'John'. The full story requires further elaboration of what counts as a clause here.

nothing requires that it be within the innermost sentence, since, unlike 'when', it binds no trace.

The difference among the implicatures, again, is accounted for by the differences among the focusing operators. (49b) does not have any; (50b) and (51b) have different ones.

The difference between these implicatures and those created in the corresponding when-questions is accounted for by the fact that the focusing operators in (50b) and (51b) are within the scope of 'why', whereas in (47b) and (48b) they are outside the scope of 'when'. As a consequence, in the why-questions, the focusing operators serve to specify an aspect of the subject matter under question, to attach uniqueness to a presupposed item. In the when-questions, they do not serve to specify an aspect of the subject matter under question: they serve as an item in the context in which that subject matter is represented, and convey an attitude of the speaker; they attach uniqueness to an interest of that speaker.[40]

The difference among the answers called for by the different why-questions is also accounted for by the occurrence of the focusing operators within the scope of 'why': since in that position they serve to specify an aspect of the subject matter under question—of the presupposition—differences among them become differences of subject matters specified, of presuppositions; and different presuppositions call for different answers.

So everything is accounted for on the assumption that 'why', unlike 'when', has no mid-sentence trace in logical form.

However, one point remains. The argument hinges on the assumption that 'why', unlike 'when', occurs in the outermost COMP. What prevents it from occurring in the innermost COMP?

Nothing!

'Why' *can* occur in the innermost COMP. But when it does, we get a set of why-interrogatives whose implicatures and answers are like those of the when-interrogatives. To see this, picture a situation in which the speaker believes that Adam and Eve and God all ate the apple and asks 'Why did ADAM eat the apple?' thereby indicating that he does not care about the others. Then picture a situation in which a speaker believes that Adam ate the apple, the banana, the orange, and the hamburger, and asks 'Why did Adam eat the

---

[40]They function like parentheticals.

APPLE?' thereby indicating that he does not care about the rest of Adam's meal.[41]

The crux of the argument was not that emphatic 'why' cannot behave like emphatic 'when' (or 'how', 'where', and so on) but that it can behave in ways that emphatic 'when' (and the others) cannot.

3   Rational Ignoramus and Why-Questions

The fact that why-questions have no mid-sentence traces has consequences for Rational Ignoramus.

Let us briefly return to the topic of attributive presuppositions. Example (7) (repeated as (52))

(52)   What is the height of the Empire State Building?

has the logical form

(53)   (What $t : t$ a distance) (t is the height of the Empire State Building)

and the attributive presupposition whose logical form is

(54)   ($\exists x : x$ a distance) (x is the height of the Empire State Building)

The connection between the attributive presupposition and the question is transparent when we look at their logical form: the only difference between (53) and (54) is their binding operator.

This means that the attributive presupposition and the question are mutually deducible by anyone who has access to these logical forms; and anyone who understands them has that access.

The transparency depends critically on the fact that the interrogative operator in (53) binds a mid-sentence trace. It is the mid-sentence trace in (53) that is the analogue of the bound variable in (54). The mutual deducibility of the question and its attributive presupposition therefore also depends on the fact that the interrogative operator binds a mid-sentence trace.

Every question whose interrogative operator binds a mid-sentence trace—i.e., every question initiated in English with 'when', 'what',

---

[41]People with sharp ears will notice a slight change in the tonality of the stress. That fact too constitutes confirming evidence: we know that logical form and phonology interact.

'where', 'how', 'which', 'who', and so forth—is transparently connected in this way to its attributive presupposition.[42] Each of them
has a logical form that fits the schema (55a) and a matching attributive presupposition that fits the schema (55b)

(55)   a. $(\exists x : x \ldots)(\ldots x \ldots)$
       b. $(\text{Wh } t : t \ldots)(\ldots t \ldots)$

As a consequence, in every case, attributive presupposition and
question are mutually deducible by anyone who understands the
question.

But in every case mutual deducibility critically depends on the
fact that the interrogative operator binds a mid-sentence trace, since
it is the trace bound to the interrogative operator that matches the
variable bound to the quantificational one.

So, as long as he limits himself to these sorts of questions, Rational Ignoramus only needs access to their logical form—that is,
only needs to understand them—and his wits, to figure out their
attributive presuppositions. The same is true for their existential
presuppositions, since logical forms display purported reference.

In short, unassisted wits and cogitation on meaning[43] alone will
tell him what he has to find out to know whether the question is
sound, and thus to know whether it is accessible to him.[44]

But nothing of the sort follows for why-questions. The interrogative operator in their logical form does not bind a mid-
sentence trace, and nothing stands to their logical form as (54) stands
to (53).

Unassisted wits and cogitation on meaning alone, therefore, will
not enable Rational Ignoramus to figure out the attributive presupposition of a why-question, even when he understands it. Or, more

---

[42]Pesetsky and others have suggested that some of these English operators do
not move into a COMP in logical form but remain in situ and that the same holds
in other languages. My main point should not be affected if they turn out to be
right, though I would then have to complicate the presentation. My point rests
on the presumption that 'why' is different from the others in that it never occurs
in situ in mid-sentence—and hence never has a trace there—whereas the others
either occur in situ or have a trace there.

[43]"Meaning" makes some people cringe. But it shouldn't in this context where
it carries very minimal commitments.

[44]Cogitation on meaning will often also tell him *whether* an attributive presupposition is satisfied: as I mentioned a while back, that sort of knowledge often
springs directly from conceptual structure, is a priori if anything is.

precisely, unassisted wits cannot lead him to that attributive presupposition in the way it can in the case of questions with bound traces. But there is no reason to believe that it can do so in any other way.

We could draw a different conclusion from the fact that why-questions do not have mid-sentence traces, namely, that why-questions simply don't have attributive presuppositions at all. That is another way of looking at the fact that nothing stands to any why-question as (54) and (53) stand to (52).

But that way of looking at the facts is of little help to Rational Ignoramus. It may force me to relabel presuppositions, but it does not change the fact that why-questions have presuppositions that cannot be discovered through cogitation on meaning alone. This can be shown very quickly.

Why-questions do have presuppositions that Rational Ignoramus can discover through cogitation on meaning alone. For instance,

(56)   Why is the circumference of the earth 250,000 stades?

cannot have a true answer unless the circumference of the earth is 250,000 stades. To know whether (56) is sound, Rational Ignoramus must know whether that presupposition is true. But he can obviously figure out that presupposition from his understanding of the question, that, is from its logical form.

What is true of (56) is generally true. Every why-question presupposes the proposition represented by deleting the why-operator from its logical form. Let us call that kind of presupposition the *propositional presupposition*. Whether we classify propositional presuppositions of why-questions with existential presuppositions of other questions is immaterial here.

But why-questions can have a true propositional presupposition and still not be sound. To believe otherwise is to believe that semantics alone can rule out brute facts, random events, things coming about without rhyme or reason, occurrences happening because of nothing in particular, capricious actions, ultimate truths, so's without why-so's. Semantics may be the handmaiden of rational theology, but it is not revealed theology! It cannot require that (56) have an answer.

So, to know that a why-question is sound, Rational Ignoramus must not only know that its propositional presupposition is true. He must know something else. But there is no reason to believe that cogitation on meaning alone can tell him what that something else is. (Whether we call that something else 'attributive presupposition' is immaterial again.)

How can that be?

A full account would require a detailed discussion of the conditions that define true answers to why-questions. I am not prepared to do that here or now. However, many a blind person—myself included—has already reported on the shape of that elephant, and its general outline is beginning to emerge.

A why-question can have a true answer only if its propositional presupposition expresses a fact. But that fact in turn must be construable as the answer to a question which is linkable to other questions by means of value adders, and not just any value adder, but a value adder that occupies a particular position in the hierarchy of value adders.[45] However, Rational Ignoramus cannot always know in advance whether a given fact can be construed that way, or how it is to be construed that way. The right value adders, predicates, determinables, and attributes must first be conceived and checked. The logical form of the why-question is no guide to these. It does not even constrain them. It has no direct conceptual relation to them. In fact, a why-question may be expressible long before the relevant value adders and attributes. 'Having mass', 'having outer electrons', 'having a logical form', 'being a combination of distinctive features', and so forth, and the value adders that link them to other determinables were conceived and received expression long *after* why-questions that called for them had been raised. The logical form of these why-questions was of no help to those who raised them. It had no direct conceptual relation to the requisite ideas.

Where does that leave Rational Ignoramus?

In the very non-plussing predicament of knowing that he does not know the answer to some why-questions, yet not knowing what he must find out in order to know whether there is anything to know at all![46]

---

[45] See footnote 18.

[46] Why-questions are not unique in this respect: 'What-is X?' questions, under certain circumstances, will raise the same predicament, but in a different way. There must be others. The topic deserves investigation. This predicament, by

What is Rational Ignoramus to do under the burden of such ignorance? My guess is that the rational thing for him to do is to
forget about the why-question and to turn to other questions instead, remembering that answers to why-questions usually emerge
from work on questions with more reliable credentials. That same
guess probably looms behind the distrust of why-questions often felt
by experimentalists, and behind the eagerness of some philosophers
to reconstrue why-questions as non-why-questions in disguise, for
example, as 'What is the cause of ... ?', 'From what laws and antecedent conditions does it follow that ... ?', 'What mechanisms are
responsible for ... ?', 'For what reason did ... ?'.

But even if my guess is right, it should not be taken as deni-
grating answers to why-questions. Those answers include some of
our most beautiful intellectual prizes. Answers to why-questions reveal the surprising in the familiar and the familiar in the surprising,
they unveil what is otherwise hidden, they link what seems otherwise unconnected; they generate new questions; they come with new
value adders. The credentials of why-questions may be unclear, but
their Peircean, Jamesian, Collingwood, and Machian value is beyond
doubt. That is probably why distrust of why-questions has never influenced theory construction for very long, and why philosophical
reconstruals have never gained wide acceptance.

---

the way, is not to be confused with what I called in "An Approach to Explanation" and "Science and the Forms of Ignorance" the p-predicament, viz., the
predicament in which one is with regard to a question q when one knows that the
presuppositions of q are true but every possible answer to q one can excogitate is
incompatible with other things one knows. Why-questions can put one in either
predicament. Questions whose presuppositions entail that at least one possible
answer is true can only put one in a p-predicament.

8

Types and Tokens in Linguistics

Introduction

Generative linguistics[1] is a perplexing field of inquiry when looked at with philosophic issues in mind. This is so not only because perplexing paradoxes bedevil the naive notions of rule, meaning, truth-condition, reference; or because a multiplicity of interests and beliefs conflict over how its subject matter should be disentangled in a principled way from other things that influence speech; but also because simple truisms on which its very possibility depends seem problematic on close scrutiny. In this paper I want to consider three of these truisms:

(1) Linguistics rests on information about types such as word types and sentence types. Since these are abstract entities, it therefore rests on information about intrinsic properties of abstract entities.[2]

(2) Some—possibly all—of the information about types that is relevant to linguistics is empirical information, that is, information that must be obtained by attending with one's senses. Typically ,that information is obtained by attending to utterances, that is, to tokens.

(3) Linguistics must concern itself with psychology since the in-

---

[1]In this paper, I shorten 'generative linguistics' to 'linguistics'.

[2]By intrinsic properties I simply mean properties whose possession does not depend on contingent relations to concrete objects via tokens. Thus the fact that a token of the word type 'dog' was uttered by Richard Nixon does not represent an intrinsic property of the type 'dog', but the fact that it is a noun, and that it is monosyllabic, and that it can occur as the subject of a sentence does represent intrinsic properties.

trinsic properties of types, and their arrangements under various languages must follow—in part at least—from facts about people's mental makeup.

Many linguists are apt to dismiss qualms about these truisms as contrived or frivolous. Their attitude is easy to understand: if (1), (2), and (3) were not true (and hence compatible), linguistics research would be impossible. But linguistics research is obviously not impossible, as attested by ongoing progress and accumulation of results, explanations, and predictions. So (1), (2), and (3) must be true and compatible. Why raise doubts about them? They have analogues in other successful disciplines. Why pick on linguistics?

And yet, consider (1) and (2). That we can get information about abstract entities at all is puzzling. It is a problem that philosophers of mathematics must also face. But the conjunction of (1) and (2) raises a problem not pertinent to mathematics but pertinent to linguistics. Philosophers of mathematics face a problem of a priori knowledge, that is, a problem raised by the possibility (or at least apparent possibility) of *nonempirical* knowledge about abstract entities. The conjunction of (1) and (2) raises a problem of a posteriori knowledge, that is, a problem raised by the possibility (or apparent possibility) of *empirical* knowledge about abstract entities. Empirical information—mentioned in (2)—is based on perceptions and perceptions require causal interactions through which the things observed affect sensory organs. But abstract entities—mentioned in (1)—cannot causally affect anything. They are not in space or time and hence do not participate in spatio-temporal episodes. Causal interactions are spatio-temporal episodes. If linguistics rests on information about abstract entities, how can that information be empirical? How could perception of anything yield information about intrinsic properties of types?[3]

Tokens can be observed. Spoken tokens[4] are events (or aspects of events) that impact our ears, produce kinesthetic sensations, involve

---

[3]The problem may be partly hidden by our use of such expressions as 'word', 'sentence', 'syllable' and others that refer indiscriminately to either types or tokens. Thus we speak of hearing words or sentences, though what affects our senses are tokens, not their types, metonymy notwithstanding. I will come back to this point later.

[4]Linguists on the whole restrict their attention to spoken language, and I will do the same in this paper.

detectable movements, and embody occurrent intentions. But according to (1), tokens are not what linguistics is primarily concerned with. Types are. However, according to (2), tokens can yield information about types. But how? It cannot be in the way facts about invisible things are accessed in the physical sciences by observing visible ones, that is, in the way physicists reconstruct aspects of invisible electron-neutron collisions from visible repercussions in a cloud chamber, or astronomers infer the rate of motion of galaxies beyond their view from spectrometer readings. Those achievements rely on causal links between things that impact senses (for instance, vapor condensing in a cloud chamber) and things thus "indirectly" observed (for instance, electrons colliding with neutrons). Causal links between spatio-temporal events make them possible. But, as already noted, types, being abstract entities,[5] cannot be—or participate in events that are—causally linked to anything, including tokens.[6]

Now consider (1) and (3). How can these two be true together? Whatever psychology is about, it is not about abstract entities. It is about mental states, mental structures, mental competences, physiology, neurology, perhaps behavior; and its procedures are designed to yield nomological generalizations and explanatory theories about these. But how can generalizations or explanatory theories about such things have any bearing on intrinsic properties of any abstract entities, or on the ways they group? Or, conversely, how can intrinsic facts about abstract entities have any bearing on generalizations or explanations about things like mental states and the like? In short,

---

[5] Viewing types as mental entities will not reconcile (1) and (2). It comes down either to the view that types can be the object of mental attitudes, which still leaves in the dark how their attributes can be inferred from attributes of tokens. Or it comes down to the view that there are mental representations and that these too have tokens and types, which simply means that a problem similar to the one raised by the juxtaposition of (1) and (2) may arise for the view that there are mental representations.

[6] Some modes of inference yield information about unobserved things from information about observed ones without presupposing causal links between the two, namely inductions from observed samples of a population to other members of that population. Inductions of that sort demand that the observed and the nonobserved make up a class across which projections of some properties are licensed, and that in turn demands that they share attributes that warrant these projections. It is doubtful that spatio-temporal and abstract entities can share projection-warranting attributes. Offhand it would seem that they can't, since such projections presuppose connections among causal histories.

how can intrinsic properties of types (or groupings of types) follow from anything about historically contingent configurations at all, be they mental, neurological, behavioral, or anything else? The link, for the reasons given above, cannot be causal. What other link could there be?

Could (2) be false? That seems incredible. The facts that linguists ferret out are contingent facts,[7] and contingent facts—except perhaps for some *recherché* and controversial metaphysical principles—are accessible only through empirical investigation. And in any case, it is undeniable that linguists attend to tokens in the course of their investigations, produce them, judge them, or have informants produce them and judge them. This is not to say that only empirical information about tokens matters to them, or that they perform statistical inductions from observed cases. Nor is it to say that they consider every token, no matter when or how produced, to be evidence. But their inductive procedures—however analyzed—do include the canon that linguistic hypotheses are refutable by empirically supported counterexamples and are corroborated by empirically confirmed consequences.

Could (3) be false? Though widely taken for granted, (3) has been denied and ignored in practice. Many linguists reject the suggestion that their theorizing should be responsive to learning theory or other branches of psychology. Linguists, like philosophers, are also still divided between supporters of versions of Platonism and supporters of versions of psychologism. Chomsky's arguments against E-language approaches, and in favor of I-language ones, are but a recent episode in that debate, and will not end it. Psychologism has an air of realism, but Platonism simplifies discourse. And Platonism sounds plausible. Think of English. It is a language that happens to be spoken by certain people during a certain historical period across a certain region. But those are contingent facts about English. Linguists are after essential facts. English might not have been spoken by these people. In some possible worlds it is not. It might not have been spoken by anyone: in some possible worlds it is not. In the first of these worlds no facts about English follow from any facts

---

[7]This is another difference between mathematics and linguistics. Though both are concerned with abstract entities, linguistics, unlike mathematics, relies not only on empirical evidence but is also after contingent truths.

about actual speakers of English,[8] and in the latter ones no facts about English follow from any facts about any human beings. Since pure linguists—as opposed to psycholinguists—working on English are after essential facts, that is, facts that hold in any possible world, including worlds in which it is not spoken, they can disregard that some of them happen to follow from facts about human beings in this world, and they can therefore ignore possible connections to psychology. The same argument for Platonism can be repeated about any language. However, it is not conclusive. It assumes the problematic thesis that English types, like numbers, exist in every possible world. More important, it leaves open whether English would be of any interest to linguists or could even be discovered if no one spoke it, that is, in a possible world in which no one does. Later I will argue that facts about English, or other languages, are of interest and are discoverable only because they follow from facts about the minds of speakers in this world.

Could (1) be false?[9] Could linguistics turn out not to be about types even though linguistics books and journals seem full of facts (or alleged facts) about types, and even though typical linguistic claims seem to mention types? For instance, it is claimed that the underlying phonological representation of 'serene' is identical to the underlying representation of the stem of 'serenity' (although their tokens are phonetically very different), that the last morpheme in 'ungrammaticality' takes adjectives into nouns (although none of the tokens is used to make an adjectival modification), that the phonetic shape of 'Flying planes can be dangerous' is associated with two different sets of thematic role assignments (although no token is), that 'He loves herself' violates gender agreement (although tokens occur probably only to mention this fact), and so on.

According to one view, mention of types is dispensable. Chomsky can be read as advocating a version of that view in *Knowledge of Language* (1985, chap. 2), when he urges that linguistics be construed as about I-language and not about E-language. Chomsky contrasts two approaches to linguistic study. Linguistic approaches that take E-language as their subject matter presuppose that each language is a system of expressions—or expressions paired with meanings—

---

[8]'English' here must be understood as a rigid designator.

[9]If (1) is false then (2) will ipso facto fail to be true, since it presupposes (1).

that is, a system of types[10]—and take on the task of characterizing these systems, that is, of discovering rules or principles from which the types of a given language can be generated, in terms of which their interconnections and individual attributes can be predicted, and through which their kinship to other languages can be made explicit. Linguistic programs that take I-language as their subject matter assume a different ontology. They start from the position that brain states are real, and that to know a language (to have an I-language) is to be in a certain brain state. And they take on the task of characterizing such states (under idealizations and by abstracting from physiological mechanisms). Thus I-language linguistics needs to admit only certain spatio-temporal things: utterances (and judgments elicited by utterances), which are spatio-temporal events, and brain states, which are states of spatio-temporal entities. The former can inform about the latter, and the latter can account for features of the former. But types play no role in I-languages.

But even subscribers to the I-language approach can, without inconsistency, subscribe to (1): (1) does not require that linguistics be concerned with anything like E-languages, nor does it rule out I-languages as legitimate subject matter. They can admit types, while denying that languages are properly individuated as sets of types. Chomsky himself actually writes of I-languages as generating classes of expressions (1985, chap. 2). And they probably should subscribe to (1). Claims made by linguists—including claims by Chomsky in technical sections of *Knowledge of Language*—almost always appeal to types, and only exceptionally mention tokens. Thus in practice, if perhaps not in theory, linguistics must be concerned with facts about types.

So we are stuck with the problems raised by (1), (2), and (3). If (1) and (2) are both true, it is despite the fact that inferences from tokens to types do not presuppose causal links. What then is the nature of these inferences? And unless better reasons are found for denying (3), we need to understand how features of the mind can have repercussions in a realm of abstract entities.

In what follows I propose a solution to these problems. That so-

---

[10] Chomsky does not use the expression 'type'; he writes instead of, for instance, 'actual or potential speech events'. He may thus not agree with the way I have extended his argument.

lution hinges critically on the presumption that theory construction proceeds on a foundation of questions. Such questions are sometimes stated but are more often simply taken for granted. Therefore their role is easily overlooked. They are nevertheless fundamental constituents of the various classificatory systems on which theories rely, and they define the domain in which any given theory operates. In this respect linguistic theorizing is like that in any of the other natural sciences. I do not defend that presumption in this paper, but by discussing its operation and by juxtaposing linguistic examples with others I hope to make it credible.

My solution hardly qualifies as a theory. It consists mostly of definitions and some illustrations to make them concrete. The relevant facts are clear. What we need are clear ways of conceptualizing them.

1   The Platonic Relationship Principle

One reason for believing that (1) and (2) can be reconciled is that linguists, in practice, often impute properties to types after observing and judging some of their tokens, and seem to do this in a principled way. Let us call the principle on which they (implicitly) rely the *Platonic Relationship Principle* to underline that it guides their attention from worldly to abstract entities. How does the Platonic Relationship Principle operate? We know that it cannot assume that types and tokens are causally related. But it must assume that they are related in some pertinent way. How?

(4)   Tokens of a type make up a quasi-natural kind, and their type is the archetype of that quasi-natural kind.

I now turn to an explanation of (4).

1.1   Quasi-natural Kinds

Quasi-natural kinds, as I use the term, are groupings, classes, assemblages, that are in many—but not all—respects like natural kinds. The notion of natural kind—insofar as it is clear at all—is loaded with historical and parochial connotations that are irrelevant for present purposes. The notion of quasi-natural kinds discards most of these connotations and preserves what I regard as essential for investigative purposes. It is free, for instance, of any association with "nature," whatever that may be; artifacts can make up quasi-natural kinds.

Quasi-natural kinds satisfy three conditions which I will label "the modeling condition," "the explainable differences condition," and "the individuation condition." I will describe each of these in turn.

The modeling condition requires that each member of a quasi-natural kind be a model of every other member of that kind. That condition enables inferences of facts about any arbitrary member from similar facts about any other member.

The notion of model on which I rely here is the notion of model appropriate for artifactual models. An artifactual model is an object so designed that, by finding the answer to some questions about it, a competent user can figure out the answer to questions about something else. So, for instance, by counting the number of smokestacks on a model of the *QE II* an initiated user can figure out the number of smokestacks on the real *QE II*; by counting the number of black spheres on a wire and wood model of methane, an initiated user can figure out the number of carbon atoms in a methane molecule. Or take maps. A map is a model of the territory it represents. By getting the answer to, for instance, (5) and (6) about the map

(5)   What is the distance between point *a* on the map and point *b* on the map?

(6)   How many contour lines occur between point *a* and point *b* on the map?

one can get the answer to the following question about the territory mapped:

(7)   What is the distance between place *A* in the territory and place *B* in the territory?

(8)   What is the difference in altitude between place *A* in the territory and place *B* in the territory?

But there are usually limits to what even an initiated reader can find out in this way. Though one can find the answer to

(9)   What is the name of the publisher printed on the map?

by looking at the map, the rules of map reading will not turn that answer into the answer to any question about the territory. And conversely, few maps, if any, yield the answer to such questions about the territory as

(10)   How many stones are there in the northern half of the territory? or

(11)   How many bicyclists were riding in the northern half of the territory on 4 July 1984 at noon?

In short, ignoring artifactness, the idea of a model comes down to the following:

(12) M is a model of O relative to a quadruple $\langle Q_m, Q_o, P, A \rangle$ if and only if, in that quadruple, Q_m is a nonempty set of questions about M; Q_o is a nonempty set of questions about O; P pairs members of Q_m with members of Q_o; and A is an algorithm that translates answers to any member of Q_m into answers to the member of Q_o paired with it by P, and translates correct answers to the former into correct answers to the latter.

Note that this concept of a model is that of a dyadic relation: no object is intrinsically a model. It takes a pair. Note also that it is a relativized notion. No pair of objects stands (or fails to stand) in the model/modeled relation absolutely, but only relative to specific sets of questions, pairings of questions, and algorithms.

Things not usually called models of each other nevertheless stand in the relation described in (12): samples of mercury, for instance. Let 'm_1' and 'm_2' designate two samples of mercury, then (13) will hold:

(13) m_1 and m_2 are two good samples of mercury only if m_1 is a model of m_2 with regard to the quadruple consisting of:

    (a) Q_{m_1}, a set of questions about m_1 that includes 'What is the boiling point of m_1?', 'What is the freezing point of m_1?', 'What is the molecular weight of m_1?';

    (b) Q_{m_2}, a set of questions about m_2 that includes 'What is the boiling point of m_2?', 'What is the freezing point of m_2?', 'What is the molecular weight of m_2?'

    (c) The pairing P_m that matches each question in Q_{m_1} with the question in Q_{m_2} exactly like it but for a switch of reference from m_1 to m_2.

    (d) The algorithm A_m that matches identical answers but for a switch of reference from m_1 to m_2.

By satisfying (13) samples of mercury do more than just satisfy (12). Those subsidiary conditions are important in what follows. I will shorten their description with the help of the following convention, on which I will also rely throughout the rest of this paper:

(14)   *The Related Questions Convention:*[11] When some $Q(n_1)$ is a question that is about something n_1, and some $Q(n_2)$ is a question that is about something n_2, and $Q(n_1)$ can be turned into $Q(n_2)$ by substituting n_2 for n_1, conflate $Q(n_1)$ and $Q(n_2)$ and refer to them as one question about both n_1 and n_2. And when the (right) answer to $Q(n_1)$ can be turned into the right answer to $Q(n_2)$ by again substituting n_2 for n_1, conflate these two answers, and refer to one answer that holds for both $Q(n_1)$ and $Q(n_2)$.

So, for instance, the facts about the boiling point in (13) can now be put by saying that m_1 and m_2 bear the same answer to

(15)   What is the (or its) boiling point?

Let us now return to those subsidiary conditions:

A. The universal generalization of (13) with respect to the positions occupied by m_1 and m_2 is also true. In other words, though some samples of mercury are mutual models relative to quadruples not sketched in (13), the quadruple sketched in (13) holds for any paired samples of mercury.

B. The universal generalization of (13) remains true when construed as a nomological, law-like generalization. Counterfactuals instantiated from it are true. If the water in the glass before me right now were a sample of mercury, it would be a model of any sample of mercury relative to the quadruple in (13).

C. P_m and A_m combine to match identical answers to identical questions.

D. Some of the questions mentioned in (13) bear answers that are amenable to explanation, that is, that can serve as object to

---

[11]The convention is stated in a way that imputes reality to questions over and above the reality of the locutions that express them. This, in the eyes of many people, may be suspect. I do not intend to address the issue here, though it is important. The convention can be easily rephrased to fit more puritanical ontologies.

sound why-questions,[12] and these why-questions in turn get identical answers. So, for instance,

(16)   What is its boiling point?

gets the same answer for every sample of mercury

(17)   356.6°C

and that answer is the object of the sound why-question (that is, a why-question that has a true 'because' answer)

(18)   Why is the boiling point 356.6°C?

which in turn gets the same answer for every sample of mercury (something about molecular bonds).

The modeling condition on quasi-natural kinds incorporates these subsidiary conditions A–D. Fully stated, it now becomes:

(19)   Every member of a quasi-natural kind is nomologically a model for every other member relative to some questions askable of each and to which each bears the same answer with the same explanation.

Using *questions projectible for N* to mention questions that render (19) true for a quasi-natural kind N, we can restate (19) as:

(20)   If N is a quasi-natural kind, then there is a nonempty set Q_p of projectible questions for N, and if the answer[13] to any of them gives rise to a why-question,[14] then that why-question is also projectible for N.

---

[12]Here and elsewhere in this paper, I am committing a sin that I have rightly condemned in other writings: the sin of disregarding that many explanations are not answers to why-questions and that many answers to why-questions are not explanations. The two notions are very loosely connected, except in philosophic literature, where they are often irresponsibly conflated. The commission of sins usually brings some pleasure. In this case, the pleasure is avoidance of circumlocution at the cost of relatively little immediate confusion.

[13]Here and elsewhere I use the locution 'the answer' in a way that suggests that questions can have only one correct answer. Whether this is true or not depends on how one individuates questions and answers. I ignore these issues too for the time being for nothing presently crucial hinges on how they get resolved. If we adopt a position according to which some questions have more than one right answer, then we must rephrase some passages more carefully, but that can be done without essential distortion of what is intended, though not without more ugly circumlocutions.

[14]The presumption behind this formulation that some answers do not give rise to why-questions is allowed deliberately: some of these answers represent brute, ultimate facts not amenable to explanation.

The explainable differences condition requires that some differences among the members of a quasi-natural kind be systematic differences, that is, differences that follow from laws, or principles, or theories, and kinds of circumstance that pertain to all its members. So, for instance, samples of mercury differ in temperature, but the temperature of each at any given time is accounted for by laws and kinds of boundary conditions common to all samples of mercury at all times. Thus,

(21)   If N is a quasi-natural kind then there is a nonempty set of questions Q_a

    (a) whose presuppositions are satisfied by every member of N;[15]

    (b) to which different members of N bear a different answer;

    (c) whose right answer in each case—that is, for each member—is the object of a sound why-question;

    (d) whose answer, in turn, in every case, follows from the same nomological principles together with contingencies peculiar to the case but of a kind applicable to all.

The point of the condition on presuppositions is to allow for failures of presupposition. The following example will show what is going on: 'What is the age of the person who was king of France in 1987?' has no answer because no king of France existed in 1987. That is a failure of existential presupposition. 'How fast did Julius Caesar fly when he crossed the Rubicon?' has no answer, not because Julius Caesar did not exist but because Julius Caesar did not fly when he crossed the Rubicon—or for that matter at any other time. That is a failure not of existential presupposition, but of something I have called elsewhere attributive presupposition. Different sorts of things satisfy different sorts of attributive presuppositions. Thus samples of mercury satisfy the attributive presupposition of 'What is its boiling point?' but not of 'What is its limit?' The situation reverses for mathematical series.

Actually (21) should be qualified. What I should really say is that there is a nonempty set of presuppositions which are satisfied by every member of N modulo reference to locations in space or in time, that is, if we abstract from certain specification of places and

---

[15]Except, of course, the existential presuppositions that refer to the member.

times. So, for instance, the sample of mercury in the dish before me right now may not satisfy the presupposition of

(22)   What was its temperature on 7 July 1924 at noon?

because it did not exist on 7 July 1924. But it must satisfy the presupposition of some questions of the form 'What was its temperature on ... ?' However, since (21) will play only a minor role in what follows, I will leave it in this relatively crude state for the present.

Let us call questions that satisfy (21) *w-projectible questions for N*. Thus (22) is a *w*-projectible question for samples of mercury, since (a) every sample of mercury satisfies its presupposition,[16] that is, has a specific temperature at specific times; (b) different samples of mercury have different temperatures at specific times; (c) whatever the temperature of a sample of mercury at a certain time may happen to be, the question

(23)   Why did it have that temperature (at that time)?

has a correct answer; and (d) at least one right answer to (23) for each sample follows from the same general principles (for instance, of kinetic theory) supplemented by boundary conditions peculiar to the sample but of a sort common to all (for instance, having to do with intermolecular bonds).

The individuation condition requires that the members of a quasi-natural kind differ from each other along common dimensions but not in ways that answer projectible questions or *w*-projectible questions. So, for instance, samples of mercury are at different places at different times and these locations are not the consequence of laws or principles common to all of them. Their parts get scattered and assembled by agents and in ways for which no single principled explanation is forthcoming. So the third condition is

(24)   If N is a quasi-natural kind, then there is a nonempty set Q_i of questions whose presupposition is satisfied by every member of N, but which are neither projectible nor *w*-projectible for N.

Let us call such questions *individuating questions for N*. So

(25)   Where was it on 7 July 1924?

is an individuating question for samples of mercury.

---

[16]Subject to the above qualification about (21).

The definition of a quasi-natural kind is then:

(26)   A class of objects constitutes a quasi-natural kind relative
        to triple $\langle Q_p/A_p, Q_w, Q_i \rangle$—in which Q_p, Q_w, and Q_i are
        nonempty sets of questions and A_p a nonempty set of an-
        swers matched with members of Q_p—if and only if it is the
        largest class of objects for which the questions in Q_p are pro-
        jectible, those in Q_w are w-projectible, and those in Q_i are
        individuating, and that bear the members of A_p as answers
        to the members of Q_p with which they are matched.

The notion of quasi-natural kind is a relative notion: no class
of things is a quasi-natural kind absolutely, and a given class may
be a quasi-natural kind relative to more than one set of questions.
When this happens, the individual members will belong to distinct
but coextensive quasi-natural kinds, like cordates and renates. They
may of course also separate into distinct quasi-natural kinds that are
not coextensive.

Some questions are ruled out as possible projectible, w-project-
ible, or individuating questions for taxonomizing the members of
some classes. For instance

(27)   How much income tax did it pay in 1924?

(28)   What nutrients does it require to survive?

are ruled out for the members of the class made up of samples of
mercury.

1.2   Archetype of a Quasi-Natural Kind

The archetype of a quasi-natural kind is an entity very similar to but
also very different from the members of that quasi-natural kind. It
is very similar to the members because it is an exact model of them
relative to the projectible questions of the kind. (By an exact model
I mean a model that bears the same answers to the same questions.)
But it is very different from them because it bears no answer at all
to any of the w-projectible questions or to any of the individuating
questions of the kind.

So, for instance, the archetype of samples of mercury is an entity
that is very similar to a sample of mercury: it bears the same answer
as any sample of mercury to questions such as

(29)   What is its boiling point? Answer: 356.6°C

(30)   What is its freezing point? Answer: $-38.87°C$

(31)   What is its molecular weight? Answer: 200.6

In other words, it is an exact model of any sample of mercury with regard to these questions. But it is very different from any sample of mercury when it comes to such questions as

(32)   What was its temperature on 7 July 1924 at noon?

(33)   Where was it on 7 July 1924?

Whereas samples of mercury bear various answers to (32) and (33) and other w-projectible and individuating questions, their archetype bears none at all. It had no temperature at all on 7 July 1924, and it was nowhere on 7 July 1924.[17] The archetype of samples of mercury has a boiling point, a melting point, a molecular weight, an index of electric conductivity, but it has no mass, no volume, no history, no location, no age. That is how it is an abstract entity: it fails to meet the presuppositions of the w-projectible questions and of the individuating questions in the same sense as the samples themselves fail to meet the presuppositions of (27) and (28).

So far I have spoken of "the" archetype of the samples of mercury, as if there is only one, as if samples of mercury (or members of other quasi-natural kinds) have—that is, exemplify—only one archetype. That is not quite right: samples of mercury and members of other quasi-natural kinds may—and do—exemplify more than one archetype. This is so because they belong to more than one quasi-natural kind and because some of these quasi-natural kinds differ from each other by being related to different sets of projectible questions. They exemplify each of the archetypes that emerge through the projectible questions from these various quasi-natural kinds. Furthermore, since distinct samples of mercury (or members of any quasi-natural kind) probably also belong to distinct and *noncoextensive* quasi-natural kinds, distinct samples of mercury probably also exemplify distinct archetypes.

Summarizing all this, the definition of an archetype is then:

---

[17]I don't mean, of course, that no appropriate or informative reply can be offered to someone who raises one of these questions about the archetype. A reply that points out that the archetype is not a thing that has a temperature at any time or location, for instance, would be appropriate and informative. What I mean is that no "direct" answer will do, no reply that gives a temperature or location for the archetype on 7 July 1924.

(34) R is the archetype of Q—where Q is a quasi-natural class
        relative to the triple $\langle Q_p/A_p, Q_w, Q_i \rangle$—if and only if R bears
        A_p as answers to Q_p and bears no answers at all to any of the
        members of Q_w or Q_i.

where we understand 'R bears A_p as answers to Q_p' to mean that R
bears the members of A_p as answers to the questions in Q_p matched
to them for Q.

And a statement of the Platonic Relationship Principle follows
readily from this definition:

(35)   If T is the archetype of the quasi-natural kind relative to
        $\langle Q_p/A_p, Q_w, Q_i \rangle$ then the answer to any question in Q_p with
        reference aimed at T, is the matched member of A_p with ref-
        erence aimed at T.

The operation of the principle is so simple and transparent that—
not surprisingly—it is hardly ever noticed. To infer the properties
of an archetype from any of its examples is often trivially easy. The
difficult job is to discover $\langle Q_p/A_p, Q_w, Q_i \rangle$ triples relative to which
individuals form revealing quasi-natural kinds.

Most interesting archetypes lack spatial or temporal locations.
But their intrinsic attributes are in principle—that is, but for limits of expressive power—exhaustively describable: each archetype is
characterized by a set of question-answer pairs, namely the set of
projectible question-answer pairs of some quasi-natural kind, and is
therefore exhaustively described—except for relational properties—
by any text that encodes the information in such a set.[18] So for
instance, one of the archetypes of samples of mercury is specified by
an array such as

(36)   a. What is its boiling point? 356.6°C
        b. What is its freezing point? −38.87°C
        c. What is its molecular weight? 200.6
           and so on

and that archetype is described by any text that describes it directly
or indirectly as bearing these answers to those questions.

---

[18]Complicated issues loom behind this claim. Demonstrably there exist nondenumerably many question-answer pairs. The claim therefore assumes that sets
of nondenumerably many questions play no role in the arrangement of things into
quasi-natural kinds or in the emergence of archetypes. But that is a topic for
another day.

Since fictitious entities too are exhaustively describable, this may suggest that archetypes are but fictions. But if archetypes are fictions, they are very unlike the garden variety of invented fictions. The latter are describable only because someone has actually described them. Archetypes are describable even if no one has described them. In fact, most will probably never be described. Our archetype of samples of mercury happens to be describable in contemporary English. It could not have been described in classical Greek. Classical Greek lacked the right nomenclature. Similar lexical shortcomings no doubt block the description of other archetypes in contemporary English. And in all likelihood archetypes exist that will never be describable in any of the languages that have or will ever be spoken by anyone. I cannot prove this, but the subjective probability is irresistible. Whether a given archetype is describable in a certain language depends on whether certain questions are expressible in that language. And some questions will never be expressible in any language that will ever be spoken by anyone.[19] Some quasi-natural kinds, and hence some archetypes, must be related to some of these questions. Even these archetypes are inherently describable. They are not ineffable. Only accidents of lexical evolution block their description. Even so, unlike garden variety fictitious entities, they are doomed never to be described. So those archetypes at least are not invented fictions. Why should any of them be?

Archetypes may nevertheless seem unreal. The archetype of the samples of mercury, for instance, presumably has a molecular weight. But can anything real have a molecular weight without being made up of molecules and hence being in space and in time? And if it is in space and in time, must it not have spatio-temporal locations, and thus satisfy the presuppositions of individuating questions about where it was when? Similar worries may come up around other archetypes, including the linguistic types to which I am about to turn. They need not concern us for the present. The crucial point, for present purposes, about the archetype of a quasi-natural kind is that it is fully characterized by an array of question-answer pairs, and that it is fully described by any text that encodes the contents of such an array, and that we have ways of referring to it. We can even

---

[19]For a sketch of an argument see "What We Don't Know When We Don't Know Why," this volume.

think of archetypes as simply such arrays. Of course, if we do this, we will have to talk about them differently. We will, for instance, have to stop saying that the archetype of samples of mercury satisfies the presuppositions of (29)–(31). No such array can. We will have to say instead that the archetype "includes" (29)–(31).[20] I will not adopt this way of speaking because I do not see the need for it. But it should be compatible with everything that matters in the rest of the paper. And it will be more pleasing to anyone who feels that my notion of archetype may have a role in theorizing about the world (the way virtual images or frictionless planes do for instance) but cannot denote any actual items in it.

1.3   Tokens and Types

We can now understand (4), which I repeat here: "Tokens of a type make up a quasi-natural kind, and their type is the archetype of that quasi-natural kind." If the first clause is true, then tokens cluster into sets each of which satisfies (26), and if the second clause is true, then each type exemplified by tokens corresponds to a set of questions whose answers are shared by that type and each of its tokens, that is, projectible questions. If both clauses are true, then the Platonic Relationship Principle is available to infer properties of types from properties of the tokens that exemplify them: the properties of the type are those born as answers to projectible questions by each of the exemplifying tokens.

But are the two clauses of (4) true? It is difficult to tell without knowing more about the triples $\langle Q_p/A_p, Q_w, Q_i \rangle$ pertinent to each case. And the number of such cases is infinite! With the information we have so far, it is even difficult to tell whether all types that

---

[20]To what do the questions and answers in such a set refer, since—on the picture now proposed—they cannot refer to archetypes? They need not refer to anything. Think of the question and answer as replaced by whatever semantic values correspond to the nonreferring part of a full question-answer pair. Or think of the question-answer pair as containing only the sense/character of some deictic instead of an actual reference.

Here and elsewhere I have used 'question' to refer to the sorts of things that are the contents of interrogative sentences in their guise as devices for expressing questions—and I have also assumed that these contents can have constituents that refer. Such a use implies many promises. Since I believe that the semantics of interrogative expressions will some day be explained, I feel fairly confident that these promises can be kept, though not today.

have tokens are archetypes, or whether only some are. Fortunately we need not find out whether (4) is true to deal with our problems about linguistics, that is, with (1) and (2) of the introduction. The important issue as far as our problem is concerned is whether linguistics operates on the presumption that both clauses of (4) are true. For that to be true, by the way, it is not necessary that linguists ever express the notions of *quasi-natural kind,* or *projectible question,* or *archetype,* that is, notions that have applications beyond linguistics. But it is required that they on occasion rely either explicitly or implicitly on the Platonic Relationship Principle in a way that implicates its erotetic aspects. And there are good reasons for believing that they do.

One perhaps strange but nevertheless good reason for holding this is that linguists seldom if ever mention tokens, or more precisely, habitually conflate mention of tokens with mention of types. That is easily explained if linguists are held to rely on the Platonic Relationship Principle. The questions that concern linguists when they focus on a token (and attending judgments) while concerned about its type, are questions that apply indifferently to the type and to the token, and whose answer is the same for both.[21] If types are what they care about, and tokens are but fleeting evidence, then only pedantry could drive them to highlight the distinction.

A more obvious reason for holding that they rely on the Platonic Relationship Principle is that it is difficult to see how else any inference from types to tokens can proceed. One view is that tokens group under types simply by resemblances with respect to certain traits, and that these traits are directly imputed to their types, without the intrusion of questions. On this view mention of questions is an uncalled-for complication. I will argue later that, on the contrary, questions play a critical role—or if not questions, at least the determinables that constitute their core. But even now we can see that this view leaves us in the dark about the kinds of resemblances that are relevant for the construction of further theories.

A further reason for holding that linguists rely on the Platonic Relationship Principle is that they conceptualize tokens in ways that make these amenable to applications of the principle, and that cannot be just an accident. Examples will show what I mean.

---

[21]They too, in effect, rely on the Related Questions Convention (14).

Tokens of the English word type represented orthographically as

(37)   bell

for instance, are presumed to form a quasi-natural kind relative to a set whose projectible questions/answers include at least

(38)   What is its underlying phonological structure? / [bəl]

(39)   How many syllables does it have? / One

(40)   What are the dorsal features of its second segment?
        / [− back], [−high], [−low]

(41)   What is its syntactic category? / Noun

(42)   What is its number? / Singular

whose w-projectible questions include:

(43)   What thematic role did it express?

(44)   How strongly was the vowel stressed?

(45)   In what speech act did it occur?

(46)   Was it being used literally?

(47)   To what object, if any, did it refer?

and whose individuating questions include

(48)   Where was it uttered?

(49)   When was it uttered?

(50)   To whom, if anyone, was it addressed?

(51)   By whom was it uttered?

And the type of these tokens bears the same answers to (38)–(42) as the tokens themselves, but fails to meet the presuppositions of (43)–(51) and the rest.

Tokens of the English sentence type orthographically depicted as

(52)   John's picture of himself is nice.

are presumed to form a quasi-natural kind relative to a set whose projectible questions include at least

(53)   What is its S-structure?
        / [$_S$[$_{NP}$[$_N$ John's][$_{NP'}$[$_N$ picture][$_{PP}$ of himself]]][$_{VP}$ is nice]][22]

---

[22]I know that this answer is controversial. That in itself is not without interest. It shows that perceptual recognition of attributes is not sufficient for theoretical— that is, nonperceptual—understanding. Theory is also required, as I discuss

(54)   What is its phonological representation? / (I omit the lengthy
        answer.)

(55)   What is the antecedent of the reflexive? / The determiner of
        the subject NP

(56)   What thematic roles are represented by which phrases? / (I
        omit the answer, again, as too lengthy and also too contro-
        versial.)

with w-projectible questions that include

(57)   What object does the subject NP refer to?

(58)   What is its truth value?

(59)   What speech act was performed through its production?

(60)   Which vowels were reduced in its production?

and so on, with individuating questions that include

(61)   Who uttered it?

(62)   When was it uttered?

(63)   Why was it uttered?

(64)   How loudly was it uttered?

        and so on.

And the type of these tokens bears the same answers to (53)–(56)
as the tokens themselves, but fails to meet the presuppositions of
(57)–(64) and the rest.

It may be objected that this way of viewing the relation between
tokens and their types is implausible and cannot accord with linguistic practice. Spoken tokens are sounds describable in acoustic terms
or articulatory gesticulations describable in physiological terms. It
is as sounds or articulatory gesticulations that they affect our senses.
But sounds and articulatory gesticulations have no grammatical or
phonological underpinnings. Therefore, the objection goes, no token
can satisfy the presuppositions of questions such as (38). Tokens
themselves do not have underlying structures. That fact may be
hidden in the 'bell' example because, in this case, the surface structure of the type is identical to the underlying structure. But is it
plausible that a token of the word spelled 'dogs' should in any sense

---

below. That holds for perceptual recognition of the properties of nonlinguistic
events as well.

have an underlying structure roughly like '/dog + es/'? Similar objections will readily come to mind about some of the questions said to be projectible for the tokens of (52).

The claim that spoken tokens are sounds describable in acoustic terms, or articulatory gesticulations describable in physiological terms, and that they affect our sense organs as such is uncontroversial. They undoubtedly even form quasi-natural kinds relative to some $\langle Q_p/A_p, Q_w, Q_i \rangle$ with other noises and articulatory gesticulations that have affected someone's senses, that is, quasi-natural kinds anchored to questions about acoustic and articulatory attributes with presuppositions also satisfied by grunts and burps and snorts and snores.[23] We have seen that members of quasi-natural kinds can belong to more than one natural kind. But that fact does not disqualify tokens from being topics of questions about phonological or syntactic attributes, and hence from also belonging to quasi-natural kinds relative to sets of such questions. Speech utterances are, after all, very different from other noises and articulatory gestures. Unlike other noises, they are produced by agents with phonological, syntactic, semantic, and pragmatic intentions. They embody and manifest such intentions. And they have attributes that encode such intentions. Their underlying phonological structure, the number and structure of their surface phonological segments, the category of their constituents, their thematic structure, their constituent structure, their logical form are among such attributes. Utterances are endowed with these attributes by their creators, that is, by their utterers. Competent (that is, linguistically proficient) listeners can detect them as intentionally present,[24] indeed must detect them as intentionally present in order to understand. Admittedly only speakers and listeners who have undergone the appropriate mental development can do this. But that is because the mental states that result

---

[23]It may be helpful to compare utterances here with inscriptions. Inscriptions too exemplify simultaneously a number of different types, that is, orthographic types, calligraphic or font types, geometric types, sample of substance types, etc.

[24]For instance, in the standard American dialect tokens of the words spelled 'sense' and 'cents' are produced so as to be acoustically almost indistinguishable. However the stop (t) between the nasal (n) and the continuant (s) in tokens of 'sense', unlike in tokens of 'cents', is not put there intentionally by speakers but is there as an effect of tongue inertia. The stop is thus acoustically present and can be heard even by American hearers. But it is not linguistically present, that is, it is either not detected by these hearers at all or detected as unintentional.

from such development are prerequisites for certain causal effects between intentional speech events and responsive attention events. It does not make those attributes any less real or true of tokens. It is also true that linguists often can impute and characterize such attributes only with the help of theories. But the same holds for the imputation and characterization of most attributes of any scientific interest, even temperature and acceleration. It does not entail that the attributes do not belong to the tokens.

The objection may, however, take another form. Tokens cannot have types as parts,[25] for tokens are temporal and their parts must be temporal, but types are atemporal. Syllables, it may be argued, are types. It follows that they cannot be parts of tokens and that no token therefore can satisfy the presuppositions of (39), and that furthermore no one—no matter how competent or theoretically sophisticated—will ever be able to detect a syllable in a token. Other versions of the argument may be constructed about other constituents recognized by linguistic theory.

But even in that form, the objection is mistaken. 'Syllable' is one of the terms which like 'word' and 'sentence' are used indiscriminately to refer to either types or tokens. Syllables—the types—are archetypes of temporal segments of tokens, and as such, as archetypes, are obviously never segments of tokens themselves (though they are nontemporal segments of types). But syllables—the tokens—are temporal parts of tokens.

These facts may elude us because of certain limitations on our ability to talk about specific tokens. For instance, in replying to the question

(65)   What is its first syllable?

raised about a specific token one cannot display the syllable itself, or point to it. It is gone! And so one must refer to it by seeming to mention the type it exemplifies. What one actually does is to produce another token (of a so-called quote name) that, depending on circumstances, will refer to either its own type or another token. Similarly, I could have mentioned 'John' as answer to (55) instead of the convoluted answer I did mention. Had I done so, I would then

---

[25]For a brilliant discussion of this objection and issues surrounding it, see Wetzel 1984, chap. 3. The view imputed to me there is a previous version of the one in this paper.

have used an expression (that is, another so-called quote name) that functions indiscriminately to mention either tokens of its own type or the type itself.[26] Such linguistic practices may be the source of confusions, but they do not indicate that tokens cannot have syllables as parts, or that no tokens of 'John' can be a part of some other token.

Two difficulties remain, however.

The first difficulty concerns types that have no tokens. Linguistic theory is not limited to types that have tokens. It is concerned with all the linguistic types, including those that will never have any tokens. It admits no essential distinction between exemplified and unexemplified types. The Platonic Relationship Principle, however, is restricted to inferences about exemplified types, and does not, by itself, account for inferences about types that have no tokens.

The second difficulty concerns the selection of projectible questions. Tokens arrange themselves into quasi-natural kinds in many different ways, that is, relative to innumerable sets of triples $\langle Q_p/A_p, Q_w, Q_i \rangle$. But only some of these arrangements yield archetypes of linguistic significance. As was already pointed out, applying the Platonic Relationship Principle is a trivial exercise. The important reasoning occurs while looking for revealing $\langle Q_p/A_p, Q_w, Q_i \rangle$ triples.

To resolve these difficulties we have to consider further aspects of quasi-natural kinds. But doing so will eventually also enable us to see how (1) and (3) are related.

2   Types and Minds

2.1   Categories

Samples of mercury are also samples of chemical substances. Chemical substances include not only mercury, but also gold, water, iron, hydrochloric acid, and so on. Together these form what I shall call a category. A category is simply a set of distinct quasi-natural kinds that are all relativized to the same projectible, w-projectible, and individuating questions. They differ through their answers to project-

---

[26]Matters are further confounded by the fact that this discussion is in writing. I count on the reader to enact the above passages as a spoken exchange taking place on a specific occasion, at a specific time, and under circumstances that disambiguate between use and mention.

ible questions. Each set has its own answers. But each set therefore
also has its own members.

Returning to our example, the chemical substances form a category. The samples of mercury are a quasi-natural kind relative to
a $\langle Q_p/A_p, Q_w, Q_i \rangle$ triple. That triple includes among its projectible
questions Q_p the familiar

(66)   What is its boiling point?

(67)   What is its freezing point?

(68)   What is its molecular weight?

        and so on.

It includes among its w-projectible questions (22) and the like,
and among its individuating questions (25) and the like.   The
samples of gold are a quasi-natural kind relative to another triple
$\langle Q_p/A_p', Q_w, Q_i \rangle$. That triple is identical to the previous one, except
that the answers A_p' to the projectible questions are different. For
samples of gold the answer to (66) is $2807°C$, the answer to (67) is
$1064.43°C$, the answer to (68) is 197, and so on. The samples of wa-
ter are a quasi-natural kind relative to a third triple $\langle Q_p/A_p'', Q_w, Q_i \rangle$,
and that triple too is identical to the previous one except that the
answers A_p'' to the projectible questions (66), (67), (68), and so on,
are different again. And the same goes for iron, hydrochloric acid,
and all the other chemical substances.

Putting all this a little more precisely, the quasi-natural kinds
of samples of chemical substances form a category[27] because they
satisfy the following definition:

(69)   A class of quasi-natural kinds forms a category relative to a
        triple $\langle Q_p, Q_w, Q_i \rangle$ if and only if it is the largest set of quasi-
        natural kinds for each of whose members the questions in Q_p
        are projectible, the questions in Q_w are w-projectible, and the
        questions in Q_i are individuating.

The notion of a category, like the notion of a quasi-natural kind,
is a relativized notion. Like the notion of a quasi-natural kind again,

---

[27]The union of the quasi-natural kinds in a category may itself be a further
quasi-natural kind. All the samples of substances, for instance, probably form a
quasi-natural kind relative to some triple or other, though not a triple defining
any of the members. Nothing in the definition of category in the text rules this
out. In other contexts this becomes important.

it is relativized to triples in which questions are essential. The triples pertaining to both notions are in fact identical but for the fact that those pertaining to categories include no answers to projectible questions.

The notion of category turns out to be crucial for resolving the difficulties described at the end of the last section. But to appreciate this we must first consider the relationship between a category and the archetypes of its members. And there is a convenient way of describing that relationship: each archetype is at a specific point in a space uniquely defined by the category.

The idea is straightforward. Each projectible question related to a category—that is, each member of Q_p in its $\langle Q_p, Q_w, Q_i \rangle$ triple—represents a dimension of a space whose points are tuples of logically possible answers to these questions. I use the phrase 'logically possible answers' instead of simply 'answers' because up to now I have used 'answer' for correct answers only, and we need a broader notion, that is, a notion according to which, for instance

(70)   Twenty centimeters

is an answer—though not a correct one—to

(71)   What is the length of Cleopatra's nose?

whereas

(72)   Three liters

is no answer at all.

So, to return to our example, the space defined by the category of chemical substances has as dimensions the projectible questions (66), (67), (68), and so on, and as points the tuples made up of logically possible answers to these questions, that is, roughly speaking, actual and conceivable boiling points, melting points, molecular weights, and so on. The ontological status of such tuples need not trouble us at present, though it admittedly raises vexing problems. It is an issue for the semantics of interrogatives and we must assume that it can be resolved.

The notion of a categorial space is obviously an abstraction from the notion of a Cartesian space. A Cartesian two-dimensional space has one dimension corresponding to the question

(73)   What is the value of x?

and another corresponding to the question

(74)   What is the value of y?

and its points are the ordered pairs made up of answers to (73) and (74).

The location of an archetype in a categorial space is simply the tuple-point corresponding to the answers that the archetype bears. So, in our example, the archetype of mercury is located at the point corresponding to the answers 356.6°C on the dimension of (66), -38.87°C on the dimension of (67), 200.6 on the dimension of (68), and so on; the archetype of gold is located at the point corresponding to the answers 2807°C on the dimension of (66), 1064.33°C on the dimension of (67), 197 on the dimension of (68), etc., and so on for the other archetypes of chemical substances.

Picturing categories and archetypes this way brings out the difference between the scientifically significant and the scientifically uninteresting quasi-natural kinds. The scientifically significant ones are those that make up categories whose spaces are the domain of laws. The scientifically uninteresting ones (except perhaps in some purely taxonomic disciplines) are the rest.

The following somewhat contrived example illustrates the point. A less contrived one would require too much time.

All the objects made up of a weight swinging under the force of local gravity (that is, simple pendulums), in a region where local gravitational acceleration is 980 cm/sec^2, at the end of a relatively weightless string 50 cm long, form a quasi-natural kind relative to a triple whose projectible questions are

(75)   What is the value of local gravitational acceleration?

(76)   What is its length?

(77)   What is its period?

with the answers to these questions respectively

(78)   980 cm/sec^2

(79)   50 cm

(80)   1.42 seconds

and whose w-projectible and individuating questions include

(81)   What is the temperature of the weight?

(82)   What holds the strands of the string together?

(83)   What is the material of the weight?

(84)   Where is it located?

and so on.

Furthermore, all the objects—whatever the length or the value of gravitational acceleration in their neighborhood—whose movements are constrained like the above ones, that is, all the simple pendulums, form the union of a category, namely the category relativized to the $\langle Q_p, Q_w, Q_i \rangle$ triple whose set of projectible questions consists of (75), (76), and (77), and whose set of w-projectible and individuating questions include (81) and the rest. That category is partitioned into quasi-natural kinds by the answers to (75), (76), and (77).

The categorial space of simple pendulums has as dimensions the questions (75), (76), and (77), and has as points the ordered triples of answers to these questions. Some of these points are occupied by archetypes and some are not. In that respect, the category is very much like any other arbitrary category, even those of no scientific interest. What gives it scientific import is that all the points occupied by archetypes in its categorial space obey a law, namely the law of the simple pendulum

(85) $T = 2\pi \sqrt{l/g}$

that is, a law whose domain is the categorial space, which systematically selects combinations of answers to (75), (76), and (77), and which includes all the archetypes of simple pendulums among the selected positions.

Objects swinging at the end of light strings under the influence of gravity form many different quasi-natural kinds and hence enter into many different categories with each other and with other objects. Each exemplifies many different archetypes located in many different categorial spaces. But they can be viewed as objects of scientific interest (that is, as simple pendulums) only in their guise as exemplifications of archetypes that conform to a law (that is, the law of the simple pendulum). This is not a peculiarity of objects swinging at the end of strings! A thing has a scientifically interesting persona, so to say, only when seen as exemplifying an archetype situated in a space where archetypes conform to law.

Normally we do not interpret laws like (85) as alluding to questions, and that may explain why we do not normally think of them as associated with categories. For most expository purposes, it is more convenient to think of them as mentioning determinables—

that is, such things as period, length, value of local gravitational acceleration—rather than questions in which these determinables are cited. However, laws such as (85) have virtues that remain obscure unless we recognize that they also mention questions. The most obvious of these virtues is that they can be used to obtain answers to some questions (answers that may be difficult to get in any other way) from answers to other questions (that may be easier to get). In "Rational Ignorance" and elsewhere I have called that being a "value adder." Value adders are subject to special criteria. Another of these virtues is that they endow theories from which they can be derived with instrumental power. Finally, they have a bearing on choice in the rational satisfaction of curiosity, that is, in the rational pursuit of answers. And in all these respects they are like laws that do not mention determinables.

The case of simple pendulums illustrates an important further fact. The law of the simple pendulum partitions the space defined by (75), (76), and (77) into two sets of points: those that conform to the law (the locus) and those that do not. In other words, it defines a sort of curve in categorial space. The archetypes of simple pendulums are all located at points on that curve. But many points on the curve are not occupied by any archetype. Archetypes, as I have been using the term, always have examples. Many points on the curve do not.

The fact can be put more generally. Laws such as the law of the pendulum are supposed to be sound and complete. Soundness and completeness are notions taken from logic: a deductive system is sound and complete in a certain domain, for instance, if and only if every one of its theorems is a valid formula in that domain and every valid formula in the domain is a theorem in the system. But the notion is easily extended. The algebraic equation

(86) $x^2 + y^2 = 25$

is a sound and complete characterization of the points on the circumference of a circle with center at the origin and radius of length 5 because every set of values that satisfies (86) designates a point on the circumference, and every set of numbers that designates a point on the circumference satisfies (86). Soundness and completeness, whatever their object, are defined by reference to pairs of properties. They hold or fail to hold depending on whether or not the two

properties are coextensive: for instance, the property of being a theorem and the property of being valid in the domain, the property of
satisfying (86) and the property of designating a point on the circumference. Sense can be made of the idea that a law such as the law
of the simple pendulum is sound and complete only if we can specify
the property that must be coextensive with the property of being a
point that conforms to the law. The property of being a point at
which an archetype happens to be located is seldom an appropriate
property. There is nothing particularly interesting about its extension and no plausible way of determining what it is. And imposing
that property would rule out most acknowledged laws, like the law
of the pendulum, as demonstrably unsound. That would conflict too
blatantly with normal practice.

So the view that the scientifically significant quasi-natural kinds
are those that generate categorial spaces governed by laws leaves
an important fact unexplicated until the conditions on soundness
and completeness for laws are spelled out. The problem is an old
one, and has many names. Many philosophers have assumed that
it should be solved in one fell swoop through one general notion of
reality that fits laws in all categorial domains. However, that may
be a mistake. Different categorial domains may require different
implementations of the notion of soundness and completeness. Their
respective archetypes are, after all, abstracted along very different
dimensions. In the next section I will consider how it might be
implemented in the case of linguistics.

But the view is clear enough to show the complex mixture of tasks
required to discover scientifically significant quasi-natural kinds. Observation of phenomena is only the most obvious among them. Questions, answers that fit them, concepts with which to embed them into
laws, expressions with which to process them, must be thought of;
those that are projectible across significant numbers and varieties
of things must be recognized; theories that reveal both sides of the
completeness and soundness requirement must be excogitated; regularities must be spotted; canonical usages that guard against the misleading associations of the current vernacular must be introduced,
and so on.[28] Since in the performance of these tasks, conceptual

---

[28]Scientists must use language and may be hampered by what is available in
their vocabulary. At any given time, that vocabulary will include words that

and terminological creativity plays an enormous part, one might be tempted to conclude that scientists rather than facts about the world are responsible for the existence of categorial spaces in which laws operate. But that is hardly plausible. Surveyors label and map the territory; they sometimes divide it; but they do not create it. Gloves are human creations, but it does not follow from this that the hands they are designed for are also human creations, or that the shape of those hands spring from the glovemaker's mind.

More important for present purposes, the view also shows that the two difficulties left unanswered by the Platonic Relationship Principle at the end of the last section are but special versions of issues that arise in every scientific field. The first is a version of the problem of soundness and completeness. The second is a version of the problem of demarcating scientifically significant quasi-natural kinds from scientifically unimportant ones. It turns out that they can be resolved together in the case of linguistics.

2.2   Linguistics

Let us turn to soundness and completeness as it applies to linguistics. I will focus for present purposes on the study of individual

---

belong to the designated nomenclature of a science, that is, words that have been introduced in the language with the explicit proviso that their extension must constitute a quasi-natural kind or a category of scientific import. (I don't mean, of course, that the proviso is stated using 'quasi-natural kind', 'category', etc., but that such terms are explicitly introduced in canonical texts under conventions that have the effect of attaching such provisos), a proviso whose implementation is subject to deliberate, and publicly acknowledged, revision or modification. That part of the vocabulary is apt to be marked and to be controllable. But other words will not have been explicitly introduced in the language at all. They will belong to the generally used, naturally acquired lexicon. And these words can be a source of difficulty. English and other languages, for instance, contain so-called natural kind terms. Those words do not have extensions that make up quasi-natural kinds or categories of scientific import, in spite of the label philosophers attach to them. Or at least there is no evidence that they do. Mere knowledge of their semantic and syntactic features, in any case, will not be enough to determine whether they do, since terms whose extension are quasi-natural kinds or categories are not likely to form, by themselves, a grammatically natural class. (If they did—if so-called natural kind terms formed a grammatically relevant category—knowledge of a language would include more knowledge of the world than anyone has!) Scientists cannot rely on such words to mention their subject matter. Thus, to perform their task, to be able to refer to quasi-natural kinds and to categories, scientists must produce and maintain control over their terminology.

languages and leave for some other occasion the study of linguistic universals.

The problem, at least as I have characterized it, arises in linguistics only if linguistics is not merely interested in types, but is interested in types that form categories, that is, views types as archetypes that are located with other types in categorial spaces. To satisfy ourselves that it is, we do not have to be convinced that linguists make explicit use of these notions but only that they analyze different types with a common set of questions. And they obviously do.

Consider for instance how they study the lexicon of a given language. They take for granted that each word in that language is open to such questions as

(87)   How many syllables does it contain?

(88)   What is its underlying representation?

(89)   What is its surface representation?

(90)   What is the onset of its first syllable?

(91)   What is its argument structure?

and so on.

Different linguists guided by different theories and different conjectures opt for different questions, but whatever questions they deem linguistically significant about a word type, they will deem the question to be not only projectible across all the tokens of the word, but to be also askable (with the expectation of different answers) about every other word type.[29]

---

[29]This claim is open to an obvious objection. There are questions such as,

(97)   What is the onset of its third syllable?

(98)   What is its gender?

that, at first glance at least, can be asked about some words but not about all. (97) can be asked about words that contain three or more syllables, but, it may seem, not about shorter ones; (98) cannot be asked of English prepositions. Such questions obviously occur in linguistics. That objection can be met in a number of ways. One way would be to admit the claim is an oversimplification, and to modify it so that linguists regard all word types as forming not one single category, but as forming a relatively small number of categories. Another way would be to deny the objection and to point out that we can and do adjust to our theoretical needs the distinction between bearing an answer and violating a presupposition. Thus for some theoretical purposes 'none' is significant as an answer to (97) and for others it isn't, just as 'zero' is an answer to 'How many

That by itself is still not yet enough to show that they treat words as members of categories.[30] They must also presume that there is a set of questions whose combined answers about any word type fully individuates that word type. They must presume that no two word types in English bear the same answer to, for instance, all of the questions (87)–(91) above. But most lexicographers and morphologists do presume that. A great deal of their effort, in fact, is spent on discovering such sets of questions.

In short, if I am right so far, linguists do in practice as well as in theory presume that word types locate themselves in categorial spaces, that is, that there is a set of dimensions, representable as questions, in which each word type will find a location, and such that each word is fully individuated by the position it occupies in that space. Let us call that space the *lexical* space of the language.

Consider now the study of the syntax of the sentence types of a given language. Linguistics here too proceeds on the presumption that there is a set of questions to which each sentence type bears an answer, and whose answers fully individuate sentence types. Typical members of such a set include

(92)   How many words does it contain?

(93)   What is the matrix verb?

(94)   What is the D-structure?

(95)   What is the S-structure?

(96)   Which phrase receives what thematic role from which predicate?

Here again, different linguists guided by different theories and

---

people live permanently at the North Pole?' but is not an answer to 'How many numbers live permanently at the North Pole?' A third way would be to include in our scheme hypothetical questions, for instance,

(99)   If it has a third syllable, what is its onset?

A fourth way would be to recognize that I have given a very sketchy account so far, and that a fuller one would incorporate erotetic structures in which some answers to some questions license further questions, while others do not. I don't want to choose here among these options because none of them is warranted for all the cases, though one at least should be warranted for each case. In short, the objection is one that calls for technical refinements rather than a change of outlook.

[30]To be more precise, I should have written "to show that they treat words as archetypes of quasi-natural kinds that are members of categories"!

different conjectures opt for different questions. But the presumption, however implemented, is tantamount to the presumption that the sentence types of a language can be located in a categorial space. Let us call that space the *sentential* space of the language.

The presumption that there is a lexical space or that there is a sentential space still do not, by themselves, raise the problem of soundness and completeness for linguistics. Three more things must be presumed by linguists.

First, linguists must presume that the laws (or rules, or constraints, to use the preferred terminology) that they try to discover will be violated by some—though not all—points in lexical space and in sentential space. In other words, they must presume that lexical theories and grammars partition lexical space and sentential space in a principled way. But they obviously expect that. This is shown by, among other things, one of the critical standards they impose on claims about such theories and grammars: such claims must not "overgenerate," and therefore must leave some points out as violations. Of course, just leaving points out as violations is not good enough, but that is immaterial right now.

Second, linguists must presume that the laws that they try to discover will license all the types (points) that have actual tokens. And they obviously do. This is shown by another critical standard that they impose on claims: such claims must not "undergenerate," that is, must not leave out any type that has tokens deemed by speakers to be well formed.[31] Of course, they can never show conclusively that a claim meets that standard, since tokens produced in the past or in the future are not available for inspection: the best they can do is to consider tokens of which they are aware and accept them as evidence.[32]

Third, linguists must presume that the laws that they try to discover will also license types (points) that have no tokens. And again,

---

[31]Utterances deemed to be ill-formed by speakers are irrelevant. They belong with grunts and snorts and other noises that may be acoustically and phonetically similar to linguistic tokens. They do not execute linguistic intentions, or execute them with only partial success.

[32]In actual practice only parts of the language are treated as relevant to any actual proposal. Most of the language is left out of consideration altogether. This probably shows that the idea of a single lexical space and a single sentential space for any language is an oversimplification. The complication called for will not affect the main points of this paper.

they clearly do. This is not shown by their use of any particular standard, but by the fact that they refrain from using certain standards, to wit, standards which would imply that only types with actual tokens are licensed. One might think they refrain from such standards only because it would make the task of linguistics impossible. The only way that task could be accomplished, under such a standard, would be by coming up with a list of all those types. The list would be shorter than a list of the tokens themselves, but it would still be impossibly long (and utterly boring!). Not only that, but it would have to include types whose tokens have left no trace and, in the case of living languages, types whose first token has not yet been produced. Somebody may some day think of a plausible theory that enumerates all and only those types, but that is unlikely. In any case, no rational linguist is currently after such a theory. On the contrary, all rational linguists operate on the principle that many types will never have tokens, and that a good theory of the lexicon or the grammar does not distinguish between those that do and those that do not. But their reasons are not merely practical. They assume that as a matter of fact the rules of language are infinitely productive or at least license an infinite number of types, even though the number of types with tokens must be finite.

It follows then that linguistics not only presupposes that there are questions relative to which types exist and have a location in categorial spaces, but it also presupposes the existence of an appropriate notion of soundness and completeness.

The problem now is to discover what that notion might be. This means discovering what attribute (or attributes) all word types or sentence types of a language share over and above the attribute of being licensed by some lexicon or grammar, proposed by a linguist, that licenses the types that happen to be attested.

One suggestion might be the attribute of being the type of a token that speakers of the language would, under conceivable circumstances, produce understandingly or hear and understand. This proposal, plausible though it may appear, is open to a number of objections. First, it raises metaphysical difficulties. Since there are types that have no actual tokens, it would require that we admit in our ontologies possible tokens, that is, possible individuals, a notion fraught with obscurities and probably incoherent. If we dismiss that objection by, for instance, indulging in possible-world metaphors, we open a second objection. The proposed attribute becomes the attribute of being a type such that there is at least one possible world in which one of its tokens is uttered and understood by a speaker of the language (in the actual world). However, any speaker of any language could, under suitable circumstances, have ended up as a speaker of a different language. Given any speaker of English, for instance, there is at least one possible world in which that speaker grows up in China and ends up as a native speaker of Chinese, and at least one possible world in which he ends up as a speaker of German, and so on. Thus pick any type of any language (actual or conceivable) and any person, there is a possible world in which (that is, conceivable circumstances under which) that person utters and understands or hears and understands a token of that type. Every type has that attribute. In fact, probably any point on any reasonable categorial space for words or sentences has it. The attribute will not do as a standard of soundness since it conflates languages, and its virtues as a standard of completeness are uninteresting.

If we try to save the proposal by restricting the range of possible worlds to the actual one, then the attribute is simply turned into that of being a type with actual tokens. And we have already seen that no rational linguist subscribes to that standard.

Another possible suggestion starts from the assumption that the maxims of scientific induction provide rules for constructing lexicons or grammars (as the case may be) from the types known to have tokens, and that lexicons or grammars constructed in this way can be ranked by maxims of simplicity. A lexicon or grammar constructed that way and selected as simplest by the maxims of simplicity would, given some reasonable further assumptions, select some superset of the set of types that have tokens. The suggestion, then, is that the attribute should be that of being encompassed by such a simplest lexicon or grammar. In practice, this would mean being encompassed by a lexicon or grammar built (according to some methodological maxims) on known or presumed exemplified types.

This proposal clearly admits types that have no tokens, and has the further virtue of making linguistic theory invulnerable to refutation by unobserved facts. It assumes, however, that we have reliable theory-independent measures of simplicity for ranking lexicons and grammars; in other words, measures of simplicity that are not inextricable parts of specific lexical theories or syntactic theories. That is a very questionable assumption. What is worse, the attribute is utterly arbitrary as a measure of soundness and completeness unless supplemented by still further assumptions. Why maximum simplicity and certification by the rules of induction? Why not maximum complexity and certification by some rules of counterinduction? Why not expressibility in iambic pentameter? The answer, presumably, is that simplicity and induction are guides to some truths. But the proposal leaves us in the dark about the nature of those truths. It simply raises the problem of soundness and completeness in a new form.

We are left, as far as I can see, with only one further reasonable suggestion, and that is that the attribute should be that of being a type generated by the lexicon or grammar (whatever the case) in a speaker's mind. That suggestion admits types that have no tokens, does not rely on an unanalyzed notion of possible tokens, and takes a stand on the nature of the truths sought by lexical and grammatical theory.

It is admittedly open to objections. With that stand on the nature of the truths sought by linguists comes the risk of increased commitment: what if no lexicon (or grammar) is represented in the speaker's mind? How do we know that any is? In other words, the proposal makes factual, not just methodological assumptions. And the factual assumption it makes involves things (minds, brains, organisms, wetware) whose archetypes (no matter how relativized) cannot be located in the categorial spaces of words and sentences. They do not belong to the subject matter of pure generative linguistics. So the proposal puts the whole linguistic enterprise at the mercy of discoveries in other fields of investigation, and the fact that this has happened to other disciplines in the past (for instance, classical thermodynamics and chemistry were at the mercy of particle physics, astronomy was at the mercy of projectile theory) does not make it more attractive.

Even so, this suggestion offers the only plausible interpretation of soundness and completeness for theories of the lexicon and for grammars. (Or, to be more precise, the only plausible interpretation of which I am aware.) And, as we have seen, linguistic practice presupposes that some interpretation exists. Without such an interpretation, the practice is ungrounded and cannot be understood as a principled partitioning of the points in its categorial spaces.

As it stands, the proposal may not seem to impose very constraining requirements. It does not say anything about the form that theories of the lexicon or grammars must have to be sound and complete. It tells us that they must generate a set coextensive with one licensed by a mental lexical structure or by a mental grammar. But if one is coextensive, no doubt infinitely many others are as well. That leaves a large field, and linguists may decide to seek only the simplest ones in it, even though there is no prior reason to believe that mental lexicons and grammars are simple by our standards.

Even so, the proposal does carry at least two kinds of methodological consequences. The first pertains to the conceptual repertoire on which the theories can draw. Theoretical lexicons and grammars can be coextensive with mental ones only if there is a match between their respective categorial spaces, that is, only if the questions with which linguists analyze types—and that means the questions through which they abstract from tokens to types—match question-representing constituents of minds. This follows from the fact that coextensiveness is defined in terms of correspondences across such spaces. But that requires that linguists discover questions that correspond to dimensions acknowledged by mental faculties. For instance, (87)–(96) are acceptable dimensions for theories of the lexicon and of the syntax only if they correspond to mental dimensions; for instance, dimensions in a space of intentions or perceptions in speakers' minds.

The second pertains to evidence. If the proposal is right, then linguistic behavior and linguistic judgments do not exhaust the evidence on which linguistics should or can proceed. Other phenomena currently studied—but with different concerns in mind—by neurologists, developmental psychologists, and—though that seems unlikely—artificial intelligencers, will also be pertinent. The study of natural languages becomes, in this respect at least, very different from the study of formal languages, and linguistics cannot simply confine itself to special versions of issues appropriate to such languages.

The Platonic Relationship Principle left us with two unresolved difficulties. First, how is it possible to infer anything about types that have no tokens? The answer can now be put succinctly. It is possible because such types, if linguistically significant, belong in categorial spaces with types that have tokens. We can discover the dimensions of these spaces by examining tokens, and we can partition these spaces in a principled way by reasoning about minds.

Second, how do the triples $\langle Q_p/A_p, Q_w, Q_i \rangle$ to which linguistically significant archetypes (word types and sentence types) are related differ from those to which linguistically uninteresting types are related? The answer to this, too, can now be put very succinctly. They differ by fitting in categorial spaces that are the domain of psychological laws.

So, (1), (2), and (3) are compatible after all and linguists who dismiss qualms about them are right in doing so.

9

The Ontology of Phonology

with Morris Halle

1 Introduction

Linguistics, like Gaul, is traditionally divided into three parts, syntax, semantics, and phonology,[1] the latter being presumably concerned with the sound aspect of language. The issues we plan to discuss in this paper concern phonology directly and the other two branches indirectly. We take phonological theory to be about the world, about reality, and thus about certain items in the world—certain "particulars," as metaphysicians[2] might put it—whose exis-

---

*We are grateful to Ned Block, Nancy Bromberger, George Boolos, Noam Chomsky, Leonard Clapp, Alec Marantz, Wayne O'Neil, and Jean Michel Roy for comments on previous drafts of this paper.

[1] See Bromberger and Halle 1989 on why phonology is fundamentally different from syntax and semantics.

[2] Though many philosophers of language have views on empirical linguistics, few, if any, have given serious attention to phonology. Recent anthologies and books on the philosophy of language either don't mentions phonology at all, or at best perfunctorily restate crude and outdated notions on the subject. This is somewhat surprising since the facts that phonology studies are critical to the individuation of expressions and to their character as objects of speech perception or outputs of speech production. But for these facts, there would by no syntax or semantics of natural languages besides sign languages (also neglected by philosophers), and philosophers deliberating about such languages would have to be silent.

There are a number of explanations for this neglect. To begin with, recent philosophers of language generally belong to an intellectual tradition that admits no essential differences between natural languages and some of their contrived extensions. This was pointed out a long time ago by Strawson (1950), though he had other shortcomings in mind. Philosophic discussions thus gener-

tence is attested to by the fact that people speak. What is the nature of these "particulars"? In the first part of our talk, we will address that question. Our answer will be that phonology is about concrete mental events and states that occur in real time, in real space, have causes, have effects, are finite in number, in other words are what metaphysicians would call "concrete particulars" closely linked to, but **distinct** from those described by traditional phoneticians. In the second part of our talk we will consider a very different answer, according to which phonology is about types, a certain species of

---

ally abstract not only from differences between English, German, Japanese, and other natural languages, but also from differences between these real languages and notational systems used in mathematics, logic, physics, chemistry, biology, linguistics, etc. Such notational systems do have a syntax (albeit usually one that has very little in common with the syntax of natural languages), a semantics, and a pragmatics, but happen to have no phonology. Their minimal units are normally ideographs which encode word-like units—rather than phonetic or even orthographic ones—open to many phonologically unrelated pronunciations (if pronounceable at all). Nothing in such notational systems corresponds to the phonologies of natural languages, and nothing about them can thus be captured in an overarching phonological doctrine linked to the overarching semantic and syntactic doctrines studied by philosophers. So it is not surprising that though Frege and his successors include signs in their Sign/Sense/Nominatum triad, they have nothing of interest to say about signs as things uttered and heard. Even philosophers who focus primarily on natural languages belong to that tradition and don't discriminate between aspects peculiar to real languages, i.e., articulated languages whose primary tokens necessarily vanish as soon as produced, and aspects peculiar to conventional notational systems with characteristically enduring tokens.

Furthermore, philosophers generally seem to believe that there can't be anything of philosophic interest about phonology. This attitude flows naturally from the previous one. The ideographs used by scientists are adopted through open and explicitly published conventions that determine everything true of them qua signs. Since they are also semantically word-like, their sub-segments have no autonomous status and raise no philosophic problems. How could there be anything of philosophic interest about the shape of simple numerals, or about the horizontal segment in an inverted A in a quantifier, or in the vertical line of the F for force? It is easy to pass from this outlook to the view that there can't be anything philosophically challenging about the spelling of words, and thence to the view that there can't be anything philosophically challenging about their pronunciation. And isn't phonology "just" about pronunciation?

Whatever the explanation for philosophers' neglect of phonology, we think that it has a cost. To begin with, we think that it is a mistake to lump all lexical systems together as forming some kind of natural family. It blurs too many differences, and attention to phonology can highlight important ones. Furthermore, we think that no theory about the relation between natural language signs and

abstract, causally impotent, non-spatio-temporal entities, possibly infinite in number, and distinct from real live utterances. Phonology, like the rest of linguistics, is normally expounded as if it were about types. But does this mean that the discipline is committed to there being such abstract entities as types? We will argue that it isn't.

In the course of our discussion we will use some technical notation but we will keep it to a minimum and will explain it as we go. We will also talk from within a framework that some linguists may reject. That can't be helped. Linguistics is in constant flux and full of controversies. Nothing of real interest in it is conclusively established once and for all and to everybody's satisfaction.

2   On the Nature of Tokens

A. The phonological representation of a token.

Let us begin by thinking about spoken tokens. And to fix ideas, let us focus on a very specific one, the one that I, the speaker,[3] will now produce:

(1)   𝕿𝖍𝖊 𝖒𝖊𝖗𝖈𝖍𝖆𝖓𝖙 𝖘𝖔𝖑𝖉 𝖘𝖍𝖊𝖑𝖛𝖊𝖘.

---

their referents (or their meaning) can be trustworthy that nonchalantly takes signs for granted. Finally, we think an adequate understanding of the ontology of language—of the objects whose existence constitutes the reality of language— must include an adequate conception of the objects investigated by phonology. More specifically, an adequate conception of language must check our tendency, when we reflect about language, to slip thoughtlessly between talk about individual utterances and talk about types, as if such slips were always innocuous and easily fixed ways of avoiding pedantry. Spoken tokens are transitory events that occur in time and space, that can be perceived, that are shaped by their speaker's occurrent intentions, and that are subject to norms fixed in their speakers mental make-up. Types—if there are types—are abstract entities, neither in time nor in space, devoid of causal histories or causal consequences, hence beyond perception. Types—if there are types—outdistance tokens. Tokens and types—if there are types—are thus utterly different. Conflating them is bound to lead to confusions and incoherence. But giving each its due, and understanding their connection, won't be possible unless we see how the type-token distinction fares in phonology, a topic which we discuss in what follows.

[3] We use the first person singular to mention Sylvain Bromberger as producer of tokens displayed during the talk in Uppsala and use the first person plural to mention ourselves, the two authors. We use script font to indicate displayed spoken tokens. Readers of the paper should thus keep in mind that the lines in script point to episodes which they can no doubt imagine but which took place in Uppsala when this paper was orally presented.

That token is now history! Only time travel could enable us to ever hear it again. We will refer to it as event (1) since we won't be able to display it again.

Actually many things happened when event (1) occurred. That is why it could be studied by more than one discipline and be analyzed differently by each. So, for instance, noises happened, and event (1) therefore could be investigated under acoustics and given an acoustical analysis. Bodily movements happened, and event (1) could therefore be studied under motor behavior and given an articulatory analysis. Brain and neurological events happened, and (1) could be looked at under neurology and given a neurological analysis. And so on.

However we exhibited event (1) to illustrate a phonological event that is an event that can be examined in the light of phonological theory and given a phonological analysis.

What would such an analysis tell us about (1)?

Well, let us look at how phonologists would represent (1) in the notation of phonology.

They would represent it as follows (the dots represent lines that we omit for present purposes):

(2)　　a.　{[ðə], Art ...} + {[mɑrtʃənt], Noun ...} + {Q, Sing ...}
　　　　　　+ {[sɛl], Vb ...} + {Q, Past ...} + {[ʃɛlf], Noun ...} +
　　　　　　{Q, Plur ...}
　　　　　　..

　　　　b.　{[ðə], Art ...} + {[mɑrtʃənt], Noun ...} + {Q, Sing ...}
　　　　　　+ {[sol], Vb ...} + {Q, Past ...} + {[ʃɛlv], Noun ...} +
　　　　　　{Q, Plur ...}
　　　　　　..

　　　　c.　ðəmɚtʃntsoldʃɛlvz

In other words, they would represent it as a sequence of lines, a "derivation." Each line would purport to stand for some fact about (1), and the ordering would purport to stand for further facts about it.

What kind of facts?

We are going to go through the derivation step by step to answer that question. But before doing so, we want to describe the general character of that answer.

My production of event (1) was an action. Like other actions, it was therefore brought about by a distinctive kind of mental set—something we will call an "intention." But this term, as we use it, is not to be taken altogether literally. We use it to refer to a familiar kind of purposive mental stance. Think of someone aiming a rifle at a target. That person moved and positioned limbs, head, eyes, etc. in certain ways. But more went on. After all, the movements were not made accidentally, or by way of checking whether the barrel is in line with the butt. The person was set psychologically in a distinct way, i.e., had distinct intentions. More specifically, a person who aims a rifle has certain effects in mind, plans moves in ways calculated to achieve those effects, and, crucially from our point of view, has the intellectual capacity to select those effects and to devise the gestures that achieve them. The uttering of (1), like the aiming of a rifle, also required a distinctive mind set, distinctive intentions on my part, intentions that I could not have formed without certain pre-existing intellectual capacities. Of course, I had many intentions when I produced it: I intended to give you an example, I intended to be understood, I intended to produce a sentence that you have probably never heard before. But only some of my intentions account for the fact that I **pronounced** (1), that (1) was an action of pronouncing something in a language I know, in my idiolect of English. Those intentions are the kinds of facts about (1) that we take (2) to represent.

B. The last line of the derivation.

Let us now look at the last line of the derivation (2), that is (2c).

(2c) **could** be construed as a phonetic transcription of the utterance (1). Formally it is a string of letters from an alphabet in which each letter traditionally stands for a speech sound.[4] Speech sounds are not unanalyzable entities. They are rather complexes of (phonetic) features. Thus each letter in (2c) stands for a particular complex of features. In (3) we have given a partial list of the feature composition of some of the component sounds of English.

---

[4]The fact that the utterance consists of sequences of discrete sounds is the insight on which all alphabetic writing systems are based. It may therefore appear to be self-evident. Yet when we last asked our colleagues working on the automatic analysis of speech, we were told that no one has yet found a reliable mechanical procedure that can segment any arbitrary utterance into its constituent sounds.

(3)   p b m f v   t d n s z   k g
        — — — + +   — — — + +   — —   continuant
        — — + — —   — — + — —   — —   nasal
        — + + — +   — — + — +   — +   voiced
        labial   coronal   dorsal   Major articulator

You will readily notice that the three sets of consonants in (3)
differ from each other in that each involves action by a different major articulator; i.e., [pbmfv] is produced with active involvement of
the lips; [tdnsz], with that of the tongue blade or coronal articulators; and [kg], with that of the tongue body or dorsal articulator.
It is the major articulator that stops the air flow from out of the
mouth in [−continuant] sounds, but allows it in the sounds that are
[+continuant].

In addition to the major articulators the production of consonants involves other articulators as well. In particular, the consonants [m] and [n] are produced with a lowering of the velum, which allows air to flow through the speaker's nasal cavities exciting thereby
the resonances of these cavities. In all other consonants, the velum
is raised, no air flows through the nasal passages and their characteristic resonances are not excited. This information is reflected
by the pluses and minuses in the second line of (3). The third line
reflects the behavior of the vocal cords. It is the vocal cords that im-
plement the feature [voiced]. They vibrate in [+voiced] sounds such
as [bmvdnzg] and they are stationary in the [−voiced] consonants
[pftsk].

We said a moment ago that (2c) **could** be construed as a phonetic transcription, that is, as a record of articulator movements
and positionings. However that is not the way we construe it! We
construe (2c) as standing for a series of intentions that generated
those movements. Each letter in (2c) stands for such an intention,
and each of these intentions called for an arrangement of articulators in the expectation of distinctive auditory effects. Each was
also the intention to act so as to produce a specific English **speech**
sound, and thus required a capacity that I acquired when I acquired
English.

Consider, for instance, the [m] in (2c). It represents an intention
(at the time) that called for simultaneously closing my mouth at the
lips, lowering my velum, adjusting the stiffness of my vocal folds, and

thereby producing a sound "m." That is why the feature notation is appropriate. However it does not represent an intention that merely called for going through all that gymnastics and produce the sound "m." I could have intended that much without intending to produce an English sound, for instance while intending to hum a tune, or imitate a cow, or express mild surprise. The 'm' in (2c) represents an intention to act so as to produce a specific **English speech** sound, a token of the phoneme /m/. And I could not have formed that intention, that mind set, had I not acquired English.[5]

The other letters in (2c) stand for similar intentions to utter speech sounds in (1). Let us call them "phonetic intentions."[6] What (2c) represents is therefore totally unlike what an oscillograph hooked to a microphone might have recorded, and this not only because some information recoverable from oscillograph records such as loudness, rate of speaking, fundamental frequency and other characteristics of the speaker's voice cannot be inferred from (2c), but crucially because it stands for a different kind of event altogether. (2c) stands for the occurrence of phonetic intentions. Oscillographs hooked to microphones record the occurrence of noises.

But why not construe (2c) as standing for the actions that produced the noises rather than for mere intentions? The symbols, after all, were introduced in the discipline for that purpose! We have at least two reasons. The first is conceptual. (2c), as we shall see in a moment, represents the result of a mental computation. And we don't think that actions can be the results of such computations. Results of computations have content. (2c) characterizes a content that was executed, but need not have been executed.[7] The second is empirical. When we execute a speech action we take into account and correct for all sorts of momentary impediments and conditions. (2c) says nothing about such corrections. It only contains linguistic information and takes into account only linguistic knowledge. As a

---

[5] Compare with the availability of click sounds as phonemes to speakers of Bantu, but only as noises to speakers of English.

[6] For a related position see Liberman and Mattingly 1985, 1989, and Bromberger and Halle 1986.

[7] Elsewhere we have called this kind of intentional content a "score," to mark the analogy with a musical score, something that can be executed through motions, but need not be executed, and often is not. Inner discourse probably stops at the formation of such "scores."

description of the articulator actions it might be false. So we use the traditional symbols, but we don't subscribe to their standard interpretation.[8]

C. The first line of the derivation.

Let us now turn to (2a), the first line in the derivation. It represents another series of intentions responsible for event (1), namely, the intentions to use certain words, e.g., the noun 'merchant', the verb 'sell' marked for past tense, etc. in a certain order. This is reflected, for instance, in (2a) by the clustering of phonetic symbols into larger bracketed word-like units.

Forming the intention to produce (1) clearly required that I know the words I used, and that I retrieve them from memory. So before discussing in more detail how (2a) relates to (1), let us look at how some linguists represent knowledge of words.

None of us is born with the knowledge of the words of our native language. That children learn words as they develop is obvious and moreover massively documented, and we all know that the process goes on through life: most of us have only recently acquired such words as *intifada, glasnost, scud*. The proposition that an essential part of learning a language consists in storing in one's memory (something representable as) a list of words, something we will call "the vocabulary", is therefore one of the most securely founded in all linguistics.

Many words that any speaker of English knows are complex in the sense that they incorporate affixes of various kinds. We illustrate this in (4)

(4)   a. shelv-es, child-ren, bough-t, sol-d
       b. pre-dis-pose, un-happy, in-secure
       c. un-poison-ous-ness, ex-pre-sid-ent, contra-in-dic-ate-d
       d. kibbutz-im, hassid-im

In linguistics the term "stem" is used to designate the element to which an affix is added and the term "morpheme" is used as a cover term for both affixes and stems. Like stems, affixes too must be learned and committed to memory (cf. (4d)).

---

[8]Our interpretation of event (1) commits us to the occurrence of the mental events we call intentions, over and above acoustical events and articulatory events. We present some of our reasons in Bromberger and Halle 1986.

A speaker's knowledge of morphemes can thus be represented as a list of items containing information about each morpheme stored in memory.

What information?

Obviously information about its meaning, its functional structure, and the thematic roles it assigns. Also about its lexical category, i.e., whether it is a noun, verb, preposition, adjective, conjunction. And certainly information pertaining to how the morpheme is pronounced, that is, phonological information. All this can be thought of as encoded in a "complex symbol", made up of elements that stand for meaning, lexical category, etc. The markers pertaining to how the morpheme is pronounced are of particular interest to us here. We will refer to them as the "identifying index." The vocabulary as a whole can be thus represented as a long list of such complex symbols, each of which contains, among other things, an identifying index.[9]

We now turn to the information in identifying indices.

Most morphemes take on the same phonetic form regardless of syntactic and/or morphological contexts. Thus the verb hint shows up in the phonetic form representable as [hInt] whenever uttered. So that string of phonetic symbols is used as its identifying index.

Other morphemes assume different phonetic forms depending on syntactic and/or morphological contexts. For instance, the stems *sell* and *shelf* were pronounced differently in (1) than in the following utterance:

(5)   The merchant sells a shelf.

The identifying index of such stems is also a string of phonetic symbols, namely [sɛl] and [ʃɛlf] in the two cases at hand. We will come back to why those particular strings.

Some morphemes, notably the English plural and past tense affixes, not only assume different phonetic forms in different contexts, but these forms can be utterly dissimilar, and sometimes they don't appear phonetically at all!

So note what happens to the plural affix in the following cases:

---

[9]In talk about identifying indices, we must take care to distinguish between what we presume to be "in the mind" of the knower and its representation in the notation of our theory. We use the term "identifying index" to refer to the representation in the notation of the theory, not what is "in the mind."

(6)   cat/s, child/ren, kibbutz/im, alumn/i, stigma/ta, geese,
        moose

and to the past tense morpheme in the following

(7)   bake/d, playe/d, dream/t, sol/d, sang, hit

Halle (1990) has dubbed morphemes like the Plural and Past
Morphemes which behave in this very irregular fashion "abstract
morphemes" and he has used 'Q', a symbol that has no direct phonetic interpretation, as their identifying index.[10]

With all this in mind, let us look again at (2a).

(2a) is a sequence of complex symbols each made up of an identifying index and other grammatical markers, all copied from the
vocabulary.

What facts about event (1) does (2a) represent?[11]

(2a) as we said before represents the intention to use certain
words, but we can now be more explicit. (2a) represents the fact
that (1) besides being produced by my phonetic intentions in (2c) was
also produced by my intention to use the words retrieved from my
vocabulary whose identifying indices (and lexical category) appear
in (2a).

But what are the phonetic symbols doing in (2a)? Take the
initial 'm' in the identifying index of 'merchant'. Does it represent
an intention, already present at that stage so to say, to produce a

---

[10]Other elements in the lexicon may also lack specific phonological content,
e.g., PRO, empty complementizers, case, expletives, etc., yet not be represented
by a complex symbol that includes any identifying index like Q. Whether or
not some morpheme must be represented with an identifying index like Q or no
identifying index at all is a contingent matter to be settled on empirical grounds.
Halle's proposal is not that we adopt a convention for the sake of giving all
complex symbols a common format. It embodies the claim that all unarticulated
morphemes are not phonologically equal.

[11]Some things we have said so far could be put in Austinian terminology (as
in Austin 1975).

(2a) modeled the formation of a *phatic* intention, that is, the intention to
produce what Austin called a phatic act, "the uttering of certain vocables or
words ... belonging to and as belonging to, a certain vocabulary, conforming to
and as conforming to a certain grammar." (We leave out "i.e., noises of certain
types" as misleading.) (2c) modeled a *phonetic* intention, i.e., the intention to
produce what Austin called a phonetic act, "the act of merely uttering certain
noises." (The "merely" is unfortunate!) (2b) then models a stage in a mental
process through which the phatic mental set gets transformed into the phonetic
mental set.

token of the phoneme /m/? Offhand that may seem reasonable. But consider then the 'ε' in the identifying index of 'sell'. It can't stand for an intention to produce a token of the phoneme /ε/. No such intention was executed in producing (1). Could I have changed my mind between the times I picked the words and pronounced them? That strikes us as a cute but vacuous idea, too literal minded about our use of "intention." As we see it, the role of the phonetic symbols in (2a) and in (2c) is very different. In (2a) they play a computational role. Formulae such as (2a) have two functions. On the one hand they model an event, represent aspects of that event. On the other hand they are used to compute other formulae in the formalism of our theory. Phonetic symbols appear in (2a) essentially to simplify computations within the theory. In (2c) they have that role but they also represent phonetic intentions. These roles, though connected, are different.

Note that in the vocabulary phonetic symbols could not stand for intentions either. The vocabulary is not a representation of intentions, but of knowledge. But its formulas too enter into computations.

D. The second line of the derivation.

Let us now look at (2b).

(2b) stands between (2a) and (2c). It is like (2a) except that some of the phonetic symbols in the identifying indices have been changed. Unlike (2c) it is partitioned, contains syntactic categories labels and occurrences of Q.

What facts about event (1) does (2b) represent?

It represents a stage between the formation of my intentions to use words, i.e., my intentions represented by (2a) and the formation of my phonetic intentions, i.e., my intentions represented by (2c). Unlike (2a) and (2c) it does not represent intentions at all, though it does represent a mental set of sorts.

Remember events (1) and (5), the actual utterances? In the earlier one I pronounced the verb one way and in the later one I pronounced the same verb very differently. The facts underlying the difference can be surmised from a vast body of evidence though they also happen to coincide with common beliefs. I know English and that means that I have not only acquired words, but have also acquired rules. In producing these utterances I applied appropriate rules, and this led to different pronunciations of the same verb.

(2b) stands for a stage in the application of these rules.

We can even tell what stage.

As noted before, the verb *sell* and the noun *shelf* appear in two distinct guises in different utterances. Specifically the *verb* sell undergoes a vowel change in the past tense, and the noun *shelf* undergoes a change of the final consonant, in the plural. In other words, in producing these words we invoke something like the rules in (8):

(8)   a. Before [Q, Past] the stem vowel is [o] in the verbs *sell*, *tell*, ...

        b. Before [Q, Pl] the stem-final consonant is [+voice] in the nouns *house*, *knife*, *life*, *wife*, *shelf*, *mouth*, ...

(2b) then represents a stage after the application of (8).

(8) are not the only rules I applied to produce (1). I also applied rules to pronounce the morphemes represented by Q in (2a). Halle (1990) has argued that the relevant rules are statable roughly as follows:

(9) $Q \mapsto /n/$ in env. $X\_\_$ Plural   if X is *child*, *ox*, ...
        $/m/$ in env. $Y\_\_$ Plural   if Y is *kibbutz*, *hasid*, ...
        $/i/$ in env. $Z\_\_$ Plural   if Z is *alumn-*, *radi-*, ...
        $/ta/$ in env. $U\_\_$ Plural   if U is *stigma*, *schema*, ...
        ϕ in env. $V\_\_$ Plural   if V is *mouse*, *moose*, ...
        $/z/$ in env. $\_\_$ Plural

(10) $Q \mapsto \phi$ in env. $X\_\_$ Past   if X is *sing*, *write*, ...
        $/t/$ in env. $Y\_\_$ Past   if Y is *buy*, *dream*, *mean* ...
        $/d/$ in env. $\_\_$ Past

So (2b) also represents a stage before the application of those rules!

But what do the phonetic symbols in (2b) represent? For that matter, what do they represent in the statement of the rules? The answer here is as before. They play a role as symbols in the formal computations of the theory. We conjecture that they also stand for something specific in the production of (1), but if they do, what they stand for is not something clearly understood at this time.

This double role assigned to phonetic symbols, we should point out, has a shortcoming: it slights certain important phenomena.

So, for instance, it does not show that between the formation of (2a)'s referent and (2c)'s referent a kind of transubstantiation occurred through which mnemonic elements were converted into articulatory ones.

3   On the Nature of Types

So far we have concentrated on a single and unique event, the utterance of (1). We have done this because we hold that phonological theory, in so far as it purports to advance knowledge at all, is about such events and about the mental conditions responsible for their occurrence. Those are the sorts of things to which it is ontologically committed, or, as some followers of Quine would put it, those are the kinds of things over which it quantifies.

Our position may strike some as prima facie implausible, as simply conflicting with too many practices of phonologists.

Thus phonologists never mention or try to explain unique events like (1). Their papers and texts mention words, phrases, sentences, phonemes, i.e., types, abstract entities outside time and space, devoid of causal histories and causal consequences. They don't mention utterances, events, or mental states. And though phonologists do sometimes elicit tokens, they do so only to obtain data about types. That is presumably why they rely on statements which abstract from whatever is peculiar to tokens and clearly fit types. In fact, most phonologists would probably not interpret (2) as about (1), the utterance produced umpteen minutes ago. How could they? How many have ever heard of that utterance! They would implicitly take (2) as about a type possibly attested by something like (1) but attestable as well by other tokens, for instance by the one that I now produce

(11)   𝔗𝔥𝔢 𝔪𝔢𝔯𝔠𝔥𝔞𝔫𝔱 𝔰𝔬𝔩𝔡 𝔰𝔥𝔢𝔩𝔳𝔢𝔰.

And that last token, as Leibniz's indiscernability of identicals tells us, is not only numerically distinct from (1), since it occurred at a different time, but is also numerically distinct from its type, which does not occur in time at all.

Furthermore, phonologists, like all grammarians, strive for theories that neither undergenerate nor overgenerate, theories that predict some items and exclude others. But the relevant items could not be tokens! If they were, any phonological theory, no matter how

absurd, could always be trivially confirmed. Imagine, for instance, a
theory which predicts that the following is in my language

(12)   𝔗𝔥𝔢 𝔭𝔩𝔪𝔬𝔱𝔭𝔣𝔲 𝔰𝔢𝔩𝔩 𝔫𝔢𝔰𝔱𝔢𝔯𝔡𝔞𝔫 𝔪𝔞𝔫𝔫 𝔰𝔥𝔢𝔩𝔣.

I would have confirmed that theory simply by having produced the
token (12)! What is more, every theory of any interest would be
demonstrably false since it would predict an infinite number of tokens
for each person, whereas the total number of tokens is bound to be
finite. Life is short! Even the most loquacious of us, no matter how
long they live, will shut up forever at some point!

That may all be true, nonetheless, we don't believe that there
are types! And so phonology can't be about types. We admit (on
empirical grounds) internalized grammars, but those exist as mental attributes of concrete, specific human individuals. We admit (on
empirical grounds) internalized vocabularies, but those too exist as
mental attributes of concrete, specific human individuals; and we admit token events (again on empirical grounds) but those are spatio-
temporally located concrete events like (1). But types, we think, belong, with useful fictions like virtual optical images, in the null class.

We can't prove that there are no types. The notion is surely not
self-contradictory, or even incoherent. Bromberger (1989) has argued
that it is a coherent and even useful one. We just don't see any reason
to think that there are any. And we don't accept that phonology
provides any evidence for them, or must presuppose their existence.

On the other hand, we do believe that phonology provides over-
whelming evidence that tokens cluster into scientifically significant
types. That does not imply that there are types besides tokens (not
even as sets, or mereological sums of tokens, though such sets and
sums may well exist). But it is sufficient to justify most of the
practices we have mentioned and to make sense of the demand that
theories should neither overgenerate nor undergenerate.

We will now explain that position in more detail.

Instead of producing (1) when I did, I could have produced a
very different token. In fact, to fix ideas, here I go:

(13)   𝔗𝔴𝔬 𝔢𝔩𝔢𝔭𝔥𝔞𝔫𝔱𝔰 𝔰𝔱𝔲𝔡𝔫 𝔦𝔫 𝔘𝔭𝔭𝔰𝔞𝔩𝔞.

And we could now go on and produce a derivation analogous
to (2) for this new token. It would be a different derivation from
(2). The last line, the first line, the intervening lines, the rules
invoked, the items said to represent morphemes retrieved from lexical

memory, all would be different. However the two derivations would have one crucial thing in common: they would incorporate answers to the same questions. Different answers, but the same questions.

In other words, event (1) was open to the questions: What morphemes were intended? What was the representation of these morphemes in memory? What articulatory gestures were intended? What rules were invoked in the course of the formation of these intentions? and so on. (2) provides the answers to these questions.[12] The last token (13) was open to the same questions. Its derivation would also provides answers to those questions, but the answers would be different. As we just said, different answers; the same questions. In fact all spoken token events are open to these questions. Some share exactly the same answers. Token event (1) and the token event (11) do. Others don't share the same answers. Token events (1) and (13) don't. Token events that share the same answers are the ones we classify as being of the same type. Those that don't, we classify as being of different types.

That is all there is to talk of types, as far as we are concerned. But that is quite a lot, as we will now show.

Note, for instance, that each token holds specific answers to these questions. We are unmitigated realists about this. We take the fact that each token holds the specific answers it does to each of these questions to constitute truths about the world, not some artifact of our way of looking at things. It is a truth about the world that the answer to "what was the first intended articulation underlying the production of (1)?" is "vibration of the vocal cord (i.e., [+voice]), constriction of the mouth cavity partially open (i.e., [+continuant]) etc." just as it is a truth about the world that the answer to "How much does Sylvain Bromberger weigh?" is "175 lbs."

Note furthermore that we also take it as a truth about the world—and a very different sort of truth—but not an artifact of our way of looking at things, that (1) has the property of holding such answers at all. We might put this somewhat more technically. It is a truth about the world that event (1) had the determinable property of having intended morphemes. And it is a truth about the world that each spoken token also does. Other events, even events

---

[12] Strictly speaking, to provide these answers it would have to be supplemented with references to the rules, as it was in the course of our discussion.

with acoustic properties, don't have that property. Noises made by our coffee pot, or coughs for instance, don't have it. That fact is of the same order as the fact that swinging pendula have periods which standing rocks don't, that positive numbers have square roots, which trees don't, that the manuscript from which we are reading has a certain weight, which the ideas we are expressing don't. Determinable properties, by the way, like period, square root, weight, and so on, are a kind of property presupposed by what-questions such as "What is the period of ...?", "What is the square root of ...?", "What is the weight of ...?" Objects that don't have the property hold no answer to the corresponding question.

(1), (5), (13), and other tokens are, of course, open to many questions besides the ones answered in derivations such as (2). They hold answers for instance to "At what time was it uttered?", "Where was it uttered?" If we were to use those to compare tokens as to type we would end up with very different typological clusters. But we don't use those. We use questions that define the field of phonology. That may sound more self-righteous than we intend, so let us put what we have in mind differently: we use the questions that make phonology **as a theoretical field** possible. That there are such questions, by the way, is also an empirical truth about the world!

An analogy that we have used elsewhere, taken from elementary chemistry, may be helpful here. Think for a moment about a sample of water, a real sample that you have "experienced" as they say in California. That sample, like our tokens, is open to a number of questions: "Where was it situated when you experienced it?", "Who owned it?", "What did you do with it?" that are of no scientific interest. But it is open to others that are of scientific interest, such as "What is its boiling point?" "What is its freezing point?" "What is its molecular weight?" Other samples of stuff get the same answers to these last questions. They comprise all and only samples of water. Still other samples, though open to the same questions, get different answers. They comprise all and only the samples of other distinct substances, e.g., samples of gold all share one set of answers, samples of mercury share another set of answers, samples of sulfuric acid share yet another set, and so on. And still other samples of stuff don't hold answers at all to these questions. Pieces of sausage, for instance, or handfuls of mud, or buckets of shoelaces. These don't make up samples of a substance at all! The scientifically interesting questions collect bits of stuff into samples of substances. Not all bits of stuff. Some bits of stuff.

But what makes these questions scientifically interesting?

That should be obvious: the fact that their answers conform to law-like, or at least computable, relationships. There are law-like, or at least computable, relationships, between boiling points, freezing points, and molecular weights. A theory can therefore be constructed on the back of these questions. And a certain attitude can be acquired. For instance, that these samples constitute a "natural" domain, a domain that includes some (water, gold, mercury, etc.) but excludes others (sausage, mud, shoe laces); and that these samples have features that demand similar explanations. Of course these attitudes are warranted only if certain facts obtain, i.e., certain law-like relationships actually hold. For all we once knew, the world might have been otherwise.

A similar story, we believe, applies to utterances. Each utterance is open to a multiplicity of questions. The scientifically interesting ones are those whose answers across tokens stand in law-like, computable relationships to each other. As we noted before, that there are such questions, if there are, is a fact about the world. An interesting fact. We believe there are.[13] If we didn't we would not spend time on linguistics. And we believe that the questions we characterized as defining the domain of phonology are among these questions. If we didn't we would not pursue phonology as we do. All of that then is implicated in our talk about types. And none of it requires us to hold that there are types over and above tokens.

We want to stress one crucial further fact about questions of scientific interest. They are not all given, they are not part of ordinary common sense, they must be smoked out, discovered, and their discovery can be an achievement more revolutionary than the discovery of a new phenomenon. Newton, for instance, discovered many things about the world, but his most important discovery (outside of optics) would not have been possible without the discovery that physical bodies have mass. That was the discovery of a new kind of

---

[13]The law-like computable relationships are those that govern the production of utterances—not of all utterances, but only of utterances produced by invoking rules and a lexicon. We can, of course, produce utterances without such invocation. The crucial fact, not revealed by simple common sense, is that we can produce utterances that do invoke them.

question (and dispositional property), revolutionary because answers to it turned out to stand in marvelous computable relation to other questions (e.g., "What force is required to accelerate such and such one foot per second per second?"). Aristotle, a very good scientist, did not have the concept of mass, and therefore could not have wondered what the mass of the moon was, could not even know that he did not know what the mass of the moon was, and, of course, could not have fathomed that the answer to that question was related in systematic ways to the answer to other question about the moon. Celestial mechanics was beyond even his imagination!

The questions that make phonology possible also had to be discovered. And their discoverers are the heroes of our field: Panini, Rask, Bopp, Saussure, Jakobson, Chomsky. Without them phonology would still consist of pedantically collecting odd curiosities. But the work of discovering the right questions is far from finished!

As we mentioned at the very outset, utterances form a natural domain with other noises, the domain of acoustical theory. To deny this would be like holding that elephants, because they have a sex life, are not, like rocks, physical objects subject to the laws of mechanics! On the other hand to deny that utterances constitute an autonomous domain, the domain of phonology, would be like holding that because elephants are subject to the laws of mechanics, like rocks, they have no sex life! And to deny a-priori that there are systematic relationships between these two domains would be like denying a-priori that there are systematic relationships between the mass of elephants and the character of their sex life. Maybe there are. And some may even be surprising.

We can now tell what we make of the fact that (2), though about (1), contained no information about time, speaker, etc. and could have served for (11) as well. (2) contains only answers to questions of interest from the position of theoretical phonology. It could serve for any token that holds the same answers to those questions. However nothing in this requires that there be types besides tokens. Talk of types then is just a façon de parler.[14]

But that still leaves us with the requirement that phonological theory should not overgenerate or undergenerate. How do we

---

[14]We ourselves resort to this façon de parler even in this paper, when, for instance, we speak of morphemes, phonemes, etc.

construe the prohibition against overgeneration? Realistically: no phonological theory is true of the world that generates derivations (combinations of answers to questions, like (2)) to which no token in our language (i.e., produced as (1) was produced) can conform.[15] Phonological theories may not ignore constraints on the production of tokens than are imposed by the internalized rules and vocabulary. There is still no need to assume types.

What of the prohibition against undergeneration? We construe that also realistically: no phonological theory can be true of the world that can't generate derivations to which tokens in our language (i.e., produced as (1) was produced) **could** conform. Phonological theories may not presume more constraints on the production of tokens imposed by internalized rules and vocabulary. There is again no need to assume types.

Our construal of these principles is stated with the aid of modalities (expressed by "could") which vex many semanticists. But that is no reason to admit types. We find admission of types unenlightening as substitutes for these modalities, and at least as vexing.

Two final comments.

Some people may object to our way of looking at phonology on the grounds that it construes phonology as about performance and not about competence.[16] If they mean that we view phonology as about processes in real time responsible for the occurrence of tokens, they are right about our view. But we don't see this as an objection. If they mean that we view phonology as having to take into account contingencies of production over and above those traceable to knowledge of language, then they misconstrue our view. We don't.

Some will object that we have loaded phonology with unwarranted assumptions. Do speakers "really" retrieve morphemes from their memory, invoke rules, go through all these labors when speaking? We think they do. In fact we would like to know more about how they do it. We may be mistaken. Time will tell. But intuition

---

[15] Admittedly this answer requires elaboration. For instance, it seems to avoid commitment to phonological types at the price of commitment to types in the notation of the theory. We think that this appearance can be dispelled, but to do so would require a long discussion of theoretical formalisms. In any case, we are not claiming that there are no abstract entities at all. We are claiming that phonology is not about types.

[16] See for instance Lindsay and Harris 1990.

won't. Clearly speakers are not aware of performing such actions. But then we perform many actions like zombies (to borrow a phrase from Ned Block). That is how we learn language, recognize faces, and solve most of our problems.

Some will object that our outlook leaves out entirely that tokens are not only uttered but are also recognized. That is indeed a big hole in our account so far. But it calls for another paper, not abstract types.

Let us then return to the topic of our title: the ontology of phonology. What must the "furniture of the world" include if phonological theory, as we conceive it, is to have a chance of becoming true of that world? It is a long list: agents, tokens, phonetic intentions, minds with vocabularies and rules, articulators, and so on, in complicated interrelations. It does not have to include types. And if, perchance, the world does include types, phonology has nothing to say about them.[17] But then, probably no branch of linguistics does.

---

[17]Chomsky, in a number of writings (e.g., 1985), distinguishes between two conceptions of language (i.e., of the objects amenable to scientific linguistics): (1) a conception of language as an (infinite) set of expressions (signs) or of expressions paired with meanings, what he calls "E-language" (actually he subsumes a number of different conceptions of language under E-language, only one of which takes language as a set of types); and (2) a conception of language as a mind/brain state attained under certain contingencies (including exposure to other speakers) and made possible by certain innate brain/mental organizations—what he calls "I-language." He has demonstrated serious shortcomings in all the studies of language offered so far that are based on an E-language concept, and has urged approaches based on the I-language concept. Our paper shares his conviction that I-language is a more appropriate object for scientific study. This is not an accident: we came to our position largely through reflections on his.

Bibliography

Achinstein, Peter. 1968. *Concepts of Science: A Philosophical Analysis.* Baltimore: Johns Hopkins Press.

Aqvist, Lennart. 1965. A New Approach to the Logical Theory of Interrogatives. Unpublished manuscript, Uppsala.

Austin, J. L. 1975. *How to Do Things with Words,* ed. J. O. Urmson and Maria Sbisa. Cambridge: Harvard Univeristy Press. 2nd edition.

Belnap, Nuel. n.d. An Analysis of Questions. Preliminary Report, System Development Corporation, Santa Monica, CA.

Bromberger, Sylvain. 1989. Types and Tokens in Linguistics. In *Reflections on Chomsky*, ed. Alexander George, 58–89. Oxford: Basil Blackwell.

Bromberger, Sylvain, and Morris Halle. 1986. On the Relationship between Phonetics and Phonology. In *Invariance and Variability in Speech Process*, ed. Joseph S. Perkell and Dennis H. Klatt, 510–520. Lawrence Erlbaum.

Bromberger, Sylvain, and Morris Halle. 1989. Why Phonology is Different. *Linguistic Inquiry* 20(1):51–70.

Chomsky, Noam. 1977. On Wh-movement. In *Formal Syntax*, ed. P. Culicover, T. Wasow, and A. Akmajian. New York: Academic Press.

Chomsky, Noam. 1985. *Knowledge of Language: Its Nature, Origin, and Use.* New York: Praeger.

Duhem, Pierre. 1914. *La Theorie Physique.* Paris: A. Hermann.

Eberle, R., D. Kaplan, and P. Montague. 1961. Hempel and Oppenheim on Explanation. *Philosophy of Science* 28:418–428.

Fowler, H. G. 1964. *Dictionary of Modern English Usage.* Oxford: Clarendon Press.

Grünbaum, Adolf. 1963. *Philosophical Problems of Space and Time.* New York: A. Knopf.

Halle, Morris. 1990. An Approach to Morphology. In *Proceedings of the North East Linguistic Society*, Vol. 1, 150–184.

Hanson, Norwood Russell. 1959. *Patterns of Discovery*. Cambridge: Cambridge University Press.

Harrah, David. 1963. *Communication: A Logical Model*. Cambridge, MA: MIT Press.

Harrah, David. 1969. On Completeness in the Logic of Questions. *American Philosophical Quarterly* 6(2):158–164.

Hempel, Carl G. 1959. The Logic of Functional Analysis. In *Symposium on Sociological Theory*, ed. Llewellyn Gross. Evanston: Peterson.

Hempel, Carl G. 1962. Deductive-Nomological vs. Statistical Explanation. In *Minnesota Studies in the Philosophy of Science III*, ed. H. Feigl and G. Maxwell. Minneapolis: University of Minnesota Press.

Hempel, Carl G. 1965. *Aspects of Scientific Explanation*. New York: Macmillan.

Hempel, Carl G. 1967. The Structure of Scientific Theories. In *The Isenberg Memorial Lectures 1965–66*, ed. Ronald Suter. East Lansing: Michigan State University Press.

Kaplan, David. 1961. Explanation Revisited. *Philosophy of Science* 28:429–436.

Katz, Jerrold J., and Paul M. Postal. 1964. *An Integrated Theory of Linguistic Description*. Cambridge, MA: MIT Press. Research Monograph No. 26.

Kim, Jagwaen. 1963. Discussion on the Logical Conditions of Deductive Explanation. *Philosophy of Science* 30:286–291.

Langacker, Ronald. 1965. French Interrogatives: A Transformational Description. *Language* 41(4):587–600.

Liberman, A. M., and I. G. Mattingly. 1985. The Motor Theory of Speech Revised. *Cognition* 21:1–36.

Liberman, A. M., and I. G. Mattingly. 1989. Specialization for Speech Perception. *Science* 243:489–494.

Lindsay, Geoff, and John Harris. 1990. Phonetic Interpretation in Generative Grammar. In *Working Papers in Linguistics*, Vol. 2, 355–369. University College, London.

Popper, Karl. 1956. Three Views Concerning Human Knowledge. In *Contemporary British Philosophy*, ed. H. D. Lewis. London: George Allen and Unwin.

Salmon, Wesley. 1989. *Four Decades of Scientific Explanation*. Minneapolis: University of Minnesota Press.

Scheffler, Israel. 1963. *The Anatomy of Inquiry.* New York: A. Knopf.

Strawson, P. F. 1950. On Referring. *Mind* 235:320–344.

Teller, Paul. 1974. On Why-Questions. *Noûs* 8:371–380.

Urmson, J. O. 1963. Parenthetical Verbs. In *Essays in Conceptual Analysis*, ed. Anthony Flew. New York: Macmillan.

van Fraassen, Bas. 1980. *The Scientific Image.* New York: Oxford University Press.

Vendler, Zeno. 1957. Verbs and Times. *Philosophical Review* 66:143–160.

Wetzel, Linda. 1984. *On Numbers.* Doctoral dissertation, Massachusetts Institute of Technology, Cambridge, MA.

Library of Congress Cataloging-in-Publication Data

Bromberger, Sylvain
    On what we know we don't know : explanation, theory, linguistics, and how questions shape them / Sylvain Bromberger.
      p. cm.
    Includes bibliographical references.
    ISBN 0-226-075397 — ISBN 0-226-075400 (pbk.)
    1. Philosophy. 2. Science–Philosophy. 3. Language and languages–Philosophy. I. Title.
B29.B7442 1992
121–dc20
                                                92–10906
                                                        CIP

♾ The paper used in this publication meets the minimum requirements of the American National Standard for Information Sciences—Permanence of Paper for Printed Library Materials, ANSI Z39.48-1984.

We gratefully acknowledge permission to publish

"An Approach to Explanation," which originally appeared in *Analytical Philosophy, vol. 2*, ed. R. J. Butler. Copyright © 1962 by Basil Blackwell, Ltd.;

"A Theory about the Theory of Theory and about the Theory of Theories," which originally appeared in *Delaware Seminar on the Philosophy of Science, vol. 2*, ed. B. Baumrin. Copyright © 1963 by University of Delaware Press;

"Why-Questions," which originally appeared in *Mind and Cosmos: Essays in Contemporary Science and Philosophy, vol. 3*, ed. R. G. Colodny. Copyright © 1966 by The Center for Philosophy of Science, University of Pittsburgh;

"Questions," which originally appeared in *The Journal of Philosophy.* Copyright © 1966 by The Journal of Philosophy;

"Science and the Forms of Ignorance," which originally appeared in *Observation and Theory in Science.* Copyright © 1971 by The Johns Hopkins Press;

"Rational Ignorance," which originally appeared in *Matters of Intelligence*, ed. L. M. Vaina. Copyright © 1987 by D. Reidel Publishing Company; and

"What We Don't Know When We Don't Know Why," which originally appeared in *Scientific Inquiry in Philosophical Perspective*, ed. N. Rescher. Copyright © 1987 by The University Press of America.